POST-PERSONAL ROMANTICISM

# Post-Personal Romanticism

Democratic Terror, Prosthetic Poetics, and the Comedy of Modern Ethical Life

*Bo Earle*

THE OHIO STATE UNIVERSITY PRESS | COLUMBUS

Copyright © 2017 by The Ohio State University.
All rights reserved.

Library of Congress Cataloging-in-Publication Data
Names: Earle, Bo, author.
Title: Post-personal romanticism : democratic terror, prosthetic poetics, and the comedy of modern ethical life / Bo Earle.
Description: Columbus : The Ohio State University Press, [2017] | Includes bibliographical references and index.
Identifiers: LCCN 2017029070 | ISBN 9780814213520 (cloth ; alk. paper) | ISBN 0814213529 (cloth ; alk. paper)
Subjects: LCSH: English poetry—19th century—History and criticism. | English poetry—18th century—History and criticism. | Terror in literature. | Romanticism.
Classification: LCC PR590 .E17 2017 | DDC 821/.709—dc23
LC record available at https://lccn.loc.gov/2017029070

Cover design by Christian Fuenfhausen
Text design by Juliet Williams
Type set in Adobe Minion Pro

♾ The paper used in this publication meets the minimum requirements of the American National Standard for Information Sciences—Permanence of Paper for Printed Library Materials. ANSI Z39.48-1992.

9 8 7 6 5 4 3 2 1

CONTENTS

| | | |
|---|---|---|
| *Preface* | | vii |
| *Acknowledgments* | | xiii |
| CHAPTER 1 | Wordsworth, Apocalypse, and Prosthesis | 1 |
| CHAPTER 2 | Blake's Infant Smile: Facing Materialism | 35 |
| CHAPTER 3 | Byron's Sad Eye: The Tragic Loss of Tragedy | 63 |
| CHAPTER 4 | Shelley's Viral Prophecy: The Erotics of Chance | 114 |
| CHAPTER 5 | Keats's Lame Flock: The Erotics of Waste | 167 |
| *Bibliography* | | 201 |
| *Index* | | 209 |

# PREFACE

> This is not a reality show. This is the real deal.
> —Donald Trump, *Meet the Press*, August 16, 2015

FOR MANY years many people have bemoaned the fact that most residents of the most powerful country in the world get most of their news of the world from comedy TV. Those who defend this state of affairs tend to do so on the grounds that some news is better than none. What's less often suggested is that regardless of whether comedy offers an easier way to get the news than conventional reporting, it might offer a better, less misleading way, a way that stands to communicate more or, rather, miscommunicate—distort, displace, and suppress—less. As I write this, one reads in mainstream press of record that Sandra Bland, a woman who recently died in prison, should be held responsible for her own death because she seemed depressed after being assaulted by police and held for three days following a minor traffic violation. The fact that a journalistically legitimate perspective on such an event could be reduced to these terms, that such a moral syllogism could be presented as self-explanatory, requiring no decoding, demonstrates a certain crisis not just in journalism but in ethical discourse generally, a need of the kind of remedial fortification that Romantic poetry has long been read as aiming to provide.

As Blake might suggest, for instance, this conjures scenes of inquisition. Foucault might add the caveat that scenes of inquisition are not the same as inquisition proper, but rather the way in which the latter has been appropriated and internalized in and by modern mass society. But this book aims to show that the Romantics needed no such correction, that, like Blake's "fearful symmetry," Romantic terror is that of a subject cowering before the arbitrary violence of modern industry and mass society, not a representation of anything supposed to transcend this context. Differentiating between inquisition and scenes of inquisition does not mean evaluating the relative terror of the two, but just that the latter is the form in which terror has presented itself since Blake's time: the form of a masquerade of terror—terror that is not fully creditable as such but no less terrifying as a result. If anything, the fact that so many can think and say otherwise today in cases like Sandra Bland's just signals modern terror's greater formal refinement. Like climate change, our capacity to dismiss modern terror in such particular cases signals how deeply ingrained it is in our background way of life. Arendt's "banality of evil" does not describe a blunt stultification and mechanization of terror but a transfiguration of what she termed "labor" generally, an intricate change in the ways and means of language and action alike. Foucault contrasted modern state coercion with medieval torture, explaining why modern state violence that lacks such banalizing refinement, that dons the cloak of actual inquisition, seems stilted, awkward, and embarrassing. But these characteristics don't mitigate terror: they just underscore its arbitrariness and compulsiveness (which is arguably to say, not the superior terror of its meaning but the superior meaninglessness of its terror). In any event, the form of terror staged is the form in which terror presents itself *for us*. The question is not whether meaning and purpose make terror more or less terrorizing but whether we must demand, like inquisitors, that terror have meaning in order to count as such. Comic art sensitizes and instructs in the ways of random accidents and of the banality, embarrassment, and awkwardness of modern outrage, whereas tragedy's reliance on singular arresting insight, Aristotle's punctual moment of definitive reversal and recognition, does the opposite.

But perhaps today we need less such instruction precisely because of our familiarity with the comic absurdities of state-sponsored violence. On the contrary, we need more such instruction; we need to become smarter, subtler readers of comedy, because such violence has become so akin to comic sideshows in the circus of popular discourse. So a basic contention of this book is that Romantic poetry responds to the fact that in modernity, significant ethical questions are decided by popular reaction not to tragedy but to comedy: Is the modern democratic experience of state-sponsored violence or climate change trivially comic or terrifyingly comic? Do these register as a reality-show diversion or a hemorrhaging of the world? This choice is the characteristic form crucial ethical questions have taken since the Romantic period. In a way, this returns us to the historical formula identified by Marx as something said by Hegel: "Hegel said somewhere that history happens twice, first as tragedy and second as farce." Well before Marx, Wordsworth was on to this crisis too in poems like "Simon Lee" and "We are Seven," poems designed to offer readers remedial practice in moral literacy. From the objective side, "We are Seven" presents readers with a basic example of what moral discourse looks like and gives them the opportunity to familiarize themselves with it, to be gently introduced to its mysterious forms and intensities. From the subjective side, "Simon Lee" appeals to readers to complete the tale the poet could not and thereby to try their own hand or voice at moral discourse and take the first baby steps at imagining what it might be like to treat this experience of radical empathy as worthy of language, as warranting explicit articulation. The basic wager of such poems is this contention: there is an experience of empathy, of emotional identification with others, a sense of others as a painful extension of oneself, that you the reader feel but have yet to articulate or even to face. Hence you need the kind of remedial help processing the feeling that this poem offers.

Eighteenth-century sentimental education had an individualized, tragic formula for such remediation. The Wordsworthian/Romantic innovation is to expand the sense of what is replicated in and by empathy to the point where distinctions among the pitiable object, the subjective emotion, and the discursive means of mediating the two begin to blur. The object of empathy according to Adam Smith is a proprietary object: a spectacle that, although painful, buttresses one's sense of one's autonomous spectatorship or what C. B. Macphearson termed "Possessive Individualism." By contrast, the empathy Wordsworth would exercise in these poems is directed not at containable objects but at *other worlds*: not just the weird pain suffered by the girl encountered in "We Are Seven" and by Simon Lee and so on, but crucially also by the ways in which such strangers respond to such pain by projecting whole worlds of terribly fragile subjective meaning and purpose. Like the insane *coup de foudre* that the crazed poet of Baudelaire's "À une passante" ("To a Woman Passerby") defies the passer-by and reader alike to deny they recognize, such dreams are, in Walter Benjamin's words, "spared rather than denied fulfillment." The terrible fragility of these hopes teaches not how or why they should be realized but, drastically more modestly, the tenuousness of world projection generally, the tenuousness of any notion of "the world" per se, in the modern context. The Black Lives Matter movement for which Sandra Bland advocated likewise appeals for the recognition not of any particular suffering but of a mere capacity for suffering, for suffering acknowledged as such, that matters in some larger world. This is made most evident by the reflexive countermovement, All Lives Matter, a rejoinder that has no significance but mere panic over broaching the question of who gets to count as living, as us "all." That is, the democratic form of the people is its own nemesis. But registering such lessons requires comic form because comedy is the form tragedy takes in modern mass society. Hegel foresaw what the aforementioned ethical crises have since made unmistakable: the disconnect between the norms of individuality and the means of the crowd is constitutive of modernity as such, that tragedy consequently cannot get beyond playing supposed definitions of us "all" against what these exclude, that we keep bumping into the same wall, and that there is no getting at the distinct terror of this repetition without acknowledging its comic form.

One also reads in the news today President Trump quoted as saying something in response to outspoken objections to nuclear arms control measures that he's often said in the past about such objections to domestic gun control: "it would be ridiculous if it were not so sad." Nothing illustrates the aptness today of Hegel's claims about the interdependence of modern democracy and terror than the routineness of police brutality and gun violence in the United States and, abroad, the increasing normalization of drone killing, indiscriminate warfare, and the proliferation of weapons of mass destruction. Indeed, the *Washington Post* reports, also this same week, that 204 days into 2015, there have been 204 "mass shootings" in the United States during this same year.[1] The report defines a "mass shooting" as one in which "four or more people are shot in a single spree or setting."[2] At four, individuals blur into a mass, and if this is the number of people who are being shot on a daily basis, if this blurring itself is quotidian, not particularly noteworthy, unworthy of representation as a significant event, then such de-individuation is ratified at that much broader level of social normativity.

Thus this report on mass shootings represents a genre of news report that is becoming increasingly familiar, particularly in association with news about climate change: the genre of self-refuting news, self-refuting in the sense that the news, the take-home message of the report, is its very *un-newsworthiness*: the news is that what seemed like a remarkable event is actually nothing of the kind but is instead entirely routine, already baked into the world as we know it, the background against which events are supposed to stand in some con-

---

1. *Wonkblog.* July 24, 2015.
2. *Mass Shooting Tracker,* http://shootingtracker.com.

trasting relief. Kenneth Burke's categories of scene and event are inverted: like the individual in the modern crowd, the distinct event is absorbed into the indifferent background. The news is not a worldly event but your obliviousness to the world. Not unlike a Romantic poem, such news can offer remedial help in catching you up to where you already are. Individuals are engendered not before but after the normalization of the mass; hence *the mass isn't composed of individuals so much as individuals are extrapolated by contrast to the mass.* This is the shell game that Hegel and the Romantic poets read here were on to long ago and that we are still struggling to grasp. Killing that happens by "sprees" and in "settings" knows no individuality of either persons or events. In the modern context, asking individuality to keep its numbers discrete is like condemning Sandra Bland for acting depressed: promulgating individuality as a terrorizing disciplinary norm. As do we who swallow such rhetoric like water. For us no less than the French revolutionaries on Hegel's account, killing is less an action than an atmosphere or climate.

In turn, our rhetoric—the medium of event and scene alike, the medium that is both our environment itself and our means of acting upon it—might register and respond to this but only by resigning to its own systemic deceptions. This requires not the rhetoric of heroically isolated tragic action but of ongoing, collective, and unremarkable comic *routines* of unmasking and remasking. So perhaps the president has the equation backwards. Perhaps the language of former presidential candidate Mike Huckabee that prompted the president's lament—language likening the arms control treaty with Iran to the Holocaust—might be better characterized as (merely) sad if it were not so (terrifyingly) ridiculous. The treaty delivers Israelis "to the doors of the ovens," Huckabee said, adding that he knows whereof he speaks because he's been to those same doors. What is decisive is not that the Holocaust is confused with a Holocaust museum but that neither commands sufficient elegiac reverence to restrict their rhetorical exploitation. The most basic contention of this book is that in Romantic and Post-Romantic mass society, tragedy is not localized but systemic, and *when tragedy becomes systemic, catharsis becomes not punctual but rhythmic*, not an arresting, penetrating recognition but an extended pattern of un- and remasking. Our rhetoric doesn't need to relearn sensitivity to tragedy but to become less arbitrarily and brutally comic, to mobilize what I present as the queer, post-personal bonds animating the social "masquerades" espoused by Shelley and Keats. Such bonds do not precede or otherwise transcend crowd life but are the latter's by-products, poetically refunctioned to awaken the crowd *from* its individuating dreams and *to* its own proper forms of feeling, aesthetic expression, and ethical agency. Against the individual's grandiose claims to singular sovereignty over such capacities, such refunctioning cannot but appear to deflate, diffuse, minimize, or, as Alan Liu following Marshall McLuan has it, "cool" their content. This is the coolness of Wordsworth reducing the drama of sentiment to that of a multiple-choice math problem ("Are we: [a] 5 or [b] 7?"), demurring to finish Simon's tale and reducing Lucy, the object of his series of lyric elegies, to a conjecture about what the mass of people disregard: "A Maid whom there were none to praise / And very few to love. . . . She lived unknown, and few could know / When Lucy ceased to be." In turn, the content of Wordsworth's grief is reduced to *the form of the event of difference*: "But she is in her grave, and, oh, / The difference to me!" She made a difference by being different, or, in any event, difference happened; there was something different once. This event of difference must transcend the logic and the present moment of the sonnet because the poet doesn't trust it to his own language and reason whose very communicability implicates it in the oblivious "many." What this cryptic gesturing from within the echo chamber at something beyond it is supposed to mean Wordsworth leaves to the reader to decide, just as he leaves the conclusion of Simon's tale to the reader. And just as the news media leave us to conclude Sandra Bland's tale: Is this an individual tragedy or a systemic one in which our very means of representing tragedy as such are crucially implicated? What difference does it make?

Only a cooling of our claims to individuating escape from the crowd might begin to mitigate the ever-accumulating disaster of history to which Benjamin's *Angelus Novus* bore witness. This overflow of the world itself, not of discrete individualities, is what Wordsworth and Romantic poetry generally would have us recollecting, discursively working and being worked by this hemorrhaging until it becomes an equally inclusive patterning of the collective, until the recognition of difference becomes a socially normative play of difference, a comic masquerade, or else not.

ACKNOWLEDGMENTS

WORK ON this book was supported by a grant from the Canadian Social Sciences and Humanities Research Council and a research leave from the University of British Columbia. I am grateful to the University of British Columbia English department for providing a most collegial and supportive work environment. Two anonymous reviewers at The Ohio State University Press provided remarkably thorough and thoughtful critiques, determining much of the final shape of this book. Lindsay Martin at OSUP has been an exceptionally generous and rigorous editor. The love of my extended family saw me through the work on this book and much else. Students I have taught provided the most insight and inspiration for the ideas explored here; this book is dedicated to them.

CHAPTER 1

# Wordsworth, Apocalypse, and Prosthesis

ON AUGUST 16, 1819, a gathering of at least 30,000 people met at St. Peter's Field in Manchester, England, to petition for democratic reform and to hear an address from Henry Hunt. They were attacked by the local militia, who killed eleven and injured several hundred. Afterwards, two of the militiamen walked over the field surveying the results of their action, and one of them commented, "This was our Waterloo." Overheard by a *London Times* reporter, the remark bestowed the name by which the day's events have been remembered: the Peterloo massacre. The name bespeaks a belief that the Napoleonic threat to English nationhood had been replaced by an equivalent, homegrown menace, but it's not obvious how this new threat was defined. To some degree of course it was defined in terms of democratic reform movement. But the militiamen evidently sufficiently equated that movement with the assembled crowd itself to read the butchering of one as the Waterloo-like conquest of the other. The militiamen could have believed themselves to have vanquished reform only by believing on some level that, as if in a political cartoon, it was reform itself that bled beneath their bayonets: there was something about the very form of the crowd that—in the militiamen's eyes—transformed fellow Englishmen and -women into the equivalent of Napoleon's army resurrected. As a matter of fact, this transformation is consistent with the views of Henry Hunt, Samuel Bamford, and other organizers of the demonstration, who likewise saw the reformist cause in/as the spectacle of the crowd itself.

Accordingly the refrain of Percy Shelley's "song" about the massacre, *The Mask of Anarchy*, is less an encomium than a statement of political purpose and identity: "Ye are many, they are few."[1] In other words, from the perspectives of reformism and reaction alike, the reform agenda itself was arguably secondary, and Peterloo was first and foremost a battle between those out to assert and those out to suppress the form of the crowd.

The challenge of the crowd form is equally evident in critical reflection on the event. According to Richard Cronin, for instance, Peterloo "was one of those events, like the Amritsar massacre, the Shapeville killings in South Africa, the killings on the campus of Kent State, and the Bloody Sunday in Londonderry, that achieve from the very first a symbolic status. Such events have the power to polarize the politics of a nation."[2] Cronin's itemized series of historical analogs does not explain so much as demonstrate the event's symbolic status. For Cronin, Peterloo was "from the very first" an event so revolutionarily singular that it precipitated an altogether new national political dispensation, yet this paradoxically relegates it to "one of those" events belonging to a familiar category. The event's very singularity qualifies it as a member of the generic series of "such events." As the *Times* anecdote suggests, it was experienced as a repetition of Waterloo *from the first*; that is, even before it was so named, and paradoxically classified as singular, repetition provided the enabling frame of Peterloo *as* singular. This embarrassing dependence of individuality on classification is arguably modern democracy's constitutive paradox. The discourse of democracy requires instances of singular individuality from which to extrapolate that otherwise elusive conceit, the collective will of "the people."[3]

Hence Cronin's retrospective depiction of Peterloo as somehow generically singular, a member of a class of the unprecedentedly unique, mirrors the organizers' own intention for the rally; that is, the retrospective recounting and prospective aim belong equally to the same continuous series, yet the coherence of this series as such depends on the conceit of the irreduc-

---

1. As James Chandler writes, "The August 16 meeting had been in preparation since Hunt's visit to Manchester in January, and the people who attended it marched to the meeting grounds in disciplined phalanxes, subdivided into platoons according to their place of dwelling in or around Lancashire. They had rehearsed, drilled, for weeks. The explicit aim of the planners was to produce a spectacle unprecedented in its display of organization and strength." *England in 1819*, 15ff.

2. *The Politics of Romantic Poetry*, 147.

3. This concern for "staging the people" as such, to borrow the title of Jacques Rancière's first book, has been a central focus of modern democratic theory from Rousseau through to Rancière himself. What Rancière calls "the archi-ethical paradigm" aims not "to improve behaviour through representation, but to have all living bodies directly embody the sense of the common"; to "fram[e] the community as artwork" (*Staging the People*, 137).

ibly unique. Bamford, for instance, wrote during planning sessions the spring prior to Peterloo that the rally "should be as morally effective as possible, and, that it should exhibit a spectacle such as had never before been witnessed in England."[4] Political and moral efficacy, achievement of the kind of transformative social consequences Cronin attributes to Peterloo, Chandler correlates less with singularity itself than with a *rhetoric* of singularity: "The explicit aim of the planners was to produce a spectacle unprecedented in its display of organization and strength, and the rhetoric of the 'unexampled' incident became very much a part of the coverage of Peterloo and its aftermath." As in Cronin's account, a subtle, implicit privileging of the authenticity of the original over successors shades Chandler's as well. Whereas the contemporary coverage and subsequent histories of Peterloo deployed merely a "rhetoric" of singularity, the organizers' collective act is credited as an actual political event rather than just a rhetoric thereof. On the one hand there is the chronological sequence—first the act and then the rhetoric of the act—but on the other hand this priority is evidently a rhetorical effect.

So the act precedes the rhetoric of the act but follows the act of rhetoric of the act. What we speak about when we speak about the act appears as such only as a consequence of such speech. This is what Jean-Jacques Rousseau, the seminal theorist of modern democratic action, meant by "the general will": the notion that whatever discrete act one undertakes, it is presupposed that one does so *as* a free agent. Individual free agency is the afterglow of religion, the supremely vexed, vestigial norm of transcendent authority that post-Enlightenment, modern democracy both demands, on the one hand, and, on the other, denies any means of definitively fulfilling. In order to count as such, an action must also issue a promise or claim to exemplify or fulfill the legitimating norm of free agency. Rousseau's general will is constitutively implicit; it never crystallizes into an explanation or justification of the what and wherefore of such agency (were it to do so, it would then be an explicit, determinate act in its own right). This implicit presupposition is a crucial feature of how actions look and feel in the modern context. Indeed Rousseau claimed that it is a *necessary* feature: as he notoriously put it, we are in this context "forced to be free." Free agency resembles a vestige of religion insofar as it is not optional; or, conversely, the very choice to opt out of free agency inevitably opts us back in, automatically installing, *not in virtue but in spite of ourselves*—in spite of the ostensible will to disown freedom or promises of freedom—a new implicit level of such promising. Here freedom is not something asserted but received, even coercively.

---

4. *Passages in the Life of a Radical*, 131.

This book construes Romanticism then as radically, even apocalyptically, undermining assumptions of historical progress in a way that it has since become impossible for us not to think of in terms of climate change. The event named *global warming* is not reducible to a particular, isolatable increase in global temperature; rather, like the self-terrorizing terms of democratic narrative, it names a feedback loop that will soon, if it has not already, become a self-fulfilling prophecy. "If it has not occurred already," Clive Hamilton wrote in his 2010 book *Requiem for a Species,* then "within the next several years enough warming will be locked in to the system to set in train feedback processes that will overwhelm any attempts we make to cut back on our carbon emissions. We will be powerless to stop the jump to a new climate on Earth, one much less sympathetic to life."[5] The problem presented by climate change is not just that a once stable, foundational aspect of nature is now subject to historical variation but that it is stuck in one very specific, systemically devastating and self-perpetuating kind of change. Of course an analogous point may be made about any number of signature modern phenomena that do not merely distort or manipulate reality, or even render it in some sense infinitely questionable or relativized, but establish autonomous structures, what Marx termed "ideology," Althusser the "ideological apparatus," Foucault the "episteme," and, most recently and expansively by Bruno Latour, simply "politics": self-sustaining systems of reality reproduction.

Where Hamilton speaks of a lack of "sympathy to life," Latour speaks in more rigorously formal terms of the effective erasure of any reality beyond what politics acknowledges. The challenge of sensitizing ourselves to the specific weight of climate change exemplifies an array of such challenges that are constitutive of the late capitalist condition. We are analogously insensitive to the weight of the indiscriminate violence, refugee crises, and torture in which the global political and economic system today is increasingly systemically implicated. These cases all face the crucial challenge to invent a new postnatural rhetoric that fosters something *like* "sympathy to life" without recourse to the foundational moral or metaphysical precepts that the term *life* traditionally entails. Any effective response to the antifoundationalist dilemma hinges on the capacity of our means of representation to register the specificity of this stuckness rather than relativizing it. This in turn presupposes a sense of the condition from which this stuckness exiled us, the perpetually displaced (indifferently elided, put to waste and/or hypostatized, appropriated) state of nature: to register the relevance or weight of this absence but to do so without thereby re-presenting it.

---

5. *Requiem for a Species,* 2.

This dual capacity entails a paradoxical, affective attunement, a distinctly modern sensitivity to numbness. Climate change offers an exemplary case for studying the challenge of cultivating this paradoxical attunement demanded by modernity generally. If science once presented us with a picture of the world in which climate figured like latitude as an invariable property of the globe, it now presents a picture in which climate varies in response to human behavior. This shift is difficult to register because even as it falls under the sway of human history, climate, unlike weather, remains phenomenally elusive, tangible only abstractly as a statistical extrapolation of weather patterns. Indeed, the reality of the event of climate change is deceptively disguised by the palpable concreteness of actual weather: the categories of context and event, frame and phenomenon, or what Kenneth Burke termed *scene* and *act*, have been inverted, leaving us phenomenally exiled from the real effects of our own history. Such migration of effective reality from the concrete to the abstract is a signature characteristic of such familiar features of modernity as consumer capitalism, financial speculation, and globalization. What is historically most distinctly revealing and salient about our experience of climate now is its very elusiveness, our very insensitivity to it. The event of climate change and the discourses surrounding it are exemplary of a moment in which sensitivity to history paradoxically becomes a sensitivity to numbness or an attunement to spectrality. The following considers British Romantic lyrics signally concerned with cultivating such sensitivity and exemplifying a rhetoric of the posthuman that, I argue, could be of particular use in our own struggle to address climate change.

The ascendance of abstraction, like climate change itself, is retraceable to the historical advent of industrialization, the moment when, according to the poet Percy Shelley, the cultural ascendance of "the calculating principle" deprived us of "the ability to imagine what we know."[6] The Romantic movement in literature is rooted not just in the same historical moment as industrialism but also in analogous inversions of Burke's "scene" and "act." Hence James Chandler casts the period in terms of an inversion of history and historicism as "the age of the spirit of the age."[7] Focusing on such inversions, the thesis of the following is twofold. First, I suggest that the British Romantics' poetic responses to this new world at the moment of its emergence still have something to teach us about how to inhabit it. Second, I hope this might shed important new light on Romanticism itself, illuminating its sensitivity to ethical compulsions exerted at the level of climate, by a reality irreducible to

---

6. *Shelley's Poetry and Prose*, 530.
7. *England in 1819*, 105–14, 161, 211.

phenomenal reality, preempting even Romanticism's signature investment in what Susan Wolfson construes terms "the questioning presence," "the interrogative processes of poetry,"[8] and what Chandler construes in terms of casuistry, the chiastic imbrication of poetry and history in "cases" defined by their interminable reversibility, "figures that cut athwart the distinction we use to contain [them]."[9] If figures of perpetual reversibility and questionability stand to mitigate the specific crisis of climatic warming, then how might this apocalyptic weight be made palpable? Instead we still want what Shelley sought: an orientation toward a an unquestionable frame of experience, "the shadows of futurity cast upon the present,"[10] the singular instance of global position, gravitational or polar orientation, the frame that, as Adorno and Horkheimer put it, was before Enlightenment registered in a sensuous language of the body and environment.

The difficulty of cultivating this paradoxical orientation exceeds that of postmodern skepticism and stands not to compromise but to radicalize the latter. In Timothy Morton's words, if "for postmodernism 'everything is a metaphor' in some strong sense," then "all metaphors are equally bad." But if in the age of climate change "there are real things for sure, just not as we know them or knew them," then "some metaphors are better than others. Yet because there is nowhere to stand outside of things altogether, it turns out that we know the truth of '"there is no metalanguage' more deeply than its inventors."[11] Climate change teaches us that postmodernist skepticism is not a universal license to doubt but stems from a specific fate, a determinate reality that makes mere normative doubt just as misplaced as normative comprehension. So Morton continues:

> The globalizing sureness with which "there is no metalanguage" and "everything is a metaphor" are spoken in postmodernism means that postmodernism is nothing like what it takes itself to be, and is indeed just another version of the (white, Western, male) historical project. The ultimate goal of this project, it seems was to set up a weird transit lounge outside of history

---

8. "If Negative Capability is defined by what it excites and declines . . . Keats's odes strengthen that capacity in their readers by requiring us to negotiate a poetic language that fixes and unfixes, forms and transforms a texture of signification. Their originating 'uncertainties, Mysteries, doubts' are sustained by the interrogative processes of the poetry itself. . . . Keats's poetry retains a mystery of signs and situation that requires negotiation through the questioning presence of a reader and achieves its fullest imaginative value in the poetics of cooperation so engendered." Chandler, *The Questioning Presence*, 331ff.

9. *England in 1819*, 554.

10. *Shelley's Poetry and Prose*, 535.

11. *Hyperobjects*, 4.

in which the character and technologies and ideas of the ages mill around in a state of mild, semiblissful confusion. Slowly, however, we discovered that the transit lounge was built on Earth, which is different from saying that it was part of Nature.[12]

The following readings mine Romantic lyric for a rhetoric attuned to the paradoxical fate of our Earth, whose singularity and concreteness are measured by their *defiance* of direct worldly apprehension and representation. More specifically I'd like to track the development of such a poetic project out of the *failure* of an early Romantic, elegiac attempt to establish the normative authority of a definitive grief and compassion: empathy as a morally foundational affect that could encompass this disoriented world and thereby redemptively reorient it, that could reintegrate all social conflict into a globally unified spectacle of normative poetic feeling.

Restoring some normative affective significance to death is a primary concern not just of Hegel but also of early Romantic lyric which registers the world-shaking implications of its loss in prevalent figural use of the globe. In "The Emigrants," for instance, Charlotte Smith casts her empathy for the revolution's victims as an empathy that pretends to bear the weight of what she terms "this suffering globe." The poet calls on an anthropomorphic deity to take pity on an equally anthropomorphized Earth, to "with mercy view / This suffering globe, and cause thy creatures cease, / With savage fangs to tear her bleeding breast."[13] But this dual personification in fact figures the poet's own absorption of her environment as a reified whole, in her words, "even as a map." Smith speaks from a god's eye perspective but as an exile of the church whose "prayer was made . . . not in domes"

> Of human architecture filled with crowds,
> But on these hills, where boundless yet distinct,
> Even as a map, beneath are spread the fields
> His Bounty clothes, divided here by woods
> And there by commons rude or winding brooks,
> While I might breathe the air perfumed with flowers
> Or the fresh odours of the mountain turf.
> (390–97)

Finally the poet identifies her song with the song of Earth itself: "I made my prayer / In unison with murmuring waves that now / Swell with dark tem-

---

12. Ibid.
13. "The Emigrant," *Selected Poems,* lines 421–23.

pests, now are mild and blue / As the bright arch above, for all to me / Declare omniscient goodness" (401–5). Darkness and brightness become one just as Smith's song of pity *for* the globe becomes one with the song *of* the globe itself. Smith's attempt at empathizing with the suffering of the world turns into a globally encompassing narcissism that leaves nothing outside herself with which to empathize.

The signature object of Wordsworthian empathy likewise is not a person's particular suffering but the systematic organization of experience in which a particular complaint figures as such. What mortifies the balladeer of Simon Lee, and cuts his tale short, is not empathy for any particular suffering or indication of Simon's helplessness, his fall from grace, or any other discrete event or feature of Simon's life. Rather, what the poet empathizes with in a way that renders him speechless is the way in which Simon's experience is systematically organized. This is what Wordsworth means by saying that the gratitude of men is sometimes harder to bear than meanness: empathizing with Simon's gratitude entails recognizing the *formal scope* of Simon's aspirations, taking the measure of Simon's world, and finding this unbearably meager. It is exactly because the object of the poet's feeling is so all-encompassing that it can be communicated only by the poet's demonstration of speechlessness, drawing readers into his world-encompassing feeling (or the feeling of a Simon's whole world, his entire scope of experience) by enjoining them to carry on the impossible task of putting it into words. Likewise in *The Prelude* and "Resolution and Independence," encountering the blind beggar and the leech gatherer, Wordsworth feels himself "admonished from other worlds," and struck dumb, with, he says, "the weight of waters."[14] Wordsworth makes his speechlessness attest to a global, *tidal* force; sympathy is not discretely pictured but figures as a function of the gravitational interplay of whole planets or worlds. The admonishment that silences him is coextensive with the tides; his silence is not an arbitrary failure of poetic speech but specifically attests to planetary forces. Where Smith pictures her positive poetic achievement in terms of the articulation of wind and water about the globe, Wordsworth makes poetic failure negatively bespeak the weight of worlds as such.

The appeal to both Wordsworth and Smith of the figure of the globe as a vehicle for articulating such sympathy may be retraceable to Edmund Burke's desire to restore a sublime weight or inertia or "cold sluggishness" to the English character, a kind of unquestionable gravitational pull to restore the traditional moral compass of the nation.[15] The formal complexity of Wordsworth's

---

14. "Resolution and Independence," line 118ff., 616–23.

15. "Thanks to the cold sluggishness of our national character, we bear the stamp of our forefathers." *Reflections on the Revolution in France* (1993), 557.

lyric expression may exceed that of Smith's, but the function of empathy seems identical: to reify others' suffering by grasping its function as a part of a whole world. Where Smith makes her poem directly and positively expressive of both the world's suffering and her empathy for it, Wordsworth's speechlessness enacts poetic incompletion in a way that stands not as metaphor but as metonym for his overwhelming grief: not as metaphorical containment of the content, meaning, and affect of grief but as metonym for the form of overflow itself. In place of expressing this grief, his emphatic failure to do so passes on the unfinished search for adequate metaphors to the reader; his speechlessness is a metonym for the prospective aim of metaphor-making rather than its achievement. If Smith's poem would stand for the beleaguered world, Simon's world according to Wordsworth is represented not by his ballad or by any other particular poem but by the very project of poetic speech, lyric expression of experience, generally. His pretense to failure, then, makes the narcissism of his empathy all the more consuming.

Despite the rigor of the blind beggar episode's negative formalism, then, Wordsworth here arguably ultimately follows Smith's restrictive economizing of affective sympathy. But in the boat-stealing episode from *The Prelude*'s first book, Wordsworth rehearses his admonishment from another world in a way that critically reflects upon this narcissism. As the scene begins, what is beyond the horizon of immediate subjective presence is explicitly dismissed as "nothing":

> A rocky steep uprose
> Above the cavern of the willow-tree,
> And now, as suited one who proudly rowed
> With his best skill, I fixed a steady view
> Upon the top of that same craggy ridge,
> The bound of the horizon—for behind
> Was nothing—but the stars and the grey sky.
> (394–400)

This self-containment gives rise to an eroticized narcissism, with the poet literally making love to the boat and lake and reveling in unchecked consumption of his present world. This bliss is exposed as a masturbatory illusion, however, when a new horizon imposes itself where the subject had assured himself there was nothing:

> She was an elfin Pinnace; lustily
> I dipp'd my oars into the silent Lake,

> And as I rose upon the stroke, my Boat
> Went heaving through the water, like a Swan,
> When from behind that craggy Steep, till then
> The bound of the horizon, a huge Cliff,
> As if with voluntary power instinct,
> Uprear'd its head: I struck, and struck again,
> And, growing still in stature, the huge Cliff
> Rose up between me and the stars, and still,
> With measur'd motion, like a living thing,
> Strode after me.
> (401–12)

As its phallic form here makes unmistakable, the uprearing head of the huge cliff, expanding with the parallax effect as the poet rows away from it, is an image of radical otherness, the return of the repressed oedipal rival and hence an otherness that was always already the self's shadow even when the latter had been blissfully oblivious to it.

In the passage's conclusion, though, this otherness turns out to enable the self to gain a new "dim undetermined sense" of itself, not in a rival self-image but as *the activity of projecting such spectacles*.

> . . . after I had seen
> That spectacle, for many days my brain
> Work'd with a dim and undetermin'd sense
> Of unknown modes of being: in my thoughts
> There was a darkness, call it solitude,
> Or blank desertion; no familiar shapes
> Of hourly objects, images of trees,
> Of sea, or sky, no colours of green fields;
> But huge and mighty Forms, that do not live
> Like living men mov'd slowly through my mind
> By day and were the trouble of my dreams.
> (417–27)

The narcissistic self-image formerly entertained was not inaccurate *as* a self-image. Instead, the initial picture was inaccurate primarily because it was *merely* a picture: it failed to account for the self as not just a narcissistically self-picturing agent but one who, in its self-picturing, is always also filling the horizon with a radical otherness that haunts the self, that no picture can capture because it is the condition of possibility of picturing per se. Readings of this passage that end by diagnosing the oedipal subtext do not preserve this radical otherness but just replace it with another picture (of, say, a psychoanalytically restricted economy).

Wordsworth thus begins to give us a sense of general economy opened up precisely by tarrying with a certain narcissistic self-containment even in the face of overwhelming self-disruption. For under such conditions this persistence of narcissism becomes revealed as a compulsive fantasy or *simulacrum* of narcissism. The sovereign excess of the general economy is mobilized by simulation of restriction. Wordsworth, in other words, here attunes us to the point Derrida emphasizes in a late interview, that the alternative to narcissistic self-enclosure is not non-narcissism—the kind of definitively consuming empathy extolled by Smith and even Wordsworth himself—but rather a narcissism whose hospitality is a function of a *self-imaging in the face of a radical asymmetry that defies reappropriation*:

> There is not narcissism and non-narcissism. There are narcissisms that are more or less comprehensive, generous, open, extended. What is called non-narcissism is in general but the economy of a much more welcoming and hospitable narcissism. One that is much more open to the experience of the Other as Other. I believe that without a movement of narcissistic reappropriation, the relation to the Other would be absolutely destroyed, it would be destroyed in advance. The relation to the Other, even if it remains asymmetrical, open, without possible reappropriation, must trace a movement of reappropriation in the image of one's self for love to be possible. Love is narcissistic.[16]

Derrida emphasized that it is finally the notion of agency itself—the notion of autonomous subjective desire, selfhood as self-causing, the anthropocentric privilege—that requires such perpetual presentation of supplementary evidence of itself. In this respect, then, there is a useful textual resource in the fact that the Anthropocene marks a shift *from* the era of the *holos* or whole *to* that of humankind. As the foundation of a new geological age, "Anthropos" ostensibly has the function of a primary cause, but it does so only in virtue of distorting the holistic world picture that represents a comprehensive and self-contained—or what George Bataille called "restricted"—economy of causes and effects to a neutral human observer. If the era of the holos was the era of the world as a holistic physical system, then *Anthropos* implies an eruption of *difference within the whole*, and that the source of this difference is none other

---

16. *Points . . .* , 199.

than ourselves. Grappling with its own otherness in a way that was unknown to the Holocene is an implicit defining feature of the Anthropocene.

Climate science offers a powerful articulation of this mutual implication of self and other in its account of the feedback loop described by Hamilton, called "the bathtub effect"[17]: an analogy meant to highlight the fact that about 45 percent of carbon emissions remain in the atmosphere long after (that is, not just decades but centuries and millennia after) they are emitted. Emissions behave like the water filling up a bathtub whose drain, even if not completely stopped, is very weak.

> For thousands of years, the trickle of $CO_2$ entering the atmosphere from natural sources was balanced by the trickle that naturally drained out. Since the Industrial Revolution, when we started burning fossil fuels, we've opened the faucet wider and wider, so the water level (or, in the real world, the $CO_2$ level) has risen. If we simply stopped opening the faucet any wider, the water would still continue to rise. If we turned it down, the water would still continue to rise, just more slowly. And if we turned it back down to the original trickle—which would mean stopping all human emissions—the water level would stop rising. But it wouldn't fall, because that tiny drain is still tiny. Most of the extra $CO_2$ we've added would stay in the atmosphere for a very long time. As a result, the planet would very likely remain in a state of higher temperature, altered weather patterns, higher sea level, and the rest for at least a thousand years, and the world would probably keep changing.[18]

The bathtub effect locates the actually inhabited world not in any "world picture" but in the midst of the ever-accumulating supplements that underwrite the projection of such pictures. By confronting us with the supplementation that such pictures would elide, the science of climate change generally, and the bathtub effect in particular, strikingly illustrate the fundamental lesson of deconstruction encapsulated Derrida's dictum "il n'y a pas de hors-texte": the picture of holistic nature, which so much environmental writing cherishes, disguises actual environmental imbalance, an ever-growing overflow of supplementation:

> Beyond and behind [the] text, there has never been anything but writing; there have never been anything but supplements, substitutive significations which could only come forth in a chain of differential references, the "real" supervening, and being added only while taking on meaning from a trace and from an invocation of the supplement, etc. And thus to infinity, for we

---

17. Cf. Andrew Revkin, "The Greenhouse Effect and the Bathtub Effect."
18. Climate Central, *Global Weirdness*, 136.

have read, *in the text,* that the *absolute* present, Nature, that which words like "real mother" name, have always already escaped, have never existed; that what opens meaning and language is writing as the disappearance of natural presence.[19]

The Anthropocene represents a transition to a world in which human action is no longer simply sanctioned by a holistic world picture but instead systematically pollutes the whole with an otherness that is the self's inexorable destabilizing shadow.

George Bataille construed this kind of self-undermining function as a "restricted economy," a system of human action beholden both to propping up an unmediated picture of its own purposes and meanings and to eliding its own mediating role. To this Bataille contrasted a "general economy" of the "sovereignty" of action as such.[20] Derrida writes that Bataille's sovereignty is a matter of the "production of useless excess," an excessive experience of "Unknowledge" released from the restricted economy or world picture built upon knowable causes, meanings, and purposes. According to Bataille, useless excess is produced by replacing the restrictive economics of knowledge with an economics precisely of their performative imitation: the imperative continually to shore up the world picture is replaced by an imperative "playfully to simulate" such shoring up. Crucially, this entails a new experience of ethical responsibility. As Derrida explains, the general economy is not chaotic, and the production of excess not arbitrary; they are bound by the ethical norm of "sovereignty" that asserts the primacy of performance over meaning:

> Sovereignty transgresses the entirety of the history of meaning and the entirety of the meaning of history, and the project of knowledge which has always obscurely welded these two together. Unknowledge is, then, suprahistorical, but only because it takes its responsibilities from the completion of history and from the closure of absolute knowledge, having first taken them seriously and having betrayed them by exceeding them or by simulating them in play.[21]

The excessiveness of the general economy stems precisely from its status as simulation; hence Bataille's crucial but easily overlooked *resistance* of what is often stereotypically construed as "romantic" pretense to transcend or dispense with economics. The general economy breaks with the restricted economy not in virtue of pretending to escape it—an escape that, one supposes,

---

19. *Of Grammatology,* 159.
20. *The Accursed Share.*
21. Derrida, "From Restricted to General Economy," 341.

must itself entail some kind of implicitly restrictive criterion of validity—but of merely (i.e., sovereignly wastefully) simulating it, making simulation an end in itself unbound to ulterior sanctioning causes and effects.

The notion that the Anthropocene might be more responsibly and sovereignly inhabited—and the baleful effects of today's restricted economies of commercial technology counteracted—through gratuitous simulation of those very economies opens intriguing new rhetorical and social possibilities for us today even while recalling a, if not the, key achievement of Romantic poetics. Even as Latour, for instance, identifies the sweepingly paralyzing effects of politics as such, he nonetheless returns to Plato's allegory of the cave to demonstrate the essentially formal, literary status not just of politics but also of its critique: the hegemonic power of politics and the critique of such power alike hinge, Latour implies, upon the form and function of allegory.

According to Latour, Plato's myth combines two incommensurable postulates: on the one hand, of an absolute disconnect between the singularity of law and the variability of social reality, and, on the other hand, of a philosopher/lawgiver who nonetheless manages to bridge this gap. For Latour these postulates are not mere propositions but entail ontological rearrangements or "shifts": each proposition smuggles in, and thereby legitimates in new terms, its own antithesis. Thus the postulate of an absolute disconnect between the world of social flux and that of immutable truth in fact includes the possibility of, to quote Plato's *Symposium*, "'Interpreting and ferrying to gods things from human beings and to human beings things from gods'"[22]; or, in Latour's words, "moving back and forth between the two houses."[23] Conversely, the postulate that such truth is preserved in the immutable state that defines it even as it is ferried into the context of social flux recasts such preservation itself as a temporal *act*, as a translation or movement across boundaries. Latour's aim is not to point out that Plato contradicts himself but to show how his myth stages conceptual oppositions in order to reshuffle their terms and implications, their ontological conditions of legitimacy, intelligibility, and authority.

In the spirit of his anti-Hegelian forerunners Althusser and Foucault, then, Latour contends that the history of modern society is a history of the exclusion of any alternative to the ideological structures he identifies: "Let us face facts," Latour writes: "there is no way out of this trap" (12).[24] But Latour's method is implicitly dialectical in its critical focus on the interplay between saying and showing, between the ideologies' ostensible propositional enunciation and the way in which such practical utterance can implicitly and practi-

---

22. Cooper, ed., *Plato: Complete Works*, 202e.
23. *Politics of Nature*, 14.
24. Ibid., 12.

cally appropriate and mobilize—or, as I would emphasize, bring into *play,* give a specifically *theatrical* efficacy to—incommensurate meanings. Latour's reading then, although evidently anti-Platonic in respect to what Plato's myth ostensibly *says,* is hardy anti-Platonic in its generous assessment of what the myth *has done,* the myth's effective social influence, the power of its restaging in the course of social history. More precisely Latour reads the myth as a *comic* (albeit also practically and theoretically supremely consequential) *play* of discursive and conceptual masks rather than a tragic foundering of discourse against the shoals of truth and logic.[25] Hence Latour focuses on techniques and technologies by which this play might be refined and enriched, not on the revelation of tragic wisdom (e.g., about the "fact" of being "trapped"): enhancing the functional "ferrying" of truth rather than its definitive revelation.

> In twenty-five centuries . . . one thing has not changed in the slightest: the double rupture, which the form of the allegory, endlessly repeated, manages to maintain as radically as ever. . . . The genius of the model stems from the role played by a very small number of persons, the only ones capable of going back and forth between the two assemblies and converting the authority of the one into that of the other. Despite the fascination exercised by Ideas (even upon those who claim to be denouncing the idealism of the Platonic solution), it is not at all a question of opposing the shadow world to the real world, but of *redistributing powers* by inventing both a certain definition of Science and a certain definition of politics. Appearances notwithstanding, idealism is not what is at issue here. The myth of the Cave makes it possible to render all democracy impossible by neutralizing it; that is its only trump card. . . . On the one hand, we have the chattering of fictions; on the other, the silence of reality. The subtlety of this organization rests entirely on the power given to *those who can move back and forth between the houses.*[26]

As the vehicle of such ferrying, then, science amounts for Latour to a "speech prosthesis" that allows humans to give their constitutively fictional speech to constitutively mute reality. Crucially, Latour's solution to the problem thus defined is to pretend neither actually to speak directly for reality nor that all speech is equally corrupt; instead Latour advocates letting the medium of speech be felt as such, noticing the specific weight and texture of words as if they were more akin to speech impediments than prosthetic mouthpieces:

---

25. I consider Hegel's defense of comedy over tragedy as a vehicle of dialectical progress and, by extension, of the kind of pragmatic discourse Latour advocates, in "Hegel's Poetics of History: Tragic Repetition and Comic Recollection."
26. *Politics of Nature,* 11–14.

We shall say, then, that lab coats have invented *speech prostheses that allow nonhumans to participate in the discussions of humans, when humans become perplexed about the participation of new entities in collective life.* The formula is long, to be sure; it is clumsy and turgid; but we find ourselves in a situation where a speech impediment is preferable to an analytic clarity that would slice off mute things from speaking humans in a single stroke. Better to have marbles in one's mouth, when speaking about scientists, than to slip absentmindedly from mute things to the indisputable word of the expert.[27]

Part of the challenge we face in discussing climate change is that speaking on behalf of a beleaguered planet requires too much of our speech. A world, as Heidegger would say, is something we speak within, not about; the very coherence of claims to diagnose and remedy a sick planet presumes an extraplanetary perspective. The other part of the challenge we face is that even as we pretend to such impossibly transcendent meaning, ours is also the era of the exhaustion of humanistic purpose, in which science has lost much of its normative social authority; and since 9/11 ethical norms generally have been increasingly undermined by global corporate capitalism and the War on Terror.

This sense of having to mean too much just as our resources for meaning are running dry, is the double bind evoked by Hegel's discussion of democratic terror. The significance of Hegel's account of modern democracy in terms of the French Revolutionary Terror becomes clearer to us with each passing year. As we've seen, this terror is not analytically explicated by Hegel so much as aesthetically symptomatized in metaphors that liken bloodletting to drinking water, and beheading to cutting cabbages: metaphors that in our own age of pervasive indifference to drone warfare and apocalyptic climate change have achieved a level of legibility Hegel couldn't have anticipated. The seminal Romantic period theorist of such displacements—of the theatrical forms of economy and the economics of aesthetics—was Edmund Burke. On May 11, 1791, during parliamentary debate on the Quebec Government Bill, Charles James Fox argued that the House of Lords was indispensable to Britain's political economy: "Nor could any government be a fit one for British subjects to live under, which did not contain its due weight of aristocracy." Fox thought this weight requisite for maintaining "the proper poise of the constitution . . . the balance that equalized and meliorated the powers of the other two extreme branches, and gave stability and firmness to the whole."[28] No government may be "fitly" British, in other words, without the participation of the aristocracy on its own terms, anchoring a political economy that otherwise risked losing

---

27. Ibid., 67.
28. Fox is paraphrased in Cannon, *Aristocratic Century,* 64.

"propriety," "poise," "stability," and "firmness." What is at once incoherent and nonetheless perspicacious in Fox's picture is that it locates the source of the normative fitness of the political economy outside that economy: the ballast of aristocracy can anchor that economy only on the strength of its very indifference to it. This picture is incoherent because it begs the question of the standard by which aristocratic distinction is to be measured; arguably, aristocracy may be made to "fit" into a generalizable equation of political legitimacy or "fitness" only by effectively canceling the distinction that is supposed to define it or, in Adorno and Horkheimer's terms, by rendering aristocracy bourgeois: "Bourgeois society is ruled by equivalence. It makes the dissimilar comparable by reducing it to abstract quantities."[29]

It is in respect to this embarrassment that the subtle acuity of the political theory of Burke, Fox's former colleague among the New Whigs, is particularly evident. Burke develops Fox's question regarding the proper contents of representation into reflections on the methodology of representation itself and finally defends the institution of aristocracy less for conducing to normatively fit political representation than precisely for resisting such representation:

> Nothing is a due and adequate representation of a state, that does not represent its ability, as well as its property. But as ability is a vigorous and active principle, and as property is sluggish, inert, and timid, it never can be safe from the invasions of ability, unless it be, out of all proportion, predominant in the representation. It must be represented in great masses of accumulation, or it is not rightly protected. The characteristic essence of property, formed out of the combined principles of its acquisition and conservation, is to be *unequal*.[30]

Although Burke characterizes the aristocracy as "the ballast in the vessel of the commonwealth," he also asserts that the absolute weight of aristocratic distinction cannot be *equated* with the relatively disproportional weighting that the British government accords the House of Lords. On Burke's account, such distinction can be preserved only by emphasizing, not disguising, the paradoxical fact that aristocratic inertia always appears in solution with its antithetical "active principle": the principle of "vigor," transformation for transformation's sake, fungibility, and exchange. Hence Burke openly affirms that such distinction is fostered in a paradoxically *active* way by the normative customs of inheritance that "perpetuate our property in our families."[31] Burke

---

29. *Dialectic of Enlightenment*, 7.
30. *Reflections on the Revolution in France*, 51.
31. Ibid., 51ff.

argues on the one hand that the "essence of property is to be *unequal*," but on the other hand that that essence is perpetuated by customs of inheritance that try to establish standards by which this inherent inequality may be relativized and hence *equitably exchanged* from one generation to the next. By characterizing property with respect to customs of inheritance, Burke focuses precisely upon the point at which *proprietary claims* become questionable and thus blur the simple distinction between aristocratic inertia and entrepreneurial activity. Thus Burke's formulation tends to accentuate the normative problem that aristocratic distinction may not *secure* the legitimacy of a political economy, without vitiating itself, and so must somehow be made to bear upon the customs by means of which it is represented and must palpably impinge upon the entrepreneurial "activeness" of representational practices generally.

Burke thus demonstrates a sensitivity to the dialectical intricacy of the problem of reification—and arguably even accomplishes a robust critical intervention—that too often eludes us centuries later. Our contemporary understanding of the term *reification* is rooted in Georg Lukács's Burkean insistence that its constitutive feature is that it is a universal rather than particular phenomenon: "where the commodity is universal it manifests itself differently from the commodity as a particular, isolated, non-dominant phenomenon."[32] Yet too often reification's baleful effects, and the values that justify counting them as baleful, have been determined in Fox's manner by criteria supposedly external to the context of reification itself. This is not a matter of failing to historicize so much as a failure to metahistoricize: what makes the reified world reified is in part that it is always already self-historicizing, viewing itself as historically contingent configuration or, as James Chandler has argued, "case." On Chandler's account, modern, Post-Romantic historiography acknowledges its dependence upon the reification it uncovers, and hence upon the "reversibility of the driving force and the driven object, vested interest and vehicle, motive and medium, norm and fact."[33] Asserting such reversibility makes historiography a matter neither of reducing historical particulars to general forces nor of enumerating them in their sheer contingency, but of finding the contingent, material particular sharing a dialectically charged intimacy with its abstract, reified counterpart. Just as reification has increased the abstraction of modern normative experience, it has proportionately increased the apparent concreteness and singularity of what defies the norm, the accidental or transgressive. Yet registering the latter requires a certain complicity in the reification it disrupts, or what Bill Brown following Arjun Appadurai has advocated as "*methodological* fetishism."[34]

---

32. *History and Class Consciousness*, 85.
33. "Moving Accidents," 170.
34. "Thing Theory," 6; cf. Appadurai, "Introduction," 5.

Burke's text uses such fetishism as a kind of allegory for the proprietary inertia that by his own account he cannot represent. Thus when Burke figures the sack of Versailles as a rape of the queen, for instance, the over-the-top rhetorical gesture is difficult to assess or weigh in the balance between the principles of enterprise and inertia. The function of injecting fiction and stylistic extravagance into his political analysis is of a piece with the function of the most remarkable formal feature of Burke's letter: the fact that it *is* a letter, an ostensibly private as opposed to public correspondence. The intended import or "weight" of Burke's *Reflections* is correlated precisely with its privacy, its rejection of public representation. Correspondingly, Mary Wollstonecraft qualifies her devastating critique of the *Reflections* by "separat[ing Burke's] public from [his] private character" and "discover[ing] . . . extenuating circumstances in the very *texture of [his] mind.*"[35] This notion of an authorial eccentricity that is irreducible to its text, and yet that, *for just this reason,* somewhat exonerates or legitimates that text, constitutes a model in its own right of the paradox at the heart of aristocratic distinction: its *functional* disequilibrium, "sluggish" resistance of transparency, refusal to equate, becomes effectively equivalent, even in the hands of a critic as acutely skeptical as Wollstonecraft, to singularly self-justifying "texture." Burke doesn't explain but allegorizes the gravitational pull to which his hysterical fantasies of the queen's rape respond, likening her to his "morning star."[36] Susan Wolfson correspondingly identifies the object of Wollstonecraft's critique as Burke's susceptibility precisely to a gravitational or magnetic pull from beyond the public activity of explicit rational explication: "The problem with Burke's glittering morning-star was . . . the magnetic adulation that corrupts the rational sphere of public life."[37] Hence Wollstonecraft effectively turns Burke's gendered contrast between the sublime and beautiful against him, faulting Burke for allowing this feminizing susceptibility to pull him from the discursive orbit of masculine rationality, or, as I will suggest, for putting this susceptibility *into discursive circulation,* giving this magnetic pull a certain cultural currency despite its constitutive resistance to the activity of rational reconstruction. This dialectical tension gives a performative dimension to Burke's economistic formulation, and a progressivism to his conservatism. Burke thus emblematizes Romanticism per se, which was basically a conservative movement that was made radically progressive or even revolutionary by the honesty with which exposed the impotence of its conservatism without taking this as a reason to renounce it.

The methodological fetishism that Brown and Chandler invoke is retraceable to Walter Benjamin, whose reading of Proustian memory, for instance,

---

35. *Vindication of the Rights of Men,* 14.
36. Burke, *Reflections on the Revolution in France.*
37. *Borderlines,* 9.

suggests that fetishizing contingency has become a kind of ethical imperative: such fetishism sacrifices the coherence of narrative and self but thereby restores *historical experience* in the form of the chance encounter which such incoherence makes possible. In Proust it is "a matter of chance whether an individual forms an image of himself, whether he can take hold of his experience." But this dissolution of experience to random chance is precisely what makes it potentially qualify as genuinely historical in the modern context in which "the shock experience has become the norm."[38] Proust "bears the marks of the situation which gave rise to it; it is part of the inventory of the individual who is isolated in many ways" and "increasingly unable to assimilate the data of the world around him by way of experience."[39] So if grasping historical reality directly is no longer possible, a "methodological fetishism" would proceed to expose the illusions of commodity fetishism by somewhat sacrificially submitting to it in order to redeem experience as the "shock experience" that ensues when the illusion founders against historical contingencies. Thus, as Brown suggests, the fetish-thing indirectly refracts historical reality: "a kind of fetishism that seems like an alternative mode of inhabiting modern culture . . . by consecrating the valueless material object, . . . confounds political economy's account of value, alienates itself from any enlightenment horror of waste, and settles happily into an unhuman (not anithumanist) history."[40]

What would the organizing principle of such a history be? How would the valueless objects it consecrates be kept from dispersing randomly? In his brief remarks on "Dream Kitsch" Walter Benjamin addresses fetishism by evoking the especially pregnant materiality that currency assumes once it becomes obsolete and loses monetary value.

> Technology consigns the outer image of things to a long farewell, like banknotes that are bound to lose their value. It is then that the hand retrieves this outer cast in dreams and, even as they are slipping away, makes contact with familiar contours. It catches hold of objects at their most threadbare and timeworn point. . . . It is the side worn through by habit and garnished with cheap maxims. The side which things turn toward the dream is kitsch.[41]

This account hinges on a Burkean dialectic: if currency is the consummate example of the way in which the commodity fetish makes material particularity into a cipher for abstract value, once that currency loses such value and can no

---

38. *Illuminations*, 168
39. Ibid., 158ff.
40. "The Secret Life of Things," 402ff.
41. *The Work of Art*, 236.

longer legitimately circulate, the currency's material form is, on the one hand, emancipated from its economic function even as, on the other hand, it remains impossible to apprehend other than in terms of economic functionality. Like the inertia Burke's text both describes and embodies, Benjamin accesses the obsolete currency's singular materiality not as something that cannot be grasped beyond economy except in the latter's own inexorable, spectral returns.

The poetic innovations of William Wordsworth pivotally draw on this paradoxical nexus between the sluggishness of Burkean property, whose value if anything is too weighty to be measured, and Benjamin's wasted bills whose only weight is the insistence of ghostly aesthetic forms lacking actual value. Wordsworth's official praise of Burke in *The Prelude* casts the latter's defense of hallowed traditions and inbred allegiances as "admonishing" and "exploding" the pretensions of upstart theory and insipid oratory, unsanctioned by and unrooted in inherited property.[42] But *The Prelude*'s deeper debt to Burke emerges at moments when Wordsworth acknowledges that such admonishment does not issue from a center of moral gravity beyond the insipid play of modern discourse and commerce but is issued *by* such discourse *upon itself* in the compulsive recoils through which discursive and commercial economy perpetually re-imposes itself. If Burke claimed that the inertia of tradition constitutes the "ballast" keeping the "vessel of the commonwealth" erect, then Wordsworth in turn suggests that it is precisely the experience of *losing* touch with this anchoring moral compass that finally allows him to register the full force of Burkean weight. Anticipating Baudelaire's description of Parisian crowds, Wordsworth describes losing himself in an urban scene so thoroughly invaded by representational activity that the scene is virtually reconstituted as a parade of reifications, a Benjaminian arcade:

> How often in the overflowing streets
> Have I gone forwards with the crowd, and said
> Unto myself, 'The face of every one
> That passes by me is a mystery.'
> Thus have I looked, nor ceased to look, oppressed
> By thoughts of what, and whither, when and how,
> Until the shapes before my eyes became
> A second-sight procession, such as glides
> Over still mountains, or appears in dreams,
> And all the ballast of familiar life—
> The present, and the past, hope, fear, all stays,

---

42. *The Fourteen-Book Prelude*, lines 512–72.

> All laws of acting, thinking, speaking man—
> Went from me, neither knowing me, nor known.
> And once, far travelled in such mood, beyond
> The reach of common indications, lost
> Amid the moving pageant, 'twas my chance
> Abruptly to be smitten with the view
> Of a blind beggar, who, with upright face,
> Stood propped against a wall, upon his chest
> Wearing a written paper, to explain
> The story of the man, and who he was.
> My mind did at this spectacle turn round
> As with the might of waters, and it seemed
> To me that in this label was a type
> Or emblem of the utmost that we know
> Both of ourselves and of the universe . . .[43]

This instance of the signature Wordsworthian experience—of being, as he puts it in "Resolution and Independence" and in *The Prelude*'s earlier boat-stealing episode, "admonished" from "some far region,"[44]—is distinguished from those other instances by the fact that the mediator of the admonishment and overwhelming Burkean weight, "the might of waters," is not some radically exotic "other"—some sublime crag or leech gatherer—on the contrary, the *all too* accessible, too transparently *legible* "label." What's crucial to recognize is that Wordsworth does not hereby foreswear or diminish but radicalizes the experience of Burkean weight: radicalizes because this weight is liberated even from Burke's relatively minimal attempts to explain and legitimize it in terms of the wisdom and enchantment of inherited custom. Here such weight presses upon Wordsworth *because* it lacks any cause he recognizes; what presses him is the recognition of the unavoidable inadequacy of the words or labels by which we perpetually attempt to legitimate such empathy to ourselves. Wordsworth recognizes that the experience of empathy is a radically disarming experience of discursive impotence, of being exposed to pressures one cannot resist but also cannot domesticate, legitimate, and reiterate in one's own terms.

Reduction of language to its barest rudiments—to talk, for instance, of "the life of things" and "the spirit in the woods"—is a feature of Wordsworthian poetics so familiar that it is difficult to read otherwise than as its own caricature. But Wordsworth's casting of the label here as the utmost that we know gives this poetics of complacency a radical turn, contending that such self-reification is inevitable: not precious or profound simplicity but inert,

---

43. *The Thirteen-Book Prelude,* lines 597–622.
44. "Resolution and Independence," *The Major Works,* lines 118–19.

compulsive necessity. Wordsworth would awaken us to the weight or compulsion of the label form *as such*. Wordsworth's minimalist turns of phrase are susceptible to caricature just to the extent that they pretend to exhibit an elegiac pathos, as in the conclusion of "Nutting" where the poet's talk of "the spirit in the woods" clearly pretends to represent the poet's guilt at having violated that spirit. But the label's weight stems not from anything beyond it but from precisely the fact that there is nothing beyond it. Vernacular "blind and mechanical habit" in fact served Wordsworth less as a vehicle of transcendence or knowledge than as ideologically depleted yet socially shared material, like the blind beggar's "label" or Shelley's "mask," with which to improvise postindividual forms of subjectivity. Thus while the sunset at the end of the "Intimations Ode" evokes the same self-deconstructing imagination that had alienated the poet from nature, the poet undermines this symbolic re-integration by the very act of calling it "another palm" in "another race." Like a stutter, the compound redundancy of these terms undoes this re-integration from within. The breakdown of the modern poetic act per se is dramatized; it is not analytically diagnosed but engaged as a practical problem, involving readers themselves in the project of *figuring* "the shock of the new" rather than merely suffering or suppressing it. This is not a project to translate shock into knowledge but to weave this gap itself into the texture of a new Wittgensteinian form of life that supplants, even while incorporating defunct vestiges of, McGann's "romantic ideology." Frank Kermode describes Wordsworthian poetics as a kind of disciplinary rehearsal and reminder of poetic impotence, "confronting the mystery of poverty" not by representing its attendant suffering but precisely by failing to do so, offering instead "a confrontation without communication, setting the word against the word."[45] Hence the label is the medium not of a tragic wisdom beyond it but of the comic wisdom precisely that there is nothing beyond it except other labels. Worldly poverty is not represented so much as performatively allegorized as the poverty of poetry, just as Burke arguably pays the most powerful homage to the weight of monarchy by allowing his theoretical defense to give way to hysterical melodrama. What both examples suggest is that Romanticism's "methodological fetishism" does not represent a retreat from but radicalization of enlightenment skepticism.

## THE COMEDY OF MODERN ETHICAL LIFE

The first part of this chapter considered Shelley's "To Wordsworth" as a radical parody disguised as elegy, playing with Wordsworthian language to the point

---

45. *The Sense of an Ending*, 171.

of mocking the very pretense to elegiac feeling. But the above readings of Wordsworth aimed to suggest that Wordsworth parodied himself in a similar way, and hence that Shelley's sonnet functions less to debunk Wordsworthian pretention—subjecting it to a determinate tragic reversal and recognition—but more to emulate a certain style, perpetuates that rhythm of superficial remnants. Hegel's metaphors of exhaustion and disenchantment enact the terrorizing dark side of modern democracy's bright promise and make history articulate not by explaining it into objective indifference but by making its music available for subjective resonance (admittedly in a typically modernist, dissonant register). Likewise, Wordsworth's bitter early sonnet, "The World Is Too Much with Us," mobilizes what the concluding chapter of this book describes as the vital potential for literary practice implicit in consumerist ideology.

> The world is too much with us; late and soon,
> Getting and spending, we lay waste our powers;—
> Little we see in Nature that is ours;
> We have given our hearts away, a sordid boon!
> This Sea that bares her bosom to the moon;
> The winds that will be howling at all hours,
> And are up-gathered now like sleeping flowers;
> For this, for everything, we are out of tune;
> It moves us not. Great God! I'd rather be
> A Pagan suckled in a creed outworn;
> So might I, standing on this pleasant lea,
> Have glimpses that would make me less forlorn;
> Have sight of Proteus rising from the sea;
> Or hear old Triton blow his wreathèd horn.
> (12–16)

A great feature of the poem is the way in which its redundancies act out the same frustration they would articulate. Not unlike the hysterics into which we find ourselves unwittingly forced when discussing political responses to climate change, Wordsworth is bombastic in his denunciation of bombast. How could we be conceivably taught, what language would be suited to instruct us, that, as Naomi Klein proclaims, *everything is changed*? What language could deliver Clive Hamilton's requiem for our species? Invariably, such prospects leave us, like Wordsworth, just stamping our feet and repeating that we are "out of tune," that "nature is not ours." But doing so only exemplifies and exacerbates the problem, since the problem is just this relationship of owning and hence buying: "getting and spending." Wordsworth wants somehow to get back to, reclaim ownership of, a condition opposed to that of getting and claiming ownership. If this is the impasse laid out by the opening octave, it is especially remarkable that the concluding sestet doesn't resolve but reiterates it. But it is a repetition with a difference. For the conclusion crucially elaborates the inescapability of possessive individualism by refining it from an impotent tantrum, a blunt and opaque repetition compulsion, to an at least formally differentiated grammar. In respect to its content, by contrast, the impasse of possessive individualism is only exacerbated by the conclusion's recourse to the subjunctive formulation, "I would rather . . . ," extending the impasse into the realm of the hypothetical. Possessive individualism preemptively structures the poet's very capacity to conceive solutions: the imagination itself, the vaunted organ of Romantic critique and emancipation, has itself been colonized by the logic of consumerist preference. Yet this redoubled failure creates, as if inadvertently, in consequence of its very excessiveness, a relatively autonomous, formal poetic dynamic of its own. Proteus surging from the sea and Triton blowing his horn rehearse Wordsworth's signature, two-step aesthetic of impulsive overflow recollected to a tempering rhythm or music.

What's remarkable here though is that the overflow and tempering music alike have been framed as constitutive symptoms of the same "savage topor" of modern consumerism that Wordsworth denounces: compulsive hungering after insipid sensation. Framed as a compulsive reflex of consumerist imagination, Wordsworth's sonnet ends as a kind of radical self-parody. In contrast to Wordsworth's signature works of self-poeticizing, like "Tintern Abbey" or *The Prelude,* this parody makes no demands on the poet's sister or friend or the rest of us to recognize, or in other words, *to buy,* the poet's claim to self-authorship. By mocking its own claim to meaning, framing it as an inadvertent and pathological compulsion, Wordsworth, despite himself, arguably demonstrates how to mean less, to consume less meaning, and thereby to address our world loss without pretending to mean more than such loss allows. The sonnet thus implicitly succeeds in comic mode where it ostensibly tragically fails. Overtly, it self-pityingly laments the impossibility of returning to the pagan "crede outworn" of myth populated by Proteus and Triton: the kind of unvarying schematic identities that characterize what Levi-Strauss termed "cold" culture, culture that endlessly rehearses certain mythological identities and scenarios, indifferent to the distinctions among individuals and generations that obsess "hot" cultures like Western modernity (and that the compulsive, neurotic narcissism of Wordsworth's sonnet so brilliantly dramatizes). In contrast to hot consumption of difference, ticking off what Hegel termed the "bad infinity" of chronological time, such lyric rehearsal of referentially opaque formal patterns recalls Levi-Strauss's cold temporality as well as Bergson's *longue durée*, even as it also vividly models the kind of extreme egalitarianism theorized by many contemporary political theorists of radical democracy. Jacques Rancière, for instance, characterizes the latter as "a new stage of equality"—the pun on stage significantly deflecting the *norm* of historical progress to the *form* of theatricality—a stage where the "different kinds of performances would be translated into one another . . . linking what one knows with what one does not know, of being at the same time performers who display their competences and visitors or spectators who are looking for what those competences may produce in a new context."[46] This pattern does not altogether displace the concern for representational content; rather it is a pattern precisely *of* displacements of the concern for such content. As in Wordsworth's self-parody, Rancière's new stage of equality remains dialectically dependent upon the mystifications of power and knowledge that they would dispel.

In their introduction to the new *Cambridge Companion to British Romantic Poetry*, Maureen McLane and James Chandler likewise consider Wordsworth's "The World Is Too Much with Us" as an exemplary instance of the class of texts their book surveys, and they do so on the same grounds I've tried to develop here. The sonnet, they explain, sets two different poetic functions in juxtaposition without resolving to one or the other. In the manner of Ricoeur's double guile and Brown's methodological fetishism, the poem on the one hand laments what Lowie and Sayre term an *exile* from history—from the event or action as such—that it is powerless adequately to represent and contain, while on the other hand it also acknowledges that it can do so only by way of the Romantic ideology, by mystifying history in the signature manner of modern consumerism. Moreover, McLane and Chandler suggest that it is precisely this juxtaposition of poetic functions—between poetry in opposition to history, standing alongside a reality it cannot represent, and poetry *as* history, demonstrating what historicity is by allegorizing precisely this representational impossibility—that makes British Romantic poetry *warrant* a "Companion" like theirs. This is to reiterate the chiasmus of literature and history with which this chapter begins: the discussion of Peterloo, but on a metaliterary level: Wordsworth's sonnet is the exemplary instance demonstrating that the class of British Romantic poetry qualifies as the kind of literary category that warrants a Companion.

---

46. Ranciere, *Emancipated Spectator,* 22.

It is fair to say that, had this Companion been published a decade ago, in the late 1990's, the claims for the distinctiveness of a Companion of "Romantic Poetry" (much less a "British Romantic Poetry") would perhaps have been less evident. But over the course of the last decade . . . there have been a number of efforts to return to poetry and poetics in the period. . . . They suggest something on the horizon that, though not yet quite distinct, may move us in a new direction over the coming decades. What that direction might be is not easy to say, but, as a very rough stab at the problem, we speculate that poetry may reassert itself within Romanticism in either of two ways: either as a principle of indeterminate form or in multiple relations to other domains. We may think of this as the difference between "poetry as . . ." and "poetry and . . . ."[47]

Above I suggest that Wordsworth's sonnet anticipates the radical ironies of Shelley's "To Wordsworth" in a way that allows the latter to work as a kind of mock elegy formally affirming the persistence of what it ostensibly mourns. Shelley's sonnet then makes us see how both poems deploy Ricoeur's "double guile" to frame Romantic ideology—the sense of exile from the present and idealization of the past—as a "discipline of necessity," necessary in its very impossibility, a discipline devoted, in eminently Wordsworthian fashion, to the texture of language, to working and being worked by words—in other words, to use Romanticism's conceit of exile to establish a home on the much more modest, fragile ground provided by that conceit's recycled remnants. If the beautiful soul is an impossible fantasy, and its ideological perpetuation necessitates an array of discursive tools, then, as Hegel showed, such necessity invites subversion and critique to show that such tools might work otherwise. If the ultimate aim of work is its liberation from any master or master purpose, then, paradoxically, this end may be purposed only by compulsive, involuntary engagement of those contingent circumstances that mastery depends on suppressing. It is in and by such work that Shelley and Wordsworth alike can be seen to return not just from historical exile in the past but also from social exile as supposed individuals, agents of single, proprietary voices, and instead to work and be worked by language conjointly.

McLane and Chandler, however, seem to discern in Wordsworth's sonnet a rather articulate metapoetic proposition, and an exceptionally audacious one at that. They seem to read the sonnet as delineating the two alternative future directions Romanticism might take going forward from *now*, describ-

---

47. *The Cambridge Companion to British Romantic Poetry*, 5.

ing what is just beyond *our* horizon today. These alternatives are coded by Wordsworth in the figures of Poseidon's sons, Proteus and Triton. Wordsworth acknowledges that the "crede" that gave reality to such figures is "outworn." Yet McLane and Chandler remark

> how interesting that he frames his wish to reinhabit this creed in terms of alternative siblings. . . . Proteus, or "first born," is Poseidon's eldest, son, but he is illegitimate. Triton is Poseidon's only legitimate son. Proteus responds to the world by assuming innumerable forms, thus remaining elusive to capture . . . the artist who enacts in his person the mimesis by which his art is constituted. . . . Proteus, we might say, embodies Shelley's polemically elastic conception of poetry as any great imaginative achievement, any triumph of *poiesis* as *making*. . . . Triton, committed to his one powerful instrument, figures what Shelley called (in that same essay) "poetry in a more restricted sense," that is, metrical language.[48]

If, as I suggested, Shelley's sonnet enacts the same necessary but impossible relation to language that Wordsworth's sonnet rehearses, then this is to say that Shelley affirms a kind of common "cause" in that shared linguistic/existential predicament: the common cause precisely of the necessary impossibility of designating narrative causes. But McLane and Chandler seem to read Wordsworth as identifying just such narrative causes, the alternative destinies—poetry as "either" radically formalist "or" simply musical language put in "relations to other domains"—laid out like a signpost: in one direction, poetry will be classified and understood in terms of one concept; in the other direction, a different concept. Thus the basic elements of McGann's Romantic ideology are neatly in place: reading the Romantics as our contemporaries by stipulating a common ground that transcends history, the abstract, conceptual domain of such narrative causes.

Whereas I read Wordsworth by way of Shelley to show how the Romantic ideology may be ironized to subvert its exile from history and beautiful soul isolation, McLane and Chandler read Wordsworth through Shelley as expounding an abstract literary historical scheme. Irony evidently plays an important role in their reading here, an irony I've postponed addressing in hopes of underscoring that the theoretical issues at stake here—formalism vs. historicism—are hardly risible. As the editors themselves say, much of what their *Companion* offers readers hinges on how its contents engage this theoretical dilemma: "The essays in this volume explore what we are provision-

---

48. Ibid., 6.

ally calling the 'Protean' and 'Tritonian' aspects of poetry. Many essays here follow the Romantics themselves by troubling the border between 'poetry as' and 'poetry and.' . . . This doubleness—poetry-in-itself v. poetry-for-itself and beyond-itself—is written into Romantic aspiration and into the essays here gathered."[49] Thus the editors' "specula[tion] that poetry may reassert itself within Romanticism in either of two ways" is replaced, two pages later, by assurance that it has already done so in both ways at once, or, more precisely, it has done so because this "doubleness" and "troubled boundary" are "written into" our own writing. The editors' introduction concludes by amplifying this view, suggesting that although Romantic poetry may count as a historical phenomenon whose comings and goings may be conjectured and schematized, it is first and foremost the very condition of the possibility of reading, here and now: "Romantic poetry, however deeply rooted in its historical and cultural moment, also remains 'ever more about to be,' in Wordsworth's phrase—ever ready to be reactivated and reimagined by the latest reader."[50] The Romantic ideology could hardly be espoused more nakedly: Wordsworth and the reader are one in their common exile from the present, transported by the magic of Wordsworth's timeless language. Yet the editors' ironic frame of this espousal sensitizes readers to this nakedness itself, revealing this ideology as a kind of "discipline of necessity." As in Shelley's sonnet's pastiche of Wordsworth, the very language of the editors' sentence *betrays* their ostensible overarching narrative according to which Romantic poetry might eventually return by either of two ways. This self-betrayal is identical to Shelley's insofar as both make the very legibility of Wordsworth's language attest to the effective reality, the actuality of something both ostensibly deny. This is the actuality of, again, that irreducible imbrication of language and history. As in Shelley's sonnet, though, irony has submitted this imbrication to crucial deflation: the editors' self-contradiction leaves us to grapple with the naked, contingent force of the words themselves rather than inviting us to grasp them as emblematic of (the triumph of) either a formalist or a historicist poetics.

The editors' ironic framing is most elegantly manifest in the way they initially introduce their decoding of Wordsworth's sonnet's inchoate theory of Romanticism's alternative destinies. After acknowledging the aspect of the sonnet on which my reading focused—its insistence on its own radical historical and discursive alienation, its incapacity just to *be* in history, let alone to represent such experience or, for that matter, to prophesy the alternative destinies of Romanticism centuries hence—the editors remark, as if in after-

---

49. Ibid., 6ff.
50. Ibid., 8.

thought, "But how interesting that he frames his wish to reinhabit this creed in terms of alternative siblings." How interesting indeed. How interesting it is, in turn, to "speculate" upon the alternative master concepts under which Romantic poetry might be theoretically rehabilitated. Rather than the idiom of authoritative literary historical analysis, the editors deploy the idiom of characters out of a Henry James novel. The editors couch the question of this normative rehabilitation in the same kind of implicitly normatively *depleted* language in which Shelley couches the avowed political concerns of his elegy: depleted in the same sense of registering subjection or enslavement to the kind of radical contingency that characterizes modernity and that makes pronouncements of any kind of normative value supposed to exceed idle, passing "interest" appear like remnants of an "outworn creed."

In other words, the editors deploy the sense of "interesting" defined by Sianne Ngai as a distinctly modern although (but also *because of*) minimal standard of aesthetic worth, minimal because the interesting designates normative value without pretending to transcend the *work* of negotiating modernity's irreducible contingency. To say that its normative status is minor is to say that, like Hegel's slave labor, it gives this contingency a relative, not absolute, normative organization. In contrast to traditional, major, or masterful categories of aesthetic value, the interesting does not disguise its own contingency, the fact that is *a symptom of* this same radical contingency that it also, nevertheless, would normatively evaluate and differentiate. The reason is that the interesting is a norm of and for the subjective experience of negotiating contingency; its normative significance would be lost altogether if it were supposed to transcend or dispel this contingency, to penetrate through to the object as such and represent a property that abided regardless of accidents of subjective perspective. "It is precisely this tension between individual and system that undergirds the interesting," Ngai writes, and makes it such an apt norm for gauging "the modern relation between individuation and standardization" and "exploring the tension between 'existence and doctrine' by staging various clashing between perceptual and conceptual systems." Ngai quotes Mikhail Epstein to the effect that "the judgment of 'interesting' is thus an effort to 'bridge the gap between reason and surprise, at once rationalizing the improbable and extending the limits of rationality.'"[51] Like Benjamin's "experience for which the shock experience has become the norm," the interesting has the same paradoxical or chiastic structure that we've been pursuing throughout this chapter and that Hegel's account of slave labor would explain: a norm *of* contingency itself, a norm without which the experience of radi-

---

51. *Our Aesthetic Categories*, 7.

cal individuality, accident, and shock would not be communicable. This is a norm, then, that counterintuitively makes the world *more complex* because it normalizes experiences of contingency to which we otherwise lack discursive access. It does not dilute and homogenize some supposedly pregiven supply of radical accidents, reducing a chaotic throng of particulars to a common standard, but gives this otherwise elusive background noise discursive recognition, makes it sharable *in and as* radical contingency. As a norm it is a mask: it does not communicate this particularity itself but covers it over. However, doing so makes tangible what we otherwise know only very abstractly. That is, again, it is a norm not of mastering power but of fragility and susceptibility: what it masks is our radical impotence to master contingency; it masks precisely the depth of our need for masks. It is the distinct kind of mask that, like the nesting doll, is constituted by the way in which it echoes beyond itself, reflecting this indigence in the rhythm of its returns. Hence what Ngai terms "the link between interest and risk":

> This risk comes from a radical receptiveness to otherness that modifies the self and, as Latour might say, overtakes it or makes it deviate from its original course of action (For Latour, the writing of "interesting" or "risky" sociological accounts—the two adjectives are used synonymously—must therefore entail paying close attention to the ways in which agency is "other-taken").[52]

In turn, by offering their analysis not just of Wordsworth's sonnet but of the current state and probable destinies of Romantic poetry under the rubric of the interesting, McLane and Chandler offer such a risky account of Romanticism, repackage canonical Romanticism, and recommend it on a risky basis of mere interest. They show how the Romantic ideology can serve to recognize and communicate such indigence rather than mystified forms of mastery and power, presenting a Romanticism not of potency but of impotence. To present that domain of works under the aegis of the interesting is to subvert its supposed canonicity. In place of the implicitly transcendent law underwriting canonical Romanticism, the editors offer that Jamesian gesture, "But how interesting . . . ," a gesture that exercises whatever normative force it does not by pretending to master contingency, like a law, but by attesting to the abiding need for norms in spite of contingency's irreducibility. To assert such a norm is not to invoke an authorizing power but, on the contrary, to test how much might be communicated without such ulterior authorization, how much fragility and indigence our communication can bear, how much, finally, we

---

52. Ibid., 137.

can bear to communicate our sheer need to communicate. So by reframing Romanticism's canonicity as its interest, the editors ask of themselves and of us what James asks of *The Portrait of a Lady*'s protagonist Isabel Archer: whether, in Ngai's terms, "such a 'frail vessel' can be strong enough to hold up the genre's heavy architecture."

But this just returns us to the Romantic ideology because there is no way definitively to answer the question; just as McLane and Chandler say, there are only ever new readings that will either corroborate their assessment of Romanticism's interest or not. What's crucial though is that, under the aegis of interest, these corroborating echoes do not assimilate readers to a transcendent law or beautiful soul but communicate a virtually unbearable bereavement thereof. Which returns us in turn to the gambit of Shelley's elegy, testing whether its narrative of loss might mobilize the deplorable depletion of the discourse of loss itself as a new means or norm of social connection. In the absence of transcendent authorization, the risk of such placing such a wager is matched by the risk of accepting it; what's normatively communicated and affirmed is principally the form itself of such risk. Like Shelley himself, McLane and Chandler make their dependence on Wordsworth's words an index of their own scholarly words' depletion, fragility, and risk. What such minor aesthetic categories lack in normative authority they repay in the concrete detail and intimacy of the social bonds they forge. As a reflection not of power but of impotence, not of mastery of but need, we cling to Wordsworth's words so compulsively and consumingly that Latour aptly calls it being "other-taken." It is just as such an "other-taking" that McLane and Chandler offer their "companion" to Romantic poetry: their authoritative guide would deprive readers of any pretention to authoritative reading and expose them instead to a compulsive attachment to the words themselves, the shareable, "companionable," masks of our common contingency. Underscoring this, the editors cite Bob Perelman's "Fake Dream," a poem about a how a couple's plans to have sex in a library are sidetracked when the poet notices a book of Wordsworth's and, in a virtual parody of the editors' own schematic analysis, begins compulsively reflecting upon the interplay between "poetry as . . ." and "poetry and . . .":

January 28: We were going to
have sex in the stacks. We

were in the 800s, standing eagerly
amid the old copies of the

Romantics. Looking at the dark blue
spines of Wordsworth's *Collected*, I thought

how the intensity of his need
to express his unplaced social being

in sentences had produced publicly verifiable
beauty so that his subsequent civic

aspirations seemed to have importance enough
for him to become Poet Laureate . . .[53]

The poet and society, the poet as society, and each of these both *in* this poem and *as* this poem: unplaced social being is sustained by its perpetual dis- and re-placement, from Wordsworth's poems to his laureateship to his place in the 800s, the place where plans for sex got misplaced only to be re-placed here in this poem, whose place might also be in the 800s, or not? Does this poem belong among the Romantics? Are they companions? Are we companions? As we saw, the high romance of Wordsworth's social concern, on the one hand, and his betrayal of this for the sake of social prestige, on the other, is the dual focus of Shelley's sonnet. The fact that this, and the analogously high romance entailed by dangerous sex, might boil down to questions about the requirements of the Dewey Decimal Classification system, perfectly exemplifies the discursive depletion Shelley's sonnet models, as well as its social contagiousness. The ideologically *inflated* fantasy of "sex in the stacks" is replaced by the deflated but compulsive interest of rehearsing this and/as chiasmus. Ultimately, however, the point is precisely that the fragile companionship established thereby just is what eros amounts to in the strict sense of forging social bonds, forging the first-person plural without which the Romantic fantasy of sex in the stacks could not be ineffectually entertained, nor could Ngai's minor aesthetic categories, by embracing just such ineffectuality, be "ours."

Nietzsche's Zarathustra heroically claims to descend from his mountain and rejoin stupefied society out of love for humankind only subsequently to deny that any act can be so neatly characterized and contained: "one thing is the thought, another thing is the deed, and another thing is the idea of the deed. The wheel of causality doth not roll between them." Zarathustra claims to act out of love for the crowd only then to splinter that claim into a series of discrete fragments, disambiguating the act from intention and memory. This self-sacrifice of the beautiful soul fantasy of personal integrity makes the form itself of this splintering available for salvaging and repurposing as an allegory of the motley crowd itself, an image in which the crowd might find itself reflected, through which it might begin to exercise its own proper kind

---

53. Perelman, xiv.

of perspective and voice. If the first-person plural may identify with neither a discrete act nor a representation of an act, if it is thus obscured by such identifications, then actual emancipation must resign to the inevitability of (or enslavement to) such misidentification in order to build upon (or work) the vestiges of such failure. The collective coalesces as discrete failures of identification coalesce into to a loosely, "minimally" integrated rhetorical series or pattern. The modern "we" just names this endless coalescence, or, precisely, companionability. Less tragically, heroically erotic than humbly, comically lovable, we perpetually salvage companionability from the vestiges of the failures of the impossible we's that we can't keep ourselves from fantasizing. The queer excess of the labor we undertake to bear our enslavement to our own impossibility mediates companionship, supplies the vectors through which companionability spreads, through which companionability is realized just *as* this spreading. Hence companionability amounts to a wager to *read itself as such*, to affirm readability, communicability, where it otherwise seems lacking. British Romantic lyric pioneered this distinctly modern, supremely fragile, and complex coordination of literacy and ethical agency. The following chapters trace how it did so and thereby also perpetuate this work.

CHAPTER 2

# Blake's Infant Smile

*Facing Materialism*

I

WILLIAM BLAKE and Sigmund Freud represent aptly incongruous bookends of the long nineteenth-century hegemony of the bourgeois subject. Whereas Freud's critique involves a radicalization of materialism, Blake defends visionary imagination precisely against the materialism of John Locke. Yet the two are not as incompatible as this contrast would suggest because both proceed less by propounding either materialism or visionary imagination per se than by rehearsing the respective dialectical processes through which these principles eat away at the illusory coherence of the atomic, bourgeois subject.

Saree Makdisi has written that "it was in the context of the revolutionary wars of the 1790s—which are often taken to mark the beginning of the 'long' nineteenth century—that Blake produced his own seemingly forgotten warning against the political, economic, cultural and psychical centralization that would necessarily accompany the bourgeois domination of both self and others."[1] In turn, in *Beyond the Pleasure Principle* (hereafter *BBP*), Freud postulates the "death drive" in an attempt to explain the repetitious traumatic war neurosis he witnesses in the wake of WWI. That trauma marks the point at which the dominant nineteenth-century model of individualistic subjectivity

---

1. *William Blake and the Impossible History of the 1790s,* hereafter *WBIH,* 6.

finally ceded to the twentieth century's signature, self-consciously and programmatically modern*ist* deconstructions of this model. According to Paul Ricoeur, it was Freud's dethroning of the bourgeois self that consummated this modernist "hermeneutics of suspicion"; but it is for just this reason that Ricoeur's construal of this consummation as a kind of "mastery" seems misguided.[2] The paradox of claiming mastery over the destruction of subjective autonomy generally is deeply characteristic of the modernism Freud ushered in, which pretended not just to expose the obsolescence of bourgeois subjectivity but thereby also to diagnose it in terms of larger extrapersonal structures of reality (from the forerunners to Freud's unconscious—Marxian class and Nietzschean genealogy—to Woolf's streaming consciousness, the mythology of Eliot and Joyce, Heidegger's history of metaphysics, Foucauldian archaeology, and so on).

Makdisi emphasizes that whereas commentators on Blake's politics have tended to lump it in with that of the dominant, Painite radical movement of the 1790s, in fact the latter is founded on the Lockean principle of possessive individual sovereignty which "is profoundly destabilized and rendered inoperative in Blake's work of the same decade" (*WBIH* 5). The agent of Blakean destabilization and incapacitation, according to Makdisi, is *desire,* a term that would become no less pivotal for Freud (or, for that matter, for the postmodernists like Lacan who sought a clean break with the system-building he thought Freud epitomized only thereby to earn the title of "the *absolute* master"[3]). As Makdisi writes, "Blake can be seen to locate the foundation of both his aesthetics and his politics, as well as his sense of being, in desire, which was taken to be the great scourge of the radical culture of the period" (7). If such desire belies the Lockean picture of the sovereign observer of empirical nature espoused by Painite radicals, an aim of the following is to show that what is in fact most subversive about both Blakean and Freudian desire is the abiding commitment to Lockean subjectivity they betray. Each proceeds by drawing from the Lockean subject itself materialist or visionary dialectics that respectively consume that subject from within. I suggest that *The Book of Thel, Visions of the Daughters of Albion,* and *Beyond the Pleasure Principle* anticipate Wittgenstein's "skeptical solution to the paradox of skepticism"[4] by liberating symptomology for visionary aesthetics without diagnostic pretense.

---

2. *Freud and Philosophy.*
3. Borsch-Jacobson, *Lacan.*
4. Kripke, *Wittgenstein on Rules and Private Language,* 69.

## II

Blake followed his *Book of Thel* immediately with his *Visions of the Daughters of Albion,* and the protagonist of the latter arguably resolves the impasse in which the conclusion of *The Book of Thel* leaves its protagonist. Whereas Thel's consuming mistrust of the natural world and even her own body is retraced to implicitly Lockean, self-exacerbating subjective isolation, Oothoon ultimately manages to overcome this isolation and espouse the radical spontaneity of the experience of "the moment of desire" and, on the basis of this sensitization to particularity, to appreciate the uniqueness of every earthly "joy" and to know that each is commonly "holy" and a part of "love." However, if this sweeping redemption of the particular is taken (as it commonly is) to resolve Thel's Lockean dilemma, then Oothoon does not resolve that dilemma but repeats it, turning away from the actual material world toward a hazy dream of grace akin to the infantile "Vale of Har" to which Thel ultimately retreats in vain flight from the world. Blake insists that Thel's dilemma cannot be resolved simply by casting the Lockean worldview and frame of experience in which it emerges as an arbitrary mistake to be corrected and thereby canceled, because such a notion of sheer dispensability, indifferently contingent error or accident, is a signal feature of that very worldview.

According to Laura Quinney, Blake was, of the Romantics, "the keenest and most systematic in his critique of materialism."[5] Most pointedly Blake mocked the latter's proponents—"Bacon, Newton & Locke," "Voltaire Rousseau Gibbon Hume"—collectively represented by the Idiot Questioner, "who publishes doubt & calls it knowledge, whose Science is Despair."[6] To say that empiricism is a science of despair is to take issue not with the accuracy of its picture of the world but with its unresponsiveness to hope and desire. Blake's critique is that this picture demands to be viewed from a perspective that itself has no place in the world, the despair-inducing because paralyzingly impossible perspective that Thomas Nagel termed "the view from nowhere."[7] This entails radical self-conflict if not self-contempt, radical in the sense that it is interminable: the amount of de-biasing necessary to neutralize the particularity of my viewpoint—that is, to make me a worthy, legitimate viewer of the empiricist picture of the world—is endless because a nonparticularized viewpoint is a contradiction in terms, for it can be found precisely "nowhere."

---

5. Quinney, *William Blake on Self and Soul,* 10.

6. Erdman, ed., *The Complete Poetry and Prose,* 142 (all subsequent Blake references are to this volume).

7. Nagle, *The View from Nowhere.*

Thus the self accrues empirical knowledge only by diminishing itself as a participant in the world; empiricism in this light is a science not just of despair but also of masochism.

Yet to say that empiricism is masochistic rather than just despairing is to register that it is an expression of desire, if a perverse one. For instance, despair may result from the picture Locke presents at the outset of his *Essay Concerning Human Understanding*, but only a powerful drive or desire, or in Locke's terms "Art and Pains," can account for the strenuous exertion of an eye perpetually straining to eliminate its blind spots:

> The Understanding, like the Eye, whilst it makes us see and perceive all other Things, takes no notice of its self: And it requires Art and Pains to set it at a distance and make it its own Object. But whatever be the Difficulties, that lie in the way of this Enquiry; whatever it be that keeps us so much in the Dark to our selves, sure I am, that all the Light we can let in upon our own Minds; all the Acquaintance we can make with our own Understandings, will not only be very pleasant, but bring us great Advantage, and direct our Thoughts in the search of other Things.[8]

Locke's stated view is that the mind's self-opacity is a basically contingent obstacle to be progressively minimized, to one's "Advantage," through enlightenment. But there's more to the Lockean account than the "Advantage" he overtly acknowledges. If every modicum of Lockean self-enlightenment opens the door to despairingly interminable self-opacity, what protects this process from paralyzing despair is an analogous structurally limitless desire for newness, not for enlightenment per se but *moments* of enlightenment, the *experience of searching out, discovering* "other Things." Beyond any and all actual discrete "Advantages," the future prospect of infinite potential moments of enlightening discovery is what counteracts despair over enlightenment's intolerance of actual selfhood. The supply of particular new moments of enlightening discovery is just as inexhaustible as the self's supply of its own, obscuring particularity, because our limitless particularity consigns us to asymptotically approaching and never arriving at "the view from nowhere" (i.e., to approaching it always *from somewhere*).

The crucial consequence of this is that Locke actually deviates from his ostensible position that the mind's self-opacity is a contingent obstacle to be progressively minimized through enlightenment. He in fact treats obstacles as the condition of possibility of insight; insight is always something *to be*

---

8. Locke, 43.

*diachronically achieved* by overcoming obstacles, not something synchronically maintained or maximized. An illustration of this distinction, and of a dialectics smuggled into an ostensible account of static natural law, is provided by Locke's own political philosophy. C. B. Macpherson offers a compelling account of how Locke's well-known derivation of a limited natural right to property from one's innate rights to sustain one's body and put it to work (provided this doesn't compromise others' right to the same) gives way to the postulate of an unlimited natural right to *appropriation per se,* even of others' labor.[9] What begins as an attempt to define and minimize the limits to property right (like the attempt to delimit the eye's blind spots, to achieve corrected vision) becomes a declaration of interminable acquisitiveness for its own sake; the concern for synchronic optimization of the balance of rights shifts to the diachronic act of appropriation, of conquering ever new vistas. Thus the Lockean empiricist subject is reflected in what Hegel will term "the beautiful soul,"[10] and Jerome McGann "the romantic ideology,"[11] or in other words the bourgeois consumerist subject who has learned not just to take the experience of actual subjective distortion as evidence of transcendently coherent agency but moreover masochistically to *court* such distortion as the condition of sustaining the transcendent agency to overcome it.[12]

Freud's discussion of the "fort-da game" suggests that such a spectral echo effect is just what subjectivity is. Freud observes a boy (in fact his grandson) whom his family praises as "good," who "never cried when his mother left him," but who

---

9. Macpherson, *The Political Theory of Possessive Individualism,* 203–20.

10. "[The beautiful soul] lives in dread of besmirching the splendour of its inner being by action and an existence; and, in order to preserve the purity of its heart, it flees from contact with the actual world, and persists in its self-willed impotence to renounce its self which is reduced to the extreme of ultimate abstraction." Hegel, *Phenomenology of Sprit,* 400.

11. This ideology is defined for McGann by an aspiration to transcendental completeness expressed through rigorous insistence on worldly incompleteness. "The earliest Romantic theories of Romanticism are always cast in polemical, incomplete, or exploratory forms. They are manifestoes, *apercus,* or 'spontaneous' and self-generated searches. These characteristics of Romantic thought, in prose and verse alike, are a sign of its aspiration toward completeness: a completeness of idea, a completeness of culture, perfection of art. In short, 'Unity of Being.' But what distinguishes Romantic forms from any synthetic representation of those forms is that the former's aspirations (and dissatisfactions) are preserved at the most radical level." McGann, *The Romantic Ideology,* 47.

12. Slavoj Žižek writes that "the apparatus of categories presupposed, implied by the scientific procedure . . . , the network of notions by means of which it seizes nature, is already present in the social effectivity, already at work in the act of commodity exchange. Before thought could arrive at pure *abstraction,* the abstraction was already at work in the social effectivity of the market. . . . In this way, the transcendental subject . . . is confronted with the disquieting fact that it depends, in its very formal genesis, on some inner-worldly, 'pathological' process." *The Sublime Object of Ideology,* 17.

had an occasional disturbing habit of taking any small objects he could get hold of and throwing them away from him, into a corner, under a bed, and so on. . . . As he did this he gave vent to a loud, long-drawn-out 'oooo.' . . . His mother and the writer of this present account were agreed in thinking that this was not a mere interjection but represented the German word "*fort*" [gone]. I eventually realized that it was a game and that the only use he made of any of his toys was to play "gone" with them. One day I made an observation which confirmed my view. The child had a wooden reel with a piece of string tied round it. . . . What he did was to hold the reel by the string and very skillfully throw it over the edge of his curtained cot, so that it disappeared into it, at the same time uttering his expressive "oooo." He then pulled the reel out of the cot again by the string and hailed its reappearance with a joyful "*da*" [there].[13]

Freud also notes that the boy makes *himself* the object of the game: "He had discovered his reflection in a full-length mirror which did not quite reach to the ground, so that by crouching down he could make his mirror-image 'gone,'" upon which he would exclaim "Baby oooo!" (14n6). For Freud, the "obvious interpretation" of the game is that it constituted "the child's great cultural achievement—the instinctual renunciation (i.e., the renunciation of instinctual satisfaction) that he had made in allowing his mother to go away without protesting. He compensated himself for this, as it were, by himself staging the disappearance and return of the objects within his reach" (14). According to Freud, the game represents a "renunciation of instinctual satisfaction" insofar as it suspends the demand for the mother in her absence, and it "compensates" for that suspension by allowing the boy to "stage" the scenario of disappearance and return.

Yet Freud's own account suggests that the achievement of renunciation, indeed the very notion of something that is lost and requires renouncing, may itself already be compensatory. As Freud puts it, the boy's recognition that an absent object may endure and eventually return is decisive because it allows the boy "himself" to "stage" or rehearse this possibility: the formerly inarticulate suffering is transposed onto a stage upon which the possibility of its alleviation is rehearsed and thus affirmed. Once the boy has recognized his experience as a function of a determinate absence, and no longer of sheer destitution, the experience itself is altered. The stage is now implicitly prepared for this specific lack's return. Thus before this return is *actualized*, the child has supposedly accomplished the affirmation of its possibility that defines his

---

13. *Beyond the Pleasure Principle*, 13ff.

"cultural achievement," has already become an agent of culturally normative desire for that end. Thus defining what's wanted itself already constitutes the most decisive step toward filling that want: the question of *actually* filling that want is virtually beside the point.

Desire that provides the basis of a kind of normative agency cannot be conflated with desire as mere destitution, not only by virtue of supplying normative meaning and purpose but also because it opens a limitless horizon of possible future wants, Locke's infinite prospect of discovering new and "other Things." What the boy stages is precisely a *self*, not just the retrieval of a specific object but how to be an *agent of such retrieval generally*, a subject situated in time and space and language and possessed of desire, who experiences the determinacy of past and present, here and there, as launchpads of desiring agency's indeterminable future. Freud's attribution of the boy's cultural achievement to a renunciation of actual instinctual demands, to learning to endure an absence he couldn't formally tolerate, interprets the child's "fort" and "da" reductively literally. Freud, the great theorist of bourgeois developmental selfhood, mistakes the specific nature of this "cultural achievement" in his rush to identify its empirical cause. The boy's real achievement is to establish himself, quite independently of any particular instinctual demands, as a wholly new kind of subject who is capable of renouncing such demands generally.

Freud mistakenly construes the boy as a moment in a causal mechanism rather than as the overarching agency framing the identification of such moments. Desiring subjectivity is a way of framing and coloring empirical events, a particular kind of attitude toward them, rather than an empirical event unto itself. But this error helpfully underscores that this more generalized staging agency has the status only of an epiphenomenon, or transcendental condition, of its actual empirical losses and retrievals. Thus Freud follows Locke in explaining experience *so* thoroughly as to elide the subject of experience.

In fact the death drive aspires to explain psychic phenomena in terms of a natural law akin to that adduced by the cathartic theory that psychoanalysis *constitutively* repudiated. Whereas the law of thermodynamics held sway over the theory of catharsis, the death drive represents Freud's discovery of an altogether new law, if not of the physical universe, at least of all organic life. As Jonathan Lear notes, Freud "made his career by finding hidden meanings--regularly tending the directions opposite to the conscious purposes and intentions of his patients."[14] Freud's return to natural law can be seen as

---

14. *Happiness, Death, and the Remainder of Life* (hereafter HDR), 83.

a traumatic repetition unto itself, and hence as implicitly enacting what the death drive theorizes. Yet to point this out is also to emulate Freud's signature attentiveness to the ways of perversity, to what Lear calls purposes "opposite to conscious purposes." If, in Freud's postulation of the death drive, this attentiveness ceded to a desire to discover and impose a new overarching law, then renouncing this law simply for being a law risks making the same legalistic error: risks analogously foreclosing nonjudgmental attentiveness to and curiosity about the perverse logic underlying this irrepressible *desire for law*. The rights of such curiosity—what Jean Laplanche terms the "fundamental rule of psychoanalysis," the "freedom" to think in defiance of all censoring authorities, "to philosophize and to dream"[15]—are promoted not by pretending to renounce and remediate nomothetic desire (as if there were a law governing law-making itself), but by restoring its attentiveness to and interchange with its dialectical counterpart, the particularities that law would organize: that indeterminately disruptive acting-out that law is meant to govern.

## III

The key catalyst of the boy's staging agency in the fort-da game is the distinction between articulate and inarticulate speech, between coherent action and mere "acting-out," between playing the fort-da game and just making the "oooo" sound. This distinction is correspondingly pivotal for the contrast of the death drive to the pleasure principle. In trauma, Freud writes, "the pleasure principle is for the moment put out of action. There is no longer any possibility of preventing the mental apparatus from being flooded with large amounts of stimulus, and another problem arises instead—the problem of mastering the amounts of stimulus which have broken in and of binding them in the psychical sense, so that they can then be disposed of" (*BPP* 33ff.). Blake's *Thel* and *Visions* likewise hinge on the contrast between action that fits into a larger system—that finds it purpose in identifying with nature, God, or narcissistically with oneself—and sheer acting out that attaches to and is redeemed by no such purpose.

Whereas Thel defends a certain anxiety and hesitancy about sexuality, *Visions* begins with Bromion's rape of Oothoon. For the latter, sexuality occurs not as the Lily promises Thel, ushering in the economical and purposeful cycle of nature, but as a violent interruption of legitimate trepidation. Hence the relation between Oothoon and her lover, Theotormon, is left to develop

---

15. *Life and Death in Psychoanalysis*, 106, 110.

(or not), not according to any law of nature or pleasure but on the basis of this traumatic distortion of how things supposedly ought to be. Blake here is critiquing not just illusions about the supposed harmoniousness or lawfulness of nature but also the supposed coherence of action generally. Blake emphasizes that the ways of actual life are irreducibly weird, unsusceptible to integration into redemptively coherent systems such as that named by "nature." In a word, the actual is the "infernal," and we inevitably misconstrue life when we view it through the lens of how it "ought" to be according to religion or abstract reason or ideologies of natural harmony. Crucially, however, this makes what is commonly construed as Oothoon's ultimate resolution of the story—her proclamation that "everything is holy"—at best more complex than it appears and at worst a symptom of the problem it pretends to resolve.

The conflict dramatized in *Visions* is anticipated in Thel's internal self-conflict. The latter is figured by contrasts between "speaking" and "weeping" and, most strikingly, between an infant's smile and its random facial spasms. In a manner that correlates with Freud's attempts both to make sense of shell shock and to construe the boy's "oooo" sounds as incipient speech, the reality of an infant's face beneath the apparent smile throws into sharp relief the unbearable purposelessness of mere acting out. Thus Thel correlates the fading semblance of a smile with death, but Blake demonstrates his acuity as an avant la lettre critic of Freud by instantly pointing out two problematic repercussions of this correlation. First, this makes sustaining life a matter of resisting reality, of preserving precisely illusions of meaning and purpose. Second, and most perversely, the key *signifier* of (the illusion of) purposeful agency becomes death itself: not the death glimpsed beneath the infant's fading smile but a fantasy of a death redeemed of such horrifying purposelessness. So Thel's laments about mortality ironically usher in dreams of death, but a death that is impossibly posthumously assured of its place in the orders of nature and God alike: "gentle may I lay me down, and gentle rest my head; / And gentle sleep the sleep of death, and gentle hear the voice / Of him that walketh in the garden in the evening time" (lines 12–14).

The poem basically recounts the failure of this self-delusion, or at least the exposure of its utter willfulness. Insofar as it enacts a willful confusion of discursive thought, Thel's wish cannot be *said* to be for anything so much as a release from discourse, for the inertia at once of the Earth that passively receives God's blessing, and of the *infancy*—or, literally, speechlessness—of the infant. Freud explained the death drive as a drive to return to some inanimate origin, and Blake here suggests why this offers a plausible principle not just of psychological pathology but of culture. The promise of such a return is seductive just to the extent that this origin can be conceived not as the incoherent acting out of an infant or a shell-shock victim but instead as a coherence so complete as to transcend the very need for purpose: as the self-containedness of Mother Earth, or of what Freud disparaged as "the oceanic feeling,"[16] which only a secretly smuggled-in redeemer could vouchsafe.

Like Freud, Blake works rigorously to dispel this deception, explicitly correlating it with the *in-phans* status of the worm who "canst not speak but . . . canst weep" (l.78). The spokesman of the worm is the clod of Earth who speaks but only to profess ignorance of why it says what it says:

> he that loves the lowly pours his oil upon my head,
> And kisses me, and binds his nuptial bands around my breast. . . .
> But how this is, sweet main, I know not and I cannot know;
> I ponder and I cannot ponder; yet I live and love.
> (87–92)

The clod speaks but only to refute itself, effectively to drain its language of meaning and reduce it to the thing-like status of, precisely, the Earth. But this reduction is taken as the sign of redemption, is correlated with erotic nuptial oil, just as Thel originally correlates returning to the Earth with a chance to "gentle sleep" and "gentle hear"—that is, to be *anointed by*—God's voice. The Earth's inert materiality *implicitly signifies* erotic and spiritual redemption. As Harold Bloom notes, this skeptical empiricist profession of ignorance disguises dogmatism, "Urizenic faith of Experience, content to abide in a Mystery."[17]

## IV

What war trauma exposed to Freud and what he devised the death drive to explain was the phenomenon of neurosis without compensatory purpose or meaning. For Freud this is to say that the repetitions of traumatic neurosis defy the pleasure principle. Such defiance is consistent with the definition of trauma as exceeding the mind's capacity to integrate stimuli into an economy of pleasure and unpleasure; the traumatic stimulus penetrates what Freud calls the mind's outer "crust" or "protective shield," exploding its economic equilibrium (*BPP* 29, 33). What is harder to explain is how the mind itself could become the *agent* of such disruption through neurotic repetition of traumatic experience. Freud suggests that the phenomena of traumatic neurosis "are

---

16. *Civilization and Its Discontents*, 11.
17. *The Visionary Company*, 52.

endeavoring to master the stimulus retrospectively, by developing the anxiety whose omission was the cause of the traumatic neurosis" (37).

Much hinges upon whether Freud's "mastery" and "dispos[al]" are read as provisional or conclusive terms. Like Freud himself, Ricoeur emphasized the definitiveness of Freudian mastery, but Jonathan Lear instead construes it as a regulative aim of which traumatic neurosis represents the perpetual, inexorable possibility of failure. The pleasure principle is the outcome of a "libidinal dialectic of development," Lear writes, by way of which the self-contained psychic economy of an "I" is established to "compensate" for the external world's "fickleness" in fulfilling my wishes.[18] This economy's apparent self-containment is only apparent, since it represents an effort to master disruptive stimuli that are by nature infinite. The appearance of homeostasis just means that this endeavor has provisionally succeeded rather than failed, not that it is completed. In this sense, the pleasure principle is less a principle than an endlessly renewed effort to compensate for ever new disruptions to itself, that is, for a fundamental *lack* of principle. The pleasure principle incorporates into ever more complex libidinal economies the disruptions to which all libidinal economies are by nature subject. It is in virtue of this project of perpetual remediation that, Lear writes, "our libidinal investments . . . are good investments: we seem to be able to take back in more than we originally gave out. What I love and what I take back in exists *for me* at a higher level of complexity than I do" (165ff.). Hence the motto of psychoanalysis—"where it was there shall I become"[19]—characterizes the "I" as an ongoing pursuit and approximation (rather than attainment) of self-containment by way of ever more richly differentiated conjugations of the "it."

Freud's theory of traumatic repetition acknowledges that underlying the economy of pleasure is an endeavor that cannot be explained economically since it precedes economy: an endeavor precisely to *install* economy as a pragmatic response (not compensation or counterbalance) to a fundamental disequilibrium or lack of economy. This recognition represents "a revolutionary moment in the history of psychoanalysis," according to Lear (*HDRL* 77), because it means that the analyst can no longer rely on the pleasure principle alone to explain the repetitions acted out in transference:

> This was Freud's structural insight in *Beyond the Pleasure Principle* . . . that life is lived under conditions of tension. . . . From a psychoanalytic point of view, this is the deepest form of human helplessness: helplessness in the face of too much energy. As Freud points out, we are vulnerable to repetitions

---

18. *Love and Its Place in Nature* (hereafter *LPN*), 163.
19. *New Introductory Lectures*, 100.

of such helplessness from the beginning to the end of our lives. But this is a peculiar kind of "repetition"—because it is a repetition of something that is itself without content. It is the breaking-through of quantity without quality. It is not a repetition of "helplessness," as though helplessness were the *content* of the experience—as when one *feels* helpless, overwhelmed, anxious; it is, rather, just helplessness breaking out again. (*HDRL* 109)

The economy of the pleasure principle is the by-product of the unending endeavor to negotiate disruptions to that same economy. Freud felt he needed to go beyond the pleasure principle in order to *explain* such disruptions, when in fact the pleasure principle is essentially predicated upon their very inexplicability: "the insight that Freud opened up but could not really grasp is that some mental activity occurs without a purpose" (80).

## V

In speaking of Freud's "libidinal dialectic of development," Lear flirts with the same language of *Bildung* Freud uses when he speaks of the boy's "cultural achievement." Such *Bildung* is likewise at least a subtext of *The Book of Thel*. Thel hears the voice of her grave, which in one sense just returns her to her starting point: the aim of life is death as a radical return to the origin. Both experiences are for Thel a matter of "hearing a voice": in the first case the voice of God walking through the Garden of Eden and in the latter the voice from her own grave. Yet the conclusion cannot be read as a complete return to the beginning insofar as the place of God has been taken by, in a sense, God's opposite: not the redeemer but her own unredeemed, radically corporal death which is signally registered through her five, self-fragmenting and self-tormenting senses. As Harold Bloom puts it, "In her first lament, Thel regretted the transience of what the senses apprehended. . . . In the chant from her grave the senses become the cause of lament" (52). But both laments are organized around the same coordinates: sensuous experience desires a redeemer from which it is intrinsically separated. The earthly existence which Thel initially wishes is no less willfully ignorant than that of the Clod. Dreaming of such existence for Thel means dreaming not of re- or absolving this self-conflict but of becoming oblivious to it. This indicates the great subtlety and psychological realism of Blake's representation of Thel's fantasy, the aim of which is not (crudely, and implausibly) to make what's known unknown but to make what's known not *matter*, or, in terms of Freudian repression, to "rob" what's known of its affective potency.[20] In turn, the effect of the poem's conclusion is not to change what Thel knows but to make it matter more, or matter more richly: to make it a matter of a more richly variegated form.

One is likewise tempted to say that Thel's experience of matter "develops" in complexity: she goes from a quite simple juxtaposition of the dead Earth with God's ethereally redemptive voice to a much more complex material experience; she again hears a voice, but this issues now from the opposite term of the initial juxtaposition, from (her own) dead Earth, her grave. This voice does not reassure, let alone redeem, but raises vexing if not paradoxical questions regarding the distinctive manner in which each of the five senses is self-frustrating. The fact that the questions are so vexing makes them akin to the vexation of the senses to which they refer. The voice from the grave marks a shift from metaphor to metonymy. Not an otherworldly voice from above to redeem the Earth below, the voice from the grave belongs to the realm of the latter: the vexing questions it poses would draw Thel into "the couches of the dead" in the same paradoxically both "infix[ing]" and "restless" way that "the fibrous roots / Of every heart on Earth infixes deep its restless twists."[21] The questions literally trace out her heart's formal divagation: the questions' inquiries into the five senses' respective modes of self-frustration represent her heart's empathetic expansion—insight into and appropriation of the matter of sensuous experience itself, its vexed restless twisting infixing in such experience rather than Thel's former dream of immediate unequivocal redemption of such experience.[22]

But it is due to its essentially paradoxical character—the fact that it is precisely the questions' self-vexations that makes them stand metonymically for the self-vexations of the senses—that Blake's poem finally has no place for the (heuristically useful) terminology of developmental *Bildung*, empathetic

---

20. In "The Neuro-Psychosis of Defense" Freud characterizes such "de-cathexis" as "*turning this powerful idea into a weak one*, in robbing it of the affect—the sum of excitation—with which it is loaded." *Standard Edition*, Vol. 3, 48.

21. In other words, this re-raises the "prior question" that W. J. T. Mitchell finds in "Thel's Motto": "the Motto's questions raise a prior question about the validity of metaphor and symbol. If we take the questions metaphorically, then we side with the eagle's wisdom at a distance; if we take them literally, we choose the immediate, 'tactile' knowledge of the mole." *Blake's Composite Art*, 85.

22. An intriguing way of illustrating such sensuous self-frustration is offered by Yale experimental psychologist Paul Bloom's recent account of *psychological* "essentialism," that is, ontological essentialism, the positing and prioritization of essences hidden behind objective appearances, as a principle not of philosophical reflection but of psychological functioning itself. Such functioning is self-frustrating (and as Bloom explores disposed to masochism) insofar as it is governed by abstract conceptual identities to which it is by its empirical nature denied access. *How Pleasure Works*.

expansion, and implicitly Lockean appropriation and insight. When Blake says in the epigram to Thel's companion piece, *The Visions of the Daughters of Albion*, that "the Eye sees more than the Heart knows," it's easy to take him to be saying that the eye provides a sort of normative compass to lead the heart to enlightenment, which would make Blake sound a lot like his nemesis Locke. The Lockean subtext is there but, implicitly in *Thel* and more fully in the *Visions*, Blake turns Locke against himself, arguing in a way that anticipates Shelley's claim in his "Defense of Poetry" that "we know more than we imagine" and have "eaten more than we can digest":[23] Thel could not but have "known" mortality in some sense at the poem's outset since she knew to see it in the rainbow, the infant's smile, the Earth, and so on. Yet a central point of the poem is to demonstrate the vast difference between such knowledge which prompts Thel's interrogation of the Lily, Cloud, Worm, and Clod and what it means for the heart actually to "infix" such knowledge in the Earth, that is, for such knowledge literally (if paradoxically) to be embodied in the heart's "restless," "twisting" "infix[ing]." Such embodiment can't be assimilated to (or, in Lockean terms, appropriated for) normative enlightenment: the knowledge that the heart achieves is its achievement of formal divagation, giving some texture to the contingent material realm to which knowledge formerly stood in formally crude, diametrical contrast. But no organizing principle of this texture, no telos directing the patterning of the heart's roots' twists, can be postulated without pretending somehow to resolve the questions posed from the grave, to dispel the "restlessness" they share with those roots.

Not unlike Thel's resistance to this restlessness, Freud resisted the possibility clearly posed in his own reflections on death that some mental activity may fail to obey any principle. Instead he advances the hypothesis that such failure is itself evidence of a deeper principle. The apparent repetitions of traumatic neurosis are thus construed not as abortive attempts to "bind" and "dispose of" the traumatic stimulus, as Freud himself suggests they could be, but as expressions of a positive compulsion *to* repeat: the traumatized mind hasn't failed to integrate the traumatic event into the purposive economy of the pleasure principle, but has been reduced to *obeying* a purpose prior to that economy, that of a drive aimed ultimately at returning to the inorganic state of being that preceded life: "*the aim of all life is death*" (46). But by Freud's own lights, this state is one of purposelessness. His resistance of his own insight is akin to Thel's insofar as it retreats to the Har-like fantasy where ostensibly purposeless thingness in fact signifies not just some purpose but the ultimate purpose.

---

23. "A Defense of Poetry," 1195.

## VI

An important and often overlooked aspect of Thel's skepticism toward the Lily et al. is that it stems just as much from an inflated sense of self as from a sensitivity to mortality. If I go, Thel asks the Lily, "Who shall find my place?" (37). A self-fetishizing ego unable to conceive its own nonexistence is the necessary correlate of anxiety about mortality; it is only against the backdrop of the former that the latter can register as such. In this sense there is no reason that the Lily et al. should not be read as egoless Buddhists instead of, as they usually are, mystified minions, except that such mystification is, Blake is suggesting, to some degree inescapable, and such egolessness is likewise inconceivable. The closest we come to the latter is the infixing of the grave's questioning.

Correspondingly, although Bromion's violence and Theotormon's resentment certainly do take self-fetishism to the extreme, the problem they pose to Oothoon is not that of simply overcoming narcissism. Rather, the problem is that of giving her narcissism some formal texture beyond that of the empty, compulsive form of egotism to which Bromion and Theotormon alike cling. There is an underappreciated resemblance between Theotormon and Thel: perhaps the best way of describing Thel's dilemma is in terms of Theotormon's name as torment by God, the God for whose blessing she searches nature in vain. Most crucially, this failure causes Thel and Theotormon alike perversely to shrink from sexuality—from experimental erotic exploration of the world of unhallowed, contingent material—and to make this renunciation *in the name of* the God who eludes them. Both are defined on the deepest level by the beautiful soul that resents and rejects the contingency and ephemerality of worldly satisfaction and instead makes a virtue of suffering, makes suffering the sign of connection to a divinity that operates according to a logic at odds with the ways of the world. Such ressentiment demands a radically empty and abstract form of egotism that does not merely scorn worldly attachments but defines itself as this agency reflexively to disown its own worldliness. Bromion represents the raging chaos of worldliness itself and hence ostensibly stands in opposition to Thel's and Theotormon's self-sacrificial devotion to higher powers. Yet Blake again acutely suggests that this ostensible difference disguises basically the same empty form of reflexive egotism whose exchangeability with that of Theotormon is underscored by the seamlessness with which the latter falls under its sway.

Bromion is identified with a raging storm, but, just as the subject producing indeterminately disruptive "oooo" sounds may be recognized as a subject only by becoming recognized as an agent of language, this identity of Bromion's hinges not merely on raging and storming but on making his raging and storming *recognized* as such by another: by, as Blake writes of Oothoon, "ren[ding an other] with his thunders" (l. 24). Bromion is an illustration of the impasse of the master in Hegel's master/slave dialectic whose identity is a function of dominating another but who thereby deprives the other of the capacity meaningfully to acknowledge this domination. When Bromion brags that his slaves are "stamped with my signet," "obey the scourge . . . worship terrors and obey the violent" (29–31), he is admitting despite himself that their capacity to "obey" his mastery has been preempted by fear of essentially arbitrary violence. Mistaking his capacity to stamp and tear bodies with a capacity to command obedience, Bromion mistakes the indifferent chaos of his rage for the effective social power of selfhood. Thus his condition is analog to that of Theotormon and Thel: he fosters actual chaos for the sake of preserving the supposed coherence of an abstract identity.

Indeed Bromion and Theotormon are arguably not mere analogs but effectively identical. Bromion's appeal for Theotormon's submission to him has the same effect it had on Oothoon, "ren[ding]" his body (34), and it is no less vain than it was in her case and in those of all his other stamped and torn slaves. Yet Theotormon is said to "fold his black jealous waters round the adulterate pair" (35). Submission to Bromion as opposed to just terror of violence is no more an option for Theotormon than for any of Bromion's slaves. What does it mean to be "jealous" of a storm's terrorizing violence? At a minimum it must entail Thel-like fantasizing of an identity beyond the chaos. But this is essentially also Bromion's fantasy: that all the overt dismembering attests to his implicit identity. Thus Blake trenchantly illuminates the underlying exchangeability of the Nietzschean "slave morality" and the dilemma of mastery: both entail a compulsively circular contrasting of worldly chaos and transcendent identity. Slave and master alike take chaos as their point of orientation only thereby to render these identities just as arbitrary and without orientation as chaos itself, such that identification, consistent with the death drive, fosters the chaos it pretends to counteract.

The vicious circle in which Bromion and Theotormon are caught, of mutually implicating chaos and nomethetic narcissism, bears some relation to Freud's own professed "desire for greatness,"[24] a desire that he himself retraces to a childhood wish to defy his father's pronouncement, "the boy will come to nothing" (166). The hypothesis is not implausible that Freud's purported "discovery" of the death drive serves this wish: it represents the fantasy of achieved greatness *cum* repudiation of nothingness. The discovery of the death drive could fulfill Freud's "desire for greatness" only on the condition that such

---

24. Freud and Crick, *The Interpretation of Dreams*, 147.

discoveries are recognized as the stuff of greatness by the culture as a whole, and Lear retraces this valorization to "an obsessional strategy being played out at the cultural level" to "hide and protect" the "assumption . . . [that] the world is itself devoid of value, purpose or meaning" (*LPN* 218). This seems paradoxical: how can valorizing the discovery of the purpose of life serve to protect the assumption that the world is purposeless? The answer, according to Lear, is that such discovery puts us in the Lockean position of neutral observers upon, rather engaged participants in, our lives. Once what it means to be living is thoroughly reducible to objective knowledge, our subjective investments in the values we attach to living become *merely* subjective investments, arbitrary and dispensable unless and until, like the baby's pre-discursive experience of making "oooo" sounds, it is assimilated to normative "culture," reified in the mechanism of "instinctual renunciation." Lear writes, "One cannot abstract from a person's subjective experience without making mysterious what it is for him to be" (*LPN* 220). In his account of the death drive Freud does this not just to his grandson but also to himself. Describing an objective world independent of the subjective activity of taking the world in, leaves Freud, in Lear's words, "passive in the face of his own thinking" (*HDRL* 135). Over a decade after writing *Beyond the Pleasure Principle* Freud observes with regard to his thoughts on the death drive that "to begin with it was only tentatively that I put forward the[se] views, . . . but in the course of time they have gained such a hold upon me that I can no longer think in any other way" (*CD* 119). The death drive does exert a real compulsion: not as function of impersonal natural law, however, but as a way of subjectively taking in the world that elides the activity itself of taking the world in. "Projection," Freud writes, is a way "of dealing with any internal excitations which produce too great an increase of unpleasure: there is a tendency to treat them as though they were acting, not from the inside, but from the outside, so that it may be possible to bring the shield against stimuli into operation as a means of defense against them" (*BPP* 33). Just as Blake's characters project identities to resist their own attentiveness to chaos only thereby to perpetuate such chaos, the death drive is a defensive projection against attentiveness to phenomena so unbearably complex as the death drive.

## VII

Might this vicious circle be broken? The dark hypothesis of *Civilization and Its Discontents* is that it might not be. Yet in *Analysis Terminable and Interminable,* Freud suggests otherwise when he writes that the practical applicability of psychoanalysis depends upon having "blockages" at hand for it to "clear away." Thus, arguably, while Freud's theoretical/speculative application of psychoanalysis preemptively reifies the field of subjective possibilities, psychoanalytic practice aims at "clearing away" just such obstructive limits and projections. In order to allow for such clearing, psychoanalytic theory pursues the paradoxical aim of defining what it is about mindedness that allows it in practice to defy any such theoretical delimitation: to, in the case of each analysand, establish irreducibly idiosyncratic criteria of psychic health. Psychoanalytic theory must etch out the possibility of a science for which validation is determined, as Lear says, "internally" to the analysand's first-person perspective (*LPN* 216). Sensitizing oneself to the way in which a subject's experience perpetually promises to break open unanticipated possibilities for itself is just what it *is* to analyze and work through resistances: "The beauty of analyzing resistances is that it opens up all sorts of possibilities that cannot be anticipated. We do not complete our sketch by filling in more detail, but by clearing away blockages to our theorizing about the mind" (*HDRL* 107).

To this end Lear proposes the concept of "break": a break is the expression not of any physical or mental substance, but of the sheerly formal condition of excess that characterizes mental life: "it is just the 'too much' of the system breaking through" (*HDRL* 113):

> A disruption in the mind may be an occasion for growth . . . it may even be a vehicle of aggression . . . but that is not why it is occurring. The fact that there is a disruption is simply one manifestation of the fact that the mind lives in conditions of excess. It is not a special teleological property of the mind. We should think of this self-disruptive force as *before* good and evil. It tends to break through established psychic structures and thus presents itself as a possibility for new possibilities. (*HDRL* 112)

Lear is skeptical about our capacity to integrate such an understanding of break into our normative evaluations without making it a limiting value unto itself. The break is not a value but a momentary suspension of limits that opens unforeseeable possibilities for living with values. Thus he writes that at such moments of break, "interpretation is, I think, inappropriate, for one should not here want to capture how things fit together. Rather, this is a moment for the analysand to experience vividly how she has managed to live with things not fitting together" (*HDRL* 126). However, the same perpetual subjection to conditions of excess pressure that makes the mind a "self-disrupting organ" must also make the mind unable to sit back and bear witness to its own self-disruptive activity. By definition the mind cannot capture the event of its own "'too much' breaking through." A mind operating under conditions of "too much" is in a sense always one step ahead of itself, practically grappling with a pressure it, for precisely this reason, cannot theoretically contain. The mind's constitutive imbalance is what the homeostatic economy of the pleasure principle violently suppresses. It is not inappropriate to speak of violence here for the same reason that it is apt for Lear to characterize the "experience of things not fitting together" as "vivid." Freud's own nomothetic "desire for greatness" illustrates a general truth in particularly stark terms: that representations of the mind are also and even more fundamentally *acts* of mind, acts whose potential autonomy any static representation necessarily circumscribes, "impoverishing," as Lear says, "the universe of possibilities." Such impoverishment is a kind of deadening, a violence against the life of mindedness, just as the experience of representational breakdown, of "things not fitting together," is the condition of fostering such life.

Freud was, as Lear says, "seduced" by his own "promise" to assimilate all psychic phenomena to a natural order. But what it is to *be* a subject is nothing other than to be perpetually pressured by the mind's inherent excess to "fit things together" into unities of ever greater complexity. It is due to this inherent excess that, as Lear puts it, "our libidinal investments are good investments.... What I love and what I take back in exists *for me* at a higher level of complexity than I do." We realize this positive return on our libidinal investments not because the world *in itself* is inexhaustibly complex but because the mind's inherent excess perpetually impels us to greater internal differentiation. Indeed, the "I" and the world originally separate only in virtue of this impulsion: "love must appreciate great structure; otherwise no I would ever differentiate itself from the world" (*LPN* 166).

So when Lear invites the analysand to use the occasion of "break" to experience what it is "to live with things not fitting together," it is perhaps more precise to say that he is inviting her to experience things fitting together with a complexity with which she could not previously have imagined things *could* fit together. The idea of an experience of the failure of things to fit together should be seen as a regulative idea, encouraging us to take in a more complex picture of the world, not as an idea constitutive of what one experiences in moments of break. After all, if, as Lear says, "I become what I take the world to be" (*LPN* 162), the opening of new possibilities for my becoming is contingent upon my taking the world to be a *world*, that is, a unity that fits together in however complex a manner. Capitalizing on the occurrence of break to experience such new possibilities doesn't require one to stop taking the world to *be* a world; it requires one to take it to be a world of sufficient complexity to accommodate such occurrences. Thus Freud's defensive projection is not retraceable only to his idiosyncratic "desire for greatness" and the culturally contingent investment in the Lockean picture of a valueless, objective world. For defensive projections of this kind will be a constant temptation to any modern subject whose fate it is to take in a world so complex as to include conceptions of an excessiveness inherent to the mind, and of a self-disruptiveness inherent to the activity itself of taking the world in.

## VIII

If the theory of the death drive helps illuminate the vicious circle in which Blake's characters are caught, I hope to show that Blake in turn helps illuminate how exactly this openness to ever-increasing levels of complexity might work. Readers of *Visions* have generally been content to find an answer in the colloquy among the three main characters contrasting Theotormon's despair over violated selfhood and Bromion's sadistic celebration of the latter, on the one hand, with Oothoon's insistence that never "can one joy absorb another," that each "different joy is holy, eternal, infinite"(124–25), on the other. Quinney, for instance, casts Oothoon's triumph basically as a matter of making a normatively winning case for enlightenment emancipation and spiritual salvation: "she implicitly distinguishes between the tyrannical self-imposition of [Bromion and Theotormon] and the visionary independence she herself exemplifies. . . . The result of Oothoon's self-assertion . . . is that she discovers her freedom and generously calls on others to embrace theirs: 'Arise and drink your bliss, for every thing that lives is holy'!" (49–50). Oothoon's emancipation according to Quinney is a direct "result" of enlightenment, of seeing through the untenability of Bromion's form of identity; indeed Quinney adds that this result is so "swift and effective" that it "allows Oothoon to look back on her deluded state" (*WBSS* 51). There is a familiar enlightenment narrative implicit in Quinney's account of suffering repaid with new health and wisdom. Oothoon's climactic, ecstatic plea for "the moment of desire! the moment of desire!" (186) would thus seem a straightforward culmination of this new wisdom that sees holiness in every distinct thing. But this remains a suspiciously formulaic way of repudiating formula. Indeed the very phrase supposed to exult in particularity—"the moment of desire!"—is repeated in a way that seems designed to call this exultation into question by underscoring its formulization. But there is an even more fundamental problem. The vicious circle enclosing any attempt to determinate any kind of identity within chaos would seem to make the straightforward affirmation of particularity no more tenable than Bromion's claim to identity. That is, Quinney's reading arguably does not resolve the problem of the vicious circularity of chaos but simply switches the valence of its valuation from negative to positive. But this is just what Bromion and Theotormon do in the name of sadistic domination and slave resentment; Oothoon's doing so in the name of the holiness of everything wouldn't in itself seem to make a decisive difference. Quinney's account of Oothoon arguably casts her as actually inhabiting Thel's compensatory dream of the Garden of Eden.

But Quinney neglects the figural aspect of Blake's response to the aforementioned crux question of these poems, which doesn't pretend to normatively resolve "the experience of things not fitting together" so much as make it more "vivid." The figure of the smile introduced at the outset of *Thel* returns in the *Visions* when Blake depicts the relationship between Oothoon and Theotormon in the wake of her rape by way of an elaborate scene that turns again on the contrast between acting and acting out. There this was invoked by the *in-phans* status of the baby and the Worm who cannot speak and yet can smile and weep. Here, Theotormon can both smile and weep, whereas Oothoon cannot weep but does smile, although in a new, enigmatic, and complex manner. Oothoon is, in Freudian terms, clearly somewhat blocked here: trauma has made one mode of expression unavailable to her and reduced her to symptomatically acting out in other ways. Oothoon's subsequent "embrace" of the holiness in everything is suspiciously sweeping and universalizing because she remains unmistakably at grips with her very particularizing trauma. Yet even though (and indeed perhaps because) she is "merely" acting out in a way that recalls Thel, Oothoon simultaneously also indicates a new way beyond chaos:

> ... Theotormon sits wearing the threshold hard
> With secret tears. ...
> Oothoon weeps not—she cannot weep! Her tears are locked up
> But she can howl incessant writhing her soft snowy limbs,
> And call Theotormon's Eagles to prey upon her flesh.
>   "I call with holy voice, kings of the sounding air!
> Rend away this defiled bosom that I may reflect
> The image of Theotormon on my pure transparent breast."
> The Eagles at her call descend and rend their bleeding prey:
> Theotormon severely smiles—her soul reflects the smile
> As the clear spring mudded with feet of beasts grows pure and smiles.
> (37–51)

Blake introduces two key points in this passage. First, that Oothoon follows Theotormon in responding to Bromion's torment by inflicting it upon herself:

she has herself "rent" just as Bromion had done to her and as Theotormon had done to himself. Oothoon and Theotormon here emblematize the repetition compulsion Freud noticed in trauma victims who instead of remediating the injury repeatedly re-inflict it upon themselves. The second feature to notice, however, is that the fact that Oothoon repeats Bromion's rending of herself allows Theotormon to *"severely smile"* at Oothoon's torment as if he were himself Bromion. Oothoon's display of self-violence—her emulation of Bromion—allows Theotormon to derive some gratifying sense of mastery and domination; that is, it allows Theotormon *also* to emulate Bromion. Bromion's violence was so devastating as to leave no plausible form of identity in its wake other than that defined by the capacity to inflict such violence.

But Oothoon here does something much more enigmatic and complex than to claim direct and self-exultant access to "the moment of desire." She diagnoses Theotormon's intolerance of worldly action as the cause of a self-haunting isolation akin to Thel's, asking: "Is it because acts are not lovely that thou sleekest solitude / Where horrible darkness is impressed with reflections of desire?" (193ff.). So when Oothoon "reflects the smile" of Theotormon which as we saw betrays the latter's identification with Bromion, she is not reflecting *merely* this identification but also the whole complex interplay of fear and desire that it conceals. Blake draws a pointed contrast between identification and reflection here and deploys an epic simile to elaborate the distinction: "her soul reflects the smile / As the clear spring mudded with feet of beasts grows pure and smiles." This is a very complex image, but its key features are clear. Casting the smile as a reflection in a spring certainly underscores the theme of narcissism that was pathologically in play in Theotormon's smile. As a spring, her soul reflects not just his smile but his *whole narcissistic subjective structure*; she does not just reflect how he appears; rather, the fact that she reflects this, that her soul is a reflecting spring, itself imitates his narcissistic, atomically individualistic way of seeing and structuring the world. Yet does Theotormon see his reflection in the spring of her soul? This seems unlikely not just because it is not her soul but her body's torment that he's smilingly attending to, but also for another striking reason. Oothoon's soul is the analog to the spring, yet this is paradoxical since Theotormon's narcissism, the very thing her soul reflects, by nature blinds him to others' souls. She has taken his whole way of viewing the world into her soul, although this is just the place of which that way of viewing is constitutively unable to acknowledge the existence.

This act of taking into one's self parts of the world—or indeed other ways of structuring the world—that discount one's self as dead, gets much closer to what Blake means by a "love" that includes a radical variety of joys than merely nominal endorsement of such love. Indeed, another key feature of the simile emphasizes how this quasi-masochistic act of submission to another—emulating another's way of structuring the world even to the exclusion of oneself—is also simultaneously a positively autonomous expression. For although the image of the reflecting spring undeniably invokes Theotormon's narcissism, although considering the spring image in light of the classical scenario of Narcissus is unavoidable, as a matter of fact Blake does not have the spring reflect a smile but rather has the spring itself smile. Moreover, this smile of the spring emerges in contrast to the mud kicked up by the feet of presumably Theotormon-like beasts. On this view, then, the smile is not continuous with but opposed to Theotormon's narcissism; the smile emerges precisely by clearing away the latter's muddy traces. A dialectical interplay is certainly in effect: the smile is something that dynamically "*grows*" as the spring's upwelling water pushes the mud clouds away, something that a spring that was never muddied could not display. In M. H. Abrams's terms, Blake pointedly casts the spring not as a mirror but a lamp, a source of autonomous expression, of purity and growth. The lamp function of a self-generating spring is most evidently in effect in the poem when Oothoon pretends to acknowledge all the diverse joys of the world and to know what it means to call them all love. Yet as Harold Bloom puts it, here Oothoon's "antinomian desire" amounts to "splendidly employed" but "vain" "rhetoric" (*Visionary Company* 56; hereafter *VC*).

But before Oothoon pretends to draw a lesson from her experience and, as Quinney says, to stand back from and critique her past—that is, while she was still stuck in the midst of experience itself—Blake's simile does not allow the lamp function to stand alone but dialectically imbricates it with the mirror function it repudiates (by pretending to stand apart from and newly illuminate it). (This repudiation is especially significant because the Narcissus scenario is so deeply linked to the way the problem of Lockean identity was explored going back to Thel.) If the muddied spring seems to smile as it is purified by upwelling water, the smile reflected (Theotormon's) is associated with the mud that the smile illuminated (Oothoon's soul's) clears away. The referents of the image of the smile are mutually exclusive, and yet the image, despite (or because of) this groundlessness, suggests that this image is more subjectively than objectively compelling in the same way that those phenomena originally invoked by Thel—the rainbow and infant's smile—are visible not in themselves but only *for* a viewer. These are ephemeral not in the objective manner Thel observes in, for instance, a cloud. The rainbow and infant's smile are compelling images of ephemerality because they never even were objective to begin with. The primary reason why an infant's smile is ephemeral is not because that face is continuously changing but because the smile was never a property merely of that face but was projected onto it by a viewer just as the phenomenon of a smile growing in a spring must be the projection of a viewer. As Hazard Adams emphasizes, to affirm the worldliness of action whose unloveliness Theotormon flees is to affirm the subjectivity of vision: "Blake views time as a huge visual pattern, and . . . chastises historians for reasoning on events. They should present acts for all to visualize, not theories about acts." Oothoon's sweeping blessing of everything is empty rhetoric because, as Quinney suggests, she stands apart from what she blesses, offering her love as propositional "theory" about action rather than "communicat[ing] vision to the reader" (73).

What I wish to emphasize is that construing the smile as visionary action is irreducible to Theotormon's Lockean "severe smile" because the former does not resist but affirms its status as semblance, because the former is in this sense less substantial, tangible, and determinate but concomitantly more complex than the latter. Thus Thel's smile might be construed as radicalizing rather than remediating the empirical skepticism to which it responds. As Saul Kripke construed Wittgenstein's notion of the "language game," it offers a "skeptical solution to the paradox of skepticism." Wittgenstein's solution is skeptical because the notion of the language game renders moot the issue of external reference or causality that the skeptical empiricist perpetually raises. Another way of understanding this solution is to say that it replaces an epistemological notion of cause with the notion of criterion applied in normative judgments, that is, judgments that do not apply objectively referential knowledge but that self-referentially draw distinctions according to norms posited by the judgments themselves. For example, in his lectures of 1932–33, Wittgenstein differentiates the way in which a symptom relates to its cause from the way in which a criterion relates to the qualities it distinguishes.[25] To diagnose a symptom's cause is to make an inference from the symptom to a discrete entity only externally or contingently related to it; thus such diagnosis adds new meaning to the symptom. So to say that a person's face is sunburned is to say his skin's redness is a symptom of the sun; the sun is only one of several possible causes of this symptom, so referring this symptom to this particular cause adds meaningful context to it. By contrast, no such strictly external inference is possible from a criterion to the things it distinguishes, because such distinction is integral to that criterion's function. So saying that a person's face is angry implies an internal relationship. The anger we identify begins and ends with the phenomenon itself; its meaning makes no reference to any independent cause. To point out that a person's face displays anger adds no

---

25. *Wittgenstein's Lectures*, 36.

meaning to what I see there since either I saw the anger there to begin with or I do not see it at all; anger and its expression are mutually implicating, according to Wittgenstein, just as a rationale presupposes the same belief it would corroborate (28): the notion that we can explain and thereby add meaning to our beliefs and normative judgments is an illusion of which Wittgenstein would disabuse us. So Wittgenstein says that "we do not see facial contortions and make inferences from them . . . to joy, grief, boredom,"[26] that is, to mental states of which they would be "symptoms." Rather, these contortions are meaningful, and, indeed, even *perceptible* as such, only in virtue of participating in the articulation of the meaning of the mental states themselves: what I see in the furrowed brow is simply part of what it is to *be* angry.

This structure is exhibited not just by the infant's smile but also by several of the other examples of ephemerality Thel listed: "the dove's voice," "the music in the air," "the dreams of infants" (10–11), and ultimately by the way in which, as we saw, the grave's voice supplants metaphor with metonymy. Akin to Wittgenstein's appeal to distinguish criterion from symptom, Frye says that Blake's case against Locke aims to liberate allegory from corporeal understanding.[27] We can hear a voice in birdsong and music in the environment's ambient noise only by virtue of anthropomorphizing, of framing our experience of these things in an essentially narcissistic manner that unduly makes allegories of indifferent events. These are not metaphors then of the ephemerality of objects in the world so much as metonyms of our feeble subjective purchase on the world, the precariousness of our projections of meaning, the Lockean isolation of Thel, an isolation so extreme that it is akin to falling into a black hole. The very pretense to objectively measure, metaphorically capture—or, as Quinney describes, stand back from and critique—such isolation betrays a kind of category mistake, a mistake regarding the order of magnitude at issue. The infant does not communicate to us any more dependably than the spring does; any smile either exhibits is a smile projected by a spectator. The same holds for an "infant's dreams," but what is especially instructive about the latter image is that dreams are just what no spectator (without an fMRI machine) can even conceive seeing, just as the soul of another is inconceivable to a narcissist. Thus to imagine an infant's dream is to project an invisibility: it has the form of projection, of imposing a meaningful image onto an indifferent object, without the content of an image, or with the content of imagelessness. Blake's image is an illustration of Locke's eye projecting its own blind spot in order to perpetuate its discoveries (to hold open the possibility,

---

26. *Remarks on the Philosophy of Psychology*, §570.
27. *Fearful Symmetry*, 16–19.

for instance, of an fMRI machine that would make an infant's "dreams" visible). It points up the activity implicitly involved in perpetuating the illusion of Lockean observational neutrality and passivity. It concomitantly points up the activity involved in perpetuating narcissistic indifference to others' souls.

Although Frye speaks of liberating allegory from empiricism, this liberation is never complete and is sustained only by sustaining allegory's intimacy with what it escapes. By making Oothoon's soul the reflecting pool of Theotormon's narcissism, Blake makes the latter's indifference to her soul not just something that she acknowledges but that constitutes the organizing principle of her soul's structure. It is Oothoon's capacity to internalize without being extinguished by such radical indifference to herself—to take into herself not merely particular, indifferent objects but a way of structuring the world that systematically excludes her, and yet not to be excluded—that makes her reflection of his smile not merely a reflection but also a lamplike expressive upwelling of spring water, an expression of love for a world "that exists on a higher level of complexity" than she does. Bloom writes that "supreme embodiment of energy as she now is, the exultant Oothoon is all but trapped among the negations of her profoundly stupid males.... The binding is what Theotormon sees, not what is, for Oothoon cries out that love is as free as the mountain wind" (*VC* 55). But if this proposition finally amounts on Bloom's own account to "vain rhetoric," then what Bloom momentously designates "*what is*"—the true underlying being that this love has realized, this "mountain wind"—must stand, as Wittgenstein would say, not as something said but something shown.

Abrams's lamp is modeled on Wordsworth's "spontaneous overflow," a "spring that brims over." It is implicitly propositional insofar as it always refers to its subjective cause; for Wordsworth and Abrams alike it is securely, "unmistakably" retraceable "to the poet."[28] By contrast, what is lamplike in Oothoon's spring is its ability to illuminate a world structured around the act of her own exclusion. Giving voice to an act that denies her any voice would be indistinguishable from inarticulate acting out *but for* the fleeting phenomenon that does not even pretend to know this exclusionary act as such but rather merely to *see*—while making no claim to Lockean identity or advantage to counter Theotormon's narcissism—the sheer aesthetic semblance of his death-dealing smile's dynamic emergence or "growth." It is the ability to grasp her own death not as knowledge but precisely as a semblance (the contrary of knowledge) of growth (the contrary of death): a semblance that wears its epistemological illegitimacy on its sleeve and hence underscores the deathlike cancellation of Lockean identity. This semblance of growth constitutes Oot-

---

28. Abrams, 47.

hoon's loving illumination, projecting an absence that no mirror could reflect, a criterion for her love akin to the facial criteria Wittgenstein discusses.

## IX

"The 'I' is an interpretation," Lear writes (*LPN* 162), and for Freud and Blake alike, to accomplish such interpretation and to achieve that "I" is to take in a world that includes a concept of that "I" itself as a self-disruptive "being unto death." But our attempts to capture this disposition inevitably obstruct it by fitting things together either too well or not well enough. Oothoon's ostensible blessing of the universe represents this kind of obstruction. Coming in the wake of her soul's complex reflection of Theotormon's severe smile, her blessing is simplifying and even quasi-nomothetic insofar as it is delivered from some remove from its object. But to resist the complexity that her own act articulates is not *only* to neither fall prey to the kind of defensive projection we find underlying Freud's hypothesis of the death drive nor to traumatically to lose one's grip on one's own "I." It is also just what it is to live with the mind's excess. A theory of how to do this need not dictate laws but just say something generalizable about the obstacles posed by generalizing too well and not well enough. If the sole purpose of understanding such obstacles is to "clear them away," it must not preemptively delimit the possibilities for such clearing but must be perpetually open to seeing what it understands disappear in ways it does not understand. This, it seems, is just what it means to follow the same "fundamental rule of psychoanalysis" that, according to Laplanche, Freud's hypothesis of the death drive implicitly exemplifies even while it explicitly subordinates mental activity generally to the imperatives of hypostatized natural law. The possibility of a psychoanalytic science can be seen to hinge, then, on perpetually "clearing away" the obstacles posed *to* its theoretical activity *by* the products of just such activity.

To become practically conducive to the "freedom to philosophize and to dream," psychoanalytic theory thus faces the same challenge as the analysand. That is, to paraphrase the Mark Strand poem I've taken as my epigraph, the challenge to be open to "righting" itself *by* "writ[ing]" itself, bringing one's own and the world's perpetual disruptions "into line," in ever new, unforeseen ways. The poet repudiates law no more than the would-be nomothetic scientist: Strand's questions are finally answered *in the affirmative* by their own articulation, the very writing of the poem's own lines. It is our interminably re-demonstrated inability to face death without precisely giving it a face, projecting a smiling order on nature's unfathomable aimlessness, even in spite of ourselves rushing in to answer what we, like Strand, Thel, and Freud alike, intend to question, that best, or most "vividly," captures all we can know of subject and object alike. To manage to hold this rushing-in in view—as the smile's fleeting illusion of "growth" holds it in view—is not to see an error corrected or the fallen redeemed but to see diagnostic metaphors become metonyms for compulsive diagnosis, and to see symptoms of narcissistic resistance become criteria of love for a world that "exists on a higher level of complexity than I do."

CHAPTER 3

# Byron's Sad Eye

*The Tragic Loss of Tragedy*

I

ROMANTICISM'S PASSION for personal liberty was always in tension with its characteristically nostalgic, elegiac, and tragic modes of representing it. Indeed this tension itself is arguably constitutive of Romanticism. According to Stuart Curran, for instance, Charlotte Smith's elegiac sonnets "actually inaugurated what we think of as the new psychological realism and emotionality characteristic of Romantic poetry" (242). Yet Curran suggests that such realism was rooted in representation not of psychology as such but of overwhelming and unfathomable grief: "The lack of rationale for her pervasive sorrow, paradoxically, made it all the more compelling" (243). Gaining selfhood is a function not just of grieving loss but also of the second-order loss entailed by the inscrutable affective power of grief. This Romantic psychology represents to Curran a universal truth, namely, "how deeply we are defined by what we have all as human beings lost . . . by what has been eroded from us and is left only in our memories to taunt us with its inevitable absence" (245).[1]

In the light of this Romantic definition of personhood in terms of an elusive, affective response to loss, it is understandable why the late-eighteenth-century fall of the Venetian Republic offered a particularly appealing object

---

1. "Romantic Elegiac Hybridity," 238–50.

for early Romantic elegy. As an artifact of historical tragedy, Venice mirrored the Romantic ideal of republican self-determination in a way that was politically untroubling, an internalized emotion rather than public action. This trope was so untroubling, in fact, that its very consumability worried later Romantics like Lord Byron who began to reflect critically upon a signature ideological configuration of modernity, what Georg Hegel termed "the beautiful soul,"[2] and Jerome McGann "the romantic ideology."[3] Both are terms for the bourgeois consumerist subject. By stoking the desire and justifying the frustrations of consumerist pursuit of the constitutively elusive dream of subjective emancipation, the Romantic ideology became a hegemonic keystone of modern commodity culture, the infinitely "recreative originality" constitutive of both the commodity and its consumer. As Colin Campbell writes,

> Romanticism provided that philosophy of "recreation" necessary for a dynamic consumerism: a philosophy which legitimates the search for pleasure as good in itself and not merely of value because it restores the individual to an optimum efficiency. . . . Romanticism has ensured the widespread basic taste for novelty, together with the supply of "original" products, necessary for the modern fashion pattern to operate . . . as crucial in connection with consumption as science and technology is for production.[4]

The progress of Byron's signature treatments of Venice, from Canto 4 of *Childe Harold* in 1817 to the drama *Marino Faliero* in 1820, traces Romanticism's seminal intervention in the paradoxes of a modern commodity culture that thrived on its own self-undermining. Byron's drama faces the paradox that the verse Romance tended to suppress: the paradox that the loss of the tragic art form constitutes a kind of second-order tragedy unto itself but one that, of course, could not be represented as tragedy without implicitly refuting

---

2. "[The beautiful soul] lives in dread of besmirching the splendor of its inner being by action and an existence; and, in order to preserve the purity of its heart, it flees from contact with the actual world, and persists in its self-willed impotence to renounce its self which is reduced to the extreme of ultimate abstraction." *The Phenomenology of Sprit*, 400.

3. This ideology is defined for McGann by an aspiration to transcendental completeness expressed through rigorous insistence on worldly incompleteness. "The earliest Romantic theories of Romanticism are always cast in polemical, incomplete, or exploratory forms. They are manifestoes, *apercus*, or 'spontaneous' and self-generated searches. These characteristics of Romantic thought, in prose and verse alike, are a sign of its aspiration toward completeness: a completeness of idea, a completeness of culture, perfection of art. In short, "Unity of Being." But what distinguishes Romantic forms from any synthetic representation of those forms is that the former's aspirations (and dissatisfactions) are preserved at the most radical level." *The Romantic Ideology*, 47.

4. *The Romantic Ethic and the Spirit of Modern Consumerism*, 201.

itself. Building upon formal experiments conducted in "Darkness" and *Don Juan*, Byron's drama suggests that the nuanced and interminable self-reflexivity of this metatragedy is such that only the comic mode can bear.

I am thus suggesting that Byron's progress from *Childe Harold* through the beginning of *Don Juan* to *Marino Faliero* broadly illustrates Hegel's contention that comedy brings to completion what tragedy leaves incomplete (a contention best known through Marx's paraphrase at the opening of *The Eighteenth Brumaire of Louis Bonaparte*). According to Hegel, tragic agency as represented by characters such as Oedipus and Antigone hinges on definitive revelations (reversals of fortune resulting in what Aristotle termed *anagnorisis*, or recognition) of underlying *fixed* truths (e.g., the unalterable facts of Oedipus's past actions, of Antigone's family bonds). The function of comic agency, by contrast, is to play precisely with the unfixability of character, to play with masks. Comic agency is a function of the formal act itself of unmasking illusion, which is to say that it presupposes the impossibility of any *definitive* unmasking. Whereas tragic agency maintains a certain epistemological function, comic agency becomes autonomously theatrical, representing the interminable formal play of self-reflection. Hence Hegel characterizes the comic self as at once both actor and spectator of its own performance: "The self, appearing here in its significance as something actual, plays with the mask which it once put on in order to act its part; but it as quickly breaks down again from this illusory character and stands forth in its own nakedness and ordinariness which it shows to be not distinct from the genuine self, the actor, or from the spectator."[5]

Before considering how Hegel and Byron respectively conceive and effect this comic response to the impasse of tragedy's obsolescence, let us first consider more closely their accounts of this impasse itself.

## II

Aristotle asserts the philosophical superiority of poetry to history in the following terms: it "is not the function of the poet to relate what has happened, but what may happen—what is possible according to the law of probability or necessity. . . . Poetry, therefore, is a more philosophical and a higher thing than history: for poetry tends to express the universal, history the particular."[6] Poetically formed, imaginative plots constitute that aspect of reality in which actions appear with a completeness and coherence that they lack in actual

---

5. *The Phenomenology of Spirit*, 450.
6. "De Poetica (Poetics)," 1451a–b.

history. This unity is achieved when the poet manages to convince us that the particular events he describes, which may count among actual historical contingencies, are in fact governed by an internal logic, a "probability and necessity" that a merely historical account of them would lack. Thus unity of action for Aristotle is a requirement of *anagnorisis* itself: it is in this unity itself that the hero and audience alike come to recognize the truth of who he is (1450a).

For Aristotle, although nature determines the necessity or probability that unifies the act in accordance with a set of naturally given "types" of character, it is poetry that allows us to recognize that necessity or probability as such. Thus the "pity and fear" inspired by dramatic illustrations of our ongoing subjection to an indomitable and less than entirely transparent nature are not arbitrary—they are not merely confused, unsettling emotions that effectively internalize that subjection—but are "cathartic" in the sense that they give us a means of what Martha Nussbaum terms "clarification,"[7] distilling some degree of practical if not intellectual order and coherence from that subjection.

It is not Oedipus but Antigone who exemplifies consummately ethical action for Hegel. Transgression, which Oedipus only retrospectively discovers defines the unity of his act, is prospectively willed by Antigone. What's more, in Antigone's case, Hegel says, "the *realization* of the purpose is the purpose of the action." Her will, this suggests, is to act less for the sake of a specific purpose and more for the sake of any purpose, simply to act purposively. Not unlike Hamlet, Antigone is troubled to find herself subject to laws that "are ethical only by accident," and she sets out to show that the actual need not be accidental but may be ethically determined: her ethical purpose is basically just to demonstrate ethical purposiveness. Since demonstrating such purposiveness requires some established ethical norm to be established that transcends the accidental circumstances to which it responds, Antigone's will to sheer purposiveness is also a will to knowledge. Antigone's act "declares that actuality is not an accident of essence, but that, in union with essence, it is not granted to any right that is not a true right."[8] Her action contains a knowledge claim, a proposition that would distinguish substance from accident.

Somewhat ironically, then, Antigone's attempt at demonstrating ethical purposiveness becomes an act of self-sacrifice for the sake of ethical knowl-

---

7. "Pity and fear are not just tools of a clarification that is in and of the intellect alone; to respond in these ways is itself valuable, and a piece of clarification concerning who we are. It is a recognition of practical values, and therefore of ourselves, that is no less important than the recognitions and perceptions of the intellect. . . . Aristotle differs with Plato not only about the mechanisms of clarification, but also about what, in the good person, clarification *is*." *The Fragility of Goodness*, 391.

8. *The Phenomenology of Spirit*, 284.

edge. Despite the crucial distinction between Antigone's self-consciousness and Oedipus's lack thereof, the ethical universality that Antigone's act would embody is finally not that merely of a self but of a self as preeminently an organ of the ethical order per se. On Antigone's own terms, distinguishing the essential and accidental is not the prerogative of individuals. The fact that Creon claims this prerogative for himself is precisely what makes his rule tyrannical, rather than ethical, in Antigone's view. If the "realization of purpose is the purpose of her action," this is a purpose that is not hers to define but that is defined for her. Ultimately, Antigone's is an *essentially* sacrificial act, not only of her self but also of Creon and of selfhood generally, for Antigone demonstrates the necessity of sacrifice not only for her self-willed purposiveness but for self-willed purposiveness generally (285).

Yet Hegel notes that in the wake of this sacrifice, a crucial if unintended vestige of selfhood remains in the self-consuming *pathos* of the individual will to purposiveness. For the agent of ethical action like Antigone, Hegel writes, "His *being* consists in his belonging to his ethical law, as his substance" (284). But by casting the substance itself in opposition to actual law, the substance appears as sheer "pathos" that demands the dissolution ("disuniting") of the individual as such (284). A fundamental lesson of Antigone's tragedy is that replacing an accidental actuality with an ethical actuality requires a will that is criminal and thus just as accidental as the law it would defy: what her crime actualizes is not just the ethical substance but also the contingent pathos and criminality of the individual will.

Hegel presents Antigone's pathos as an actual barrier to ethically normative, mutual recognition among individuals. Remarkably, Hegel sees Antigone's tragedy as poetically clarifying her pathos as ethically void, an indifferent, dispensable foil for her actual ethical achievement, which is to demonstrate the need for replacing such arbitrary and hermetic, criminal pathos with the legal status of personhood as the basis for ethical life. The community creates the individual, not as the autonomous self but as the ethical shape of legal personhood. For Hegel, Antigone's tragic heroism is that it poetically articulates and privileges this shape over her indifferent or "blank" pathos: "that very necessity of blank Destiny, is nothing else but the 'I' of self-consciousness. . . . To be so acknowledged is its substantiality . . . in legal right it has a positive value" (290–91).

In *Lord Byron's Strength* (hereafter L), Jerome Christensen construes such strength in terms that echo Hegel's account of Antigone: it constitutes a normative power, a capacity generically recognizable as a "strength," but it is the power to effect radical, irreducible distinction. If Antigone's strength is her normatively recognizable capacity to assert the sheer form of "I" in action,

Byron's strength, according to Christensen, was to make writing a means of "consequential action," of no purpose beyond the assertion of individual authorship, in a modern, commercial context inherently hostile to such individuality.[9] Thus, whereas George Gordon Byron announces in the first canto that he is undertaking the poem in order to represent "consciousness awaking to her woes" (1.92), writing the poem only leads Byron to concede that this representational project, the attempt to hold apart author and character, himself and Harold, expression and signification, is "unavailing" (3, prefatory letter to Hobhouse). *Childe Harold* is commonly construed along these lines as Byron's provocative deconstruction of narrative epic by lyric, replacing the explanatory, rationalizing scheme of the former with the sublime subjectivity of the latter. Jerome McGann, for instance, writes:

> Harold . . . becomes sharply defined . . . as a character, whereas Byron's moral life is left a congeries of contradictory impulses and unfulfilled potentials. . . . Byron's very indeterminateness gives him a depth and complexity that Harold does not have; it permits him to display with great vigor a variety of passing moods and attitudes, whereas for Harold such contrarieties are impossible. In him nothing is passing or transient, all has come to be.[10]

Instead of Antigone's strength, Christensen's account of Byronic "strength" retraces this subjectivizing indeterminacy to a Hamletian suspicion of normative reason: while "strength . . . as a creatural capacity to take consequential action . . . had not thrived under the attentions of the doctors of enlightenment" (xv), Byronic poetry manages to exercise a strength of its own because it responds to this systemic neglect

> not so much with a rightness that fits the occasion (that would be a historicist standard) but with a rightness that decides the occasion (and that, I take it, is a rhetorical standard). What distinguishes the strong poet from the strong man, then, is the transformation of a creatural capacity for consequential action into a rhetorical capacity for consequential action (because it is radically creatural and therefore taken without regard to person, such action may appear criminal or violently satirical). What distinguishes the Romantic poet from all others (and this is the application that Romanticism makes of the baroque, that Byron makes of *Hamlet,* and that I make of Walter Benjamin) is the assertion that the creatural, in all the degraded

---

9. *Lord Byron's Strength,* xviii and passim.
10. *Fiery Dust,* 83.

outcastness of its relentlessly allegorical and ineradicably political destiny, *is* the rhetorical. (xviii)

According to Christensen, Byron replaces reifying representations of aristocratic autonomy with a new, performative, rhetorical enactment of it. In turn, Christensen construes the distinctive consequentiality of deconstructive criticism in terms of its capacity to disclose reality as text. Byron refuses to reduce his actions to transparent meanings, to "sacrificially objectify" their contingent particularity, their weighty opacity, but leaves it to his readers to make sense of his text just as Hamlet, after disallowing any determinate cause to attach to his actions, leaves it to Horatio to "report me and my cause aright."[11] Honoring the very inscrutability of this task, and its resistance to rational analysis, itself becomes the prince/lord's distinct cause.

But, in a paradox that arguably defines deconstruction's distinctive brand of performativity, this effectively amounts to disclosing the repetition involved in all pretense to distinct significance. Hamlet asserts his distinction from the regime of Claudius by leaving it to Horatio to reforge the link that Hamlet broke between Hamlet's particular actions and any generalizable cause, by injecting into that regime, and forcing it to come to terms with, a radical disjointedness (just as the ghost had arguably done to Hamlet himself and to which Hamlet's raving appears to testify). If Byron's link to Hamlet consists in repetition of this maneuver by exclusively textual means, then that link effectively consists in Byron's repetition and extension of Hamlet's deconstruction or disjoining of any such links between discrete particulars. Thus Christensen, by adding that he is, in making this argument, doing the same to Walter Benjamin as Byron did to Hamlet, posits a classic deconstructive community: an alliance of irreducible particulars, a series of instances of radical difference united exclusively by that difference, which is to say a text. Fostering such a series of radically distinct particulars may constitute "strength" rather than liability by sustaining Antigone's sheer, "blank" form of the "I" in a modern context in which, in Georg Lukács's terms, the "commodity form" has become "universal," "penetrat[ing] society in all its aspects and . . . remould[ing] it in its own image," allowing nothing to escape the preemptive homogenization of experience, or "reification," which it entails.[12] Hence for Christensen even modern literary writing becomes, to the extent that the "literary" itself is a consumer category, an automated routine as reified in character and disciplinary in function as stenography and sacrifice. The ostensibly literary mobilizes particularity and variability only to enable their ritualistic sacrifice to the

---

11. Shakespeare, *The Tragedy of Hamlet*, 5.2.338.
12. "Reification and the Consciousness of the Proletariat," 85.

commodity form. This disciplinary dialectic preempts consequential action, and hence finally history per se, because, as Jacques Derrida says, this dialectic "appropriates" or "relieves" difference and allows only inane repetition.[13]

The question of whether the strength of Byron's writing's radical self-differentiation defies commercial reification resolves to more general questions: How can an instance of such difference be confirmed, even recognized as such, without thereby involving it in the same reifying procedures it would defy? If, like linguistic signs, moments in the series are finally defined by mutual difference, does this not make them each essentially both arbitrary and interdependent rather than radically sovereign? At the very least it seems safe to say that forcing us to grapple with these questions must count among the principal Hamletian effects of Byron's work.

In a signature verse of *Childe Harold*, Byron describes a kind of literary practice that seems to suggest the "strong" "consequentiality" Christensen espouses:

> 'Tis to create, and in creating live
> A being more intense, that we endow
> With form our fancy, gaining as we give
> The life we imagine, even as I do now.
> What am I? Nothing; but not so art thou,
> Soul of my thought! With whom I traverse earth,
> Invisible but gazing, as I glow
> Mix'd with thy spirit, blended with thy birth,
> And feeling still with thee in my crush'd feelings' dearth.
> (3.6)

This view of a poetry that actively creates the forms through which the world is experienced is expounded again in stanzas 7, 12, and 14. It recalls William Wordsworth's aspiration to "create the taste by which he is to be relished."[14] Correspondingly, just as in the "Intimations Ode," the loss of glory is the condition of a kind of poetic self-recovery, Byron suggests that an apparently compromising fate is the condition of poetic assertions of radical autonomy. Resignation may occasion rather than forestall subjective autonomy because, Byron suggests, freedom is not a simple subjective state but an effect of rhetorical redescription of such states: "untaught in youth my heart to tame, / My springs of life were poison'd. 'Tis too late! / Yet am I chang'd though still enough the same / In strength to bear what time can not abate, / And feed on

---

13. "The Ends of Man," 121.
14. To Lady Beaumont, 21 May 1807. Alan G. Hill, ed. *The Letters of William Wordsworth*, 103.

bitter fruits without accusing Fate" (3.7). However, Byron proceeds to use this conception of poetic autonomy to distinguish himself precisely from its most obvious proponent, Wordsworth. Specifically, Byron leverages this conception of autonomy in order to contrast the latter's putative transcendentalism with what he calls the "fiery dust" of Jean Jacques Rousseau, the "apostle of affliction," who "from woe wrung overwhelming eloquence":

> This hallowed, too, the memorable kiss
> Which every morn his fevered lip would greet,
> From hers, who but with friendship his would meet;
> But to that gentle touch, through brain and breast
> Flash'd the thrill'd spirit's love-devouring heat;
> In that absorbing sigh perchance more blest,
> Than vulgar minds may be with all they seek possest.
> (3.79)

After McGann's groundbreaking 1968 book, *Fiery Dust*, the figure of "fiery dust" has emblematized Byron's resistance of representation. Arguably, that figure has paradoxically served precisely to represent that resistance.[15] But Byron's commentary on these lines offers important and neglected clues to the figure's actual consequence:

> This refers to the account in his "Confessions" of his passion for the Comtesse d'Houdetot . . . and his long walk every morning for the sake of the single kiss which was the common salutation of French acquaintance.—Rousseau's description of his feelings on this occasion may be considered as the most passionate, yet not impure description and expression of love that ever kindled into words; which after all must be felt, from their very force, to be inadequate to the delineation: a painting can give no sufficient idea of the ocean. (3.79n)

What is supposedly so special about Rousseau's fire is that it is willed out of dust itself: dustiness is made redemptive by the autonomously creative "heat" of his own passion. But it is just such autonomous creativity that Byron's talk

---

15. By indulging in such shorthand, Romantic criticism itself risks succumbing to Christensen's disciplinary stenography. Nonetheless, paradox arguably is the perfect vehicle for making McGann's point, since, by drawing our attention to a performative contradiction, it presses representation into a performative or lyric mode. I recognize the same potential below in Theodor Adorno's promotion of "necessary semblance" (*Negative Dialectics*, 93). Finally, however, my argument will be that, in respect to practical consequence, *Childe Harold* doesn't realize this theoretical possibility for the same reasons that threaten the critical potency of Adorno and Christensen.

of sublime ineffability would seem to disavow. What part can such pious speechlessness have in Christensen's rhetorical self-determination? If Rousseau can make "the common salutation of French acquaintance" into a most intense expression of love, why shouldn't he (and Byron) be able to "kindle" the same into the generic medium of language? Mimicking the same simplistic sublimation that he rejects as "vulgar" arguably serves to demonstrate Byron's independence from both critical positions: valorizing or dismissing such sublimity amounts to so much dust that Byron's virtuoso parroting would set afire. But if Byron repudiates an unjust caricature of Wordsworth only to proceed to mimic just that caricature, then his engagement with Wordsworth threatens to devolve into a kind of shadowboxing, whereas the fact that Rousseau gives actual salutations to his actual beloved is the condition of setting that dust aflame.

It can seem like an acknowledgment of precisely this problem, then, when Canto 3, stanza 7, construes Cantos 1 and 2 as failed and this failure as self-prepared, not as naturally or otherwise externally caused. In the subsequent stanza the poet draws an explicit parallel between Harold's transformation or fate and his own (as described in stanza 7):

> He of the breast which fain no more would feel,
> Wrung with the wounds which kill not, but ne'er heal;
> Yet Time, who changes all, had altered him
> In soul and aspect as in age: years steal
> Fire from the mind as vigour from the limb;
> And life's enchanted cup but sparkles near the brim.
> (3.8)

In contrast to stanza 7, though, here the transformation and fate are externally imposed on Harold by an objective force, namely, the inexorable movement of time. Harold is presented as a victim of time, even if there is nothing unique in that, whereas in the preceding stanza the poet presents himself as the product of the workings of his own "untamed" heart (3.7). Likewise, when it is said of Harold that "*The very knowledge* that he lived in vain. . . . Did yet inspire a cheer, which he forbore to check" (3.16, my emphasis), this vanity is clearly not a matter of rhetorical self-determination: it is an imposition of the world upon the subject, which the subject is proud to recognize. The "cheer" this vanity inspires signals a return to the self-satisfied, stoic vanity with which Canto 1 began ("Nor mote my shell awake the weary Nine / To grace so plain a tale— this lowly lay of mine" (1.1). False modesty thinly veils the poet's overweening pride in knowing what is lost to him and his text. In the light of this knowledge it becomes immaterial whether Byron's critique does justice to Wordsworth or whether it was even intended to do so. Byron's pride is precisely in knowing himself to be thoroughly indifferent to such questions.

Yet, paradoxically, to demonstrate indifference to Wordsworth is precisely what Byron cannot do without. Hence Byron's stance toward Wordsworth is characterized by the same ambivalence as his stance toward Napoleon in the Waterloo stanzas. Here Byron does not glorify Napoleon's martyrdom but emphatically sympathizes with it. Incongruously, Byron professes a sentimental empathy for Napoleon, or, as he puts it, a privileged access to his "breast's" (3.41n) secrets. Byron underscores the paradox this entails by specifying that it is precisely "sympathy for men" that Napoleon distinctively "wanted" (3.41n). In fact self-identification via self-contradiction becomes routine in Canto 3: while stanza 104 seems to reiterate the point of the note to stanza 99 about the pseudo-Wordsworthian nature sublime's transcendent indifference to humans, stanzas 105 to 107 reverse that point, in the manner of 99 and 103, by glorifying Edward Gibbon's incisive knowledge and irony, and Voltaire's "titanic doubt" (3.105), calling the latter a "Proteus" (3.106) "multiplying mankind's talents" (3.107).

This pattern might demonstrate the practical requirements of sustaining Christensen's rhetorical autonomy. But it also suggests that what McGann identifies as the subtle deconstruction of Harold's epic by the lyrical play of Byronic subjectivity conceals a numbing mechanization. By compulsively seeking ever new material to debunk, completely irrespective of that material's relation to the last thing debunked, such subjectivity seems prone to the same "sacrificial objectivism" with which Christensen contrasts it. If it makes no difference whether Byron defines himself by redefining Wordsworth's poetics itself or a caricature thereof, then rhetorical self-determination comes remarkably cheap; indeed, it would appear no less arbitrary and empty than the commodified literariness such self-determination supposedly overcomes. In the manner of Christensen's stenographic dialectic—literature that mobilizes the form of the particular only in order to ritualistically sacrifice it to the form of the commodity—Byron arguably does not liberate particularity but compulsively consumes it; he does not autonomously enact defiance but accepts it as an objective necessity.

On this reading Byron does not recall Hamlet so much as Macbeth, and, as if to acknowledge this, Byron makes the correlation between Harold's fatalism and his will to know explicit at the same time that he begins the series of allusions to *Macbeth* that punctuate Cantos 3 and 4. Canto 3.18 likens Napoleon to Macbeth, while Harold at Waterloo pondering the fall of Napoleon is cast as the "old man" in the play's parable who "ponders the fall of a falcon" (Duncan) "to a mousing owl" (Macbeth).[16] Like a falcon falling prey to a mousing owl and a great man falling prey to a common one, Byron considers how fame and glory that were years in the making can fall prey to a random hours of weakness and mediocrity: "How in an hour the power which gave annuls / Its gifts, transferring fame as fleeting too" (3.18). Correspondingly, Byron emphasizes the traumatized condition of society ravaged by war. He speaks of "the very life in our despair" (3.34), evoking the all-consuming, constitutive degradation that Theodor Adorno termed "false life."[17] Antiquated values like chivalry and glory no longer have the power to redeem such a life; therefore only a definitive fall into infamy can adequately demonstrate that one is at least not deceived by "fleeting" popular fame. Byron suggests that the sole possible redemption consists perversely in renouncing redemption; having integrity means finding complacence a "bane" (3.42) and resolutely devoting oneself to disruption for disruption's sake.

Correspondingly, when, at the poem's apparent climax, Byron announces, "My pilgrim's shrine is won" (4.175), this is not due to his having learned or grown, but just the opposite. Byron effectively rejects the idea upon which the whole project of a modern pilgrimage seemed premised, the idea that experience has anything to teach in the first place. The ocean figures as the nonhuman medium of this disclosure: "I was as it were a child of thee, / And trusted to thy billows far and near, / And laid my hand upon thy mane—as I do here" (4.184). Whereas in the note on Rousseau, Byron's reference to the ocean's ineffable grandeur represented an instance of autonomous rhetorical play, here that figure has tellingly come to represent a reality that circumscribes such autonomy, that does not submit to being rhetorically decided. Having brushed up against this obdurate reality, and unlearned the conceit that it has any lesson to impart, the poet's cause has expired, and with it the poem: "The torch shall be extinguish'd which hath lit / My midnight lamp—and what is writ, is writ" (4.185). The subsequent stanza suggests that, like a kind of scar, Byron's "writ" finally does not make sense of Harold's experience but reduces to a mark of sheer, inscrutable "pain":

> Ye! Who have traced the Pilgrim to the scene
> Which is his last, if in your memories dwell
> A thought which once was his, if on ye swell
> A single recollection, not in vain
> He wore his sandal-shoon, and scallop-shell;

---

16. See Shakespeare, *Macbeth*, II.iv.11–14.
17. Adorno, *Minima Moralia*, §18.

Farewell! With *him* alone may rest the pain,
If such there were—with *you*, the moral of his strain!
(4.186)

Byron proposes that the reader redeem the oceanic "pain" the poem represents as a subjectively, "moral[ly]" significant "strain." On Byron's own terms, however, this is an impossible proposition, since the source of this "pain" is, as we have seen, precisely the inaccessibility of such redemption. In other words, Byron's conclusion does not, as he claims, let Harold's pain "rest" "with him alone." On the contrary, by issuing this false promise, Byron would inflict this pain anew upon the reader. Less like a healed scar, then, Byron's writ functions as a traumatic symptom that, per Sigmund Freud, does not relieve but revisits the cause of the trauma over and over again.

So "what is writ, is writ" ad infinitum, and the liberating strength of Byron's lyric deconstructions becomes difficult to distinguish from deadeningly compulsive repetition. Christensen argues that instead of the "project of deadly enlightenment," Byron, not unlike Martin Heidegger, "has only an ethic: to 'speak out'" (*L* 314). Byron would liberate us from deadening, empiricist representation—what Wordsworth called "murder[ing] to dissect"[18]—by sensitizing us to the compulsion or "command" (*L* xvii) issued by the shear "speak[ing] out" of language, the thinging of the thing. Thus Christensen says Byron "accords an ethical disposition to a sheer 'drop of ink'" (*L* 314). On this point, comparison with Adorno is particularly instructive. For Adorno postwar life was irremediably "damaged" because Auschwitz effected a trivialization of death that precludes redemptive reconstruction, or sublimation. After Auschwitz, all attempts to grant history any kind of narrative sense amount to an "outrage" of complacent anachronism.[19] Hence, Adorno posits a "new imperative" never to act in a manner commensurate with a repetition of Auschwitz.[20] Adorno argues that our abhorrence of Auschwitz may be preserved from commodification, and this imperative fulfilled, not by virtue of commitment to any truth, even poetic truth, but only by the renunciation of truth for the sake of "semblance" as semblance.[21] Adorno does say that our "false life" has the same "right" to poetry that a tortured man has to screaming, but

---

18. Stephen Gill, ed., "The Tables Turned," in *The Major Works*, 131.
19. Adorno, *Negative Dialectics*, 365.
20. Ibid.
21. "What finite beings say about transcendence is the semblance of transcendence; but . . . it is a necessary semblance. Hence the incomparable metaphysical relevance of the rescue of semblance, the object of esthetics" (ibid., 93).

a right predicated upon torture is not a right that one could choose to exercise, and hence properly speaking not any right at all.[22] Rather than identifying an actual right, Adorno's formulation suggests that meaningful subjective agency may yet find a vehicle in what he calls the "primacy of the object"[23]—the prerogative of sheer empirical contingency over rationalizing representation—just as Christensen recovers a possibility for consequential agency from Byron's "drop of ink."

Christensen's account of Byron as a new Hamlet notwithstanding, the ethical aesthetics staked out by Byron and Adorno commonly confront a Macbethian problem. The espousal of radical aesthetic opacity and semblance as semblance arguably conceals a will to know that the need for autonomous self-accounting is behind us, that Hamlet's injunction to Horatio to tell his story has been suspended due to the sublime inscrutability of a tortured man's scream, to the chastening knowledge that that scream is not available to us but as semblance. Macbeth yearns, he says, to "know by worst means the worst."[24] Macbeth's incongruously penetrating formulation foreshadows what his fate confirms: that "the worst" is not something that one merely knows; or as Edgar puts it in *King Lear*, that "the worst is not yet so long as we can say 'this is the worst.'"[25] Macbeth's final, infantile challenge to Macduff of a test of strength is a last-ditch attempt to verify the prophecy when all other resources of verification have been exhausted, to continue to prop up the sheer form of knowing precisely by sacrificing himself as an agent of knowledge. Taking Edgar's insight to its logical conclusion, Macbeth would have the loss of his capacity to assess that "this is the worst" certify that the worst is in fact at hand. Hence, as Macbeth anticipated, "the worst" that he knows and the "worst means" by which he knows it are finally one and the same. In other words, as we noted at the outset, while accepting fate for what it is could enable rhetorical self-determination, Macbeth and Byron alike define a Macbethian fate as the annihilation of any self to be determined. In turn, like Macbeth staring at the dagger, Adorno would have Hamlet's terrible injunction to go on explaining dispelled by the sublime primacy of the object, a supposed command or law internal to objectivity, to the consciousnessness or dementia of primal screams.

Accordingly, William St. Clair's recent catalogue of Romantic period publications suggests that the possibility of Byronically strong action was at least conditioned, and arguably created, by the unprecedentedly widespread pirating of Byron's work—that is, by a kind of action that was not only out of

---

22. Ibid., 362.
23. Ibid., 183–97.
24. Shakespeare, *Macbeth*, III.iv.134–35.
25. Shakespeare, *King Lear*, IV.i.30–31.

Byron's control but that also exemplified the same commodification that his lyric practice would elude. An anonymous "Clergyman" prefaced Hodgson & Co.'s 1822 edition of *Don Juan* by remarking that "this work . . . seems . . . a sort of common property among the booksellers: for we have had editions of all sorts and sizes; from the original superb quarto, to the shabby 'two penny trash,' or weekly installments of about twenty four duodecimo, badly printed pages."[26] On the one hand, such wholesale commercial appropriation of Byron's text arguably liberated Byron to undertake his rhetorical self-determination without the taint of commercialism and allowed for a clear division of labor between speaking out and selling out. On the other hand, however, this division itself arguably reiterates and even more deeply entrenches the commodity form. Byron's pirates self-consciously traded not merely in the text that Byron produced but in the Byronic self that that text evoked. Accordingly, one publisher suggests that what consumers of the pirate editions purchased was the residual semblance of resisting commodification: "When I published *English Bards and Scotch Reviewers*, few except gentlemen had read the work, but in cheap form it was soon in the hand of every mechanic in the kingdom."[27] The retail commodity vitiates (or renders inconsequential) the distinction between consequential selfhood and its reification. Indeed, it was Byron's pirates who first publicly represented Byron as "Byron," who first construed Byron's text as a distinct consequence of a specifically Byronic agency or "strength," advertising the identity of *Don Juan*'s formerly anonymous author by way of an illustration in 1821 and by name in 1822.[28] Every market requires a standard of exchange. As the basis—the capital reserve or security—of a black rather than licit market, Byronic strength arguably amounts not to a subversion of the commodity form but just an alternative instantiation of it; and, according to Adorno and Max Horkheimer's *Dialectic of Enlightenment*, it is the essence of that logic overtly to offer alternatives only in order covertly to assimilate/eliminate them.[29]

---

26. William St. Clair, *The Reading Nation in the Romantic Period*. "Clergyman," quoted in preface, 685.

27. Benlow, *A Scourge for the Laureate*. Quoted in St. Clair, *The Reading Nation in the Romantic Period*, 676.

28. St. Clair, 683.

29. It is for just this reason, for instance, that Peter Manning's criticism of Martin Phillip's *Byron: A Poet before His Public* argues past Manning's intended target. Manning takes Martin to task for accusing Byron of, essentially, selling out. Manning does so on the grounds that it was precisely by selling out in the distinctive manner he did that Byron so successfully catered to the market in aristocratic nostalgia of his time: "An evaluative critic such as Philip Martin who finds Byron's closeness to his audience the symptom of his inauthenticity blinds himself to the nature of Byron's force: only through the double quality of a production tied to the market yet continuously read as the sign of a status (as aristocrat and poetic genius) beyond it can Byron

If this is in fact the case, however, then the question arises whether *Childe Harold*'s allusions to *Macbeth* do not in fact effect an analogous haunting. After all, isn't it a clear aim of Shakespeare's play is to disclose the fraud of Macbeth's claim to "strength"? To retrace this claim to fear of women, of men, of contingency, and of the demands of temporal action generally: of the insuperable otherness in the temporal world that, like "Banquo's issue,"[30] just keeps coming and coming without end?

Certainly. But there are two important, countervailing factors to consider. First, by *Childe Harold*'s Canto 3, stanza 113, which echoes Macbeth's concession that his rebellion has come at the cost of self-imposed dementia (of "filing" his own "mind" [III.i]), the formal pattern of Byron's self-contradictory poetics arguably is too well established to allow such recognition any practical consequence.[31] While, in respect to their discrete content, the above questions, must be affirmed, functionally this fact also, and more consistently with Byron's procedure thus far, amounts to just another, redundant layer of self-contradiction. The very resoluteness of Byron's defiance makes it perversely similar to obedience. Like Macbeth, Byron has arguably gone too far to turn back; after blood has followed blood enough times, the formal cycle has assumed a life of its own, and the prophecy has become self-fulfilling. Correspondingly, the most compelling reason why Byron's allusions to Macbeth corroborate rather than undermine the parallel between the two is that, as we have seen, perspicacious self-insight is not what Macbeth lacks but is itself what seals his fate. It is precisely Macbeth's knowledge of the true nature of what he is letting happen to himself, even as he lets it happen, that makes his fate what it is.

---

be grasped" (Peter Manning, "Childe Harold in the Marketplace: From Romaunt to Handbook," 189–90). But the purpose of criticizing someone for selling out is not to say that he is being facile or dumbing himself down. Whether the commodity desires and whether satisfactions in question are complex or simple, self-conscious or naive, is beside the point. Rather, the aim of such a criticism is to say that circulating in the marketplace is that person's determining purpose, that being bought and sold is their primary function. One need not be moralistic or evaluative to make such an observation. On the other hand, lashing out at such a red herring suggests a kind of unprovoked, Macbethian panic, as if Byron's power warranted not just analysis but also reverence or fear. In Karl Marx's account, of course, projection of such implicitly magical power is the essence of commodity fetishism. It seems to me that this is a risk run by any postulation of an ethical disposition whose effects are literary but whose source is extraliterary, like in a drop of ink. This is arguably Byronism's defining pitfall, and I suggest below that Macbethian panic is an apt description of Childe Harold's final and best-known canto.

30. Shakespeare, *Macbeth*, act III.i.64.
31. Compare Byron, *Childe Harold*, 3:113; and Shakespeare, *Macbeth*, 2.1.66.

If Christensen's sacrificial objectivism, like Adorno and Horkheimer's *Dialectic of Enlightenment,* functionally depends upon absorbing ever new moments of individuality, then the latter must continually reappear in order that they may be sacrificed. In order to confirm that blood follows blood, what is required is the absence of blood; blood must be drawn ever anew. So, if self-insight costs Macbeth his life, who or what pays for the identification with Macbeth enacted by Byron's text? Relatedly, what exactly is sacrificed in order to secure the investments of traders in Byronic strength? How exactly does Byron's text uniquely offer such security? Arguably it is finally precisely the reader's function—the function of making critical observations such as those regarding Byron's *Macbeth* allusions—that is sacrificed in order to preserve the consequentiality of Byronic strength. It is the consequentiality of critical reflection itself that Byronism sacrifices. But in order to do so, Byron's text must first provoke and exercise such reflection. Thus, what is commonly construed as Byron's deconstruction of narrative by means of lyric arguably ultimately serves the all-too-uniform repetitions of a specifically Byronic, sacrificial dialectic. Subjective indeterminacy, and the textual procedures that produce it, issue in metaphysical assurance that Byronic strength, the capacity to think and act consequentially, is, like a dagger, within reach and may be grasped and owned like any other retail property. But, as Macbeth's dagger and Karl Marx's account of commodities suggest, such transcendent assurance is not wholly transcendent but costs real blood and demands the sacrifice of the same practical consequentiality that is ostensibly secured.

In *Childe Harold*'s concluding and most famous section, the critique that I have been developing is arguably advanced by the poem itself. Stanzas 93 and 94 resurrect the Macbethian theme from Canto 2 of "blood following blood" and establish it as a frame through which to understand modernity's abandonment of aristocratic values in favor of the values of self-renunciation, self-imposed suffering: "inborn slaves, who wage / War for their chains . . . and still engage / Within the same arena where they see / Their fellows fall before, like leaves of the same tree" (4.94). Sixty-five years before Nietzsche, Byron effectively delineates the latter's theory of ressentiment. Byron calls modern, Christian culture a race to the bottom, in which each tries to bring himself lower than the last, falling one after the other "like leaves of the same tree." Thus in stanza 108 Byron evokes a critical perspective upon history as a whole: "'Tis but the same rehearsal of the past, / . . . And history, with all her volumes vast, / Hath but one page" (4.108). This mimetic self-sacrifice Byron terms "man's worst—his second fall"; the pun on "second" implying both subsequent in time and also duplicative, redundant (4.97). After the fall into sin, man takes a second fall into self-renunciation, contempt for his own potential distinctness, in resentful pursuit of an illusory power over others which "built" a second, Miltonic "adamantine wall," not between man and God but "between / Man and his [own] hopes" (4.97).

Moreover, Byron proceeds to rejoin his apostrophe to "Time"—now, however, not as the ultimate end to which all life refers and which the tomb embodies better than any poem could (as suggested in stanzas 108–10), but as the recipient of Byron's astonishingly sovereign "gift" (4.130). Christensen emphasizes the role of the gift in Byron's lordship as an act that cannot be cashed out into any neutral currency of exchange, of abstract reasons or causes, but compels—or, as Christensen puts it, "commands" (*L* xvii)—a specific act in return, is an "enchanted" "cause" unto itself (*L* 19). Byron's gift is, of course, his poem, but more specifically it is the "forgiveness curse" (4.135) that his poem announces. Stanzas 129–30 label "Time" man's "Nemesis," determining man's ultimate fate, or the fate of all fates. But the radical claim of Byron's "curse" is to pass preemptive judgment upon Time itself, deeming it out of joint not merely as a matter of fact but as a matter of principle: perversion is an inexorable, universal condition of being, applying to all action, from the "loud roar of foaming calumny" to the "lie of silence" (4.136).

Yet the function of the forgiveness curse, what makes forgiveness in this connection a curse, is arguably precisely that it denies man's fate any meaningfully tragic content. If my fate represents the sum total of who I am, depriving me of nothing that was ever really mine, then any suggestion of tragedy that might attach to that fate is illusory. Hence the final effect of the forgiveness curse is to leave nothing to forgive. Concomitantly it is to change the narrative form of history from that of tragedy to that of comedy, where the importance of the punch line consists not in the way that it definitively reverses one truth into another, incongruent, truth, but in the way that it indefinitely, comically pierces illusions. This is the ultimate consequence Byron claims for his poem: not simply to challenge prevailing truths but to redefine such challenges, no longer as tragic reversals but as comic debunkings, for tragedy is itself comically unmasked as comedy.

Byron figures this redefinition as the form of text per se. His poem, like all texts, has a permanency that makes it transcend all other elements and artifacts of human life: his text articulates what is truly the final word on the human condition. But finally this truth cannot be limited to his specific text, since, as text, it transcends the very act of judgment by which he or anyone else would discriminate that text from others. The final word is simply words; the indifferent "leaves from the same tree" are disclosed as indifferent pages of the same text. The "loud roar of foaming calumny" and the "lie of silence" become the material not of Hamletian ethical tragedy but of monotonous and interminable textual comedy.

Yet the poet calls his text a gift of love, which will "breathe when I expire . . . and move / In hearts all rocky now the late remorse of love" (4.137). In keeping with Christensen's claim for the ethics implicit in Byron's ink, this gift could provide an ethical dimension to this textualized world. But, in stanzas 137 and 138, as in 134, the poet also claims that his text transcends time, is "unearthly" (4.137). Correspondingly, Byron's love, although ostensibly linked to forgiveness, cannot but be met with "remorse" (4.137) in the one who receives it: for the earthly "unearthly" love is an empty, mocking gift. Elaborating the contrast between this eternal unity and temporal disjointedness, Byron proceeds to model history per se on the ancient Roman Coliseum ruled by "the bloody Circus' genial laws": "What matters where we fall to fill the maws / Of worms—on battle-plains or listed spot? / Both are but theatres where the chief actors rot" (4.139). Stanzas 148 to 151 invoke the legend of Caritas Romana to redefine "blood debt" from the bloody Circus's law of inane violence, and cyclic revenge, to the Christian morality of forgiveness. Yet, consistent with his characterization of the forgiveness curse from the beginning, Byron construes it not in temporal human terms but as a radical transcendence, a Christian redemption or "freeing" of souls that amounts to a "reversal" of Nature's "decree" (4.151).

Consistent with this renunciation of temporal existence, on the one hand, and intimation of immortality, on the other, Harold's absence from Canto 4 is made continuous with and exemplary of the fate of all mortal existence: self-negation is just another instance of what Byron refers to as the Hamletian "fardels" (4.166) that the mortal heart must bear. But this Hamlet allusion is tellingly conflicted: such sacrifice could never be another such a fardel since Hamlet's fardels are precisely "the whips and scorns of *time*," "the shocks that *flesh* is heir to": the burdens entailed by accepting temporal life rather than exposing oneself to "what dreams may come" after death.[32] Like Macbeth and unlike Hamlet, Byron makes self-loss not the antithesis but the very aim of self-becoming. Correspondingly, nonsensical Hamlet allusions function to reduce the temporal performance of *Childe Harold* to a compulsive acting out analogous to Macbeth's challenge to Macduff.

Thus, while Christensen's antirepresentational ethics of predicament is arguably a potentiality of Byronic irony, I would suggest that Byron's actual text, consistent with his comic leveling, preemptively trivializes this potentiality and denies it precisely the consequentiality that Christensen is after. For

---

32. Shakespeare, *Hamlet*, 3.1.65–71.

instance, consider Byron's rewriting of the Caritas Romana in the subsequent stanzas on St. Peter's Basilica. Here the sublime edifice is supposed to give us to ourselves, make us become who we truly are. But the transcendent autonomy of the artwork ultimately represents an objective truth indifferent to the contingent individual: a conception of art that baroque and fascist architecture most palpably suggest. Stanzas 155 to 163 evoke essentially the same submission of the temporal subject before the transcendent object as Coleridge's *Hymn before Sunrise*. As usual with Byron, one might question whether here he is not so much representing a Coleridgean aesthetic as staging the production of such an aesthetic. But, as we have seen, by this point the poem has drained its own ironizing strategies of critical potency, making this question moot. Once the ethical tragedy of a world consumed by the "loud roar of foaming calumny" and the "lie of silence" has given way to the textual comedy of a world consumed by the "loud roar of foaming calumny" and the "lie of silence," there is in effect no more conscience left to catch, no practical lessons to learn, but only empty "words, words, words."[33] Edmund Burke analogously criticized the French Revolution as a "profane burlesque," and, as if articulating Burke's fears for a dehistoricized future, Macbeth grafts Hamlet's textual regress onto an all-consuming temporal regress: "There would have been a time for such a word. / Tomorrow, and tomorrow, and tomorrow / Creeps in this petty pace from day to day / To the last syllable of recorded time, / . . . It is a tale / Told by an idiot, full of sound and fury, / Signifying nothing."[34] Byron would deconstruct even such an utterly deconstructed tale in order, like Heidegger, to hear a distinct "speaking out" beyond the inane sound, fury, and roar: a time beyond this time, a Being beyond beings. The dream of another, grander unity in which one might yet fit licenses the skeptic's resentful re-exposures of unfitness or disjointedness in the actual temporal world. But, in order that the "human thought" of such a unity may be cleansed of its human temporality, "human hands," the agents of our poetic production and so many other of our time-bound deeds, must be thoroughly repudiated, and so are estranged, made to tremble in Macbethian panic (4.163).[35]

---

33. Shakespeare, *Hamlet*, 2.2.193.

34. Burke, *Reflections on the Revolution in France*, ed. Mitchell, 69; Shakespeare, *Macbeth*, 5.5.18–28.

35. What I have called the confluence of Adornoian humility and Coleridgean sublimity James Chandler characterizes in terms of the repudiation of "historicism" and "intentionality" common to M. H. Abrams's Arnoldian objectivism, Bloomian psychologism, and poststructuralist study of intertextuality. Chandler compellingly argues that Romantic allusion in fact exhibits both historicism and intentionality by incorporating Augustan allusion, rather than repudiating it, into "the subject matter of the Romantic's craft," thereby making history integral to the Romantic's intentional work, itself, not its naturalized object ("Romantic Allusiveness,"

Correspondingly, when, in stanzas 174 and 175, Byron announces, "My pilgrim's shrine is won" (4.175), this cannot be due to his having learned anything new, but just the opposite. Byron effectively rejects the idea of *Bildung* upon which the whole project of a modern pilgrimage seemed premised, the idea that experience has anything to teach in the first place, that it may offer anything for consciousness to "awake to" (1.92). Like the endpoint of deconstructive criticism, the endpoint (or "stop") of the pilgrimage is a kind of degree zero, a revelation of text's opaque, "inky" (*L* 314) essence, cleansed of all the misconceptions that motivated the pilgrimage to begin with. Stanzas 157 and 158, or stanzas 179 to 184, figure the ocean as nonhuman medium of this disclosure, giving us the pulpy essence to take in hand: "I was as it were a child of thee, / And trusted to thy billows far and near, / And laid my hand upon thy mane—as I do here" (4.184). Correspondingly, when Byron pretends to conclude *Childe Harold* with a farewell, the latter in fact amounts less to an intentional act, a meaningful gesture, than testimony to the fact that the cause of the poem has expired, and with it the poem: "The torch shall be extinguish'd which hath lit / My midnight lamp—and what is writ, is writ" (4.185). Meaning is left to the reader to create by turning Harold's sheer "pain" into a significant memory of some kind:

> Ye! Who have traced the Pilgrim to the scene
> Which is his last, if in your memories dwell
> A thought which once was his, if on ye swell
> A single recollection, not in vain
> He wore his sandal-shoon, and scallop-shell;
> Farewell! With *him* alone may rest the pain,
> If such there were—with *you*, the moral of his strain!
> (4.186)

"Memories" and "recollection," Byron here claims, are the proper means of reception of the poem, where it should be allowed to linger and "dwell." In turn they are the means by which the oceanic "pain" (or terror) the poem represents is to be redeemed as a subjectively, "moral[ly]" significant "strain." There are two ways of understanding such significance. Byron could be enjoining us to harness ourselves to the terror of the poem just as he harnessed himself to

---

461–87, 486). Chandler doesn't discuss Byron in relation to this conception of Romantic allusion; my reading of *Childe Harold*, however, suggests that Byron's emphatic embrace of Augustan poetics in defiance of his contemporaries may be seen as part of a strategy of reactionary resistance against the craft, or normative work, of historicism entailed not only by Romanticism but ultimately perhaps also by Augustan poetics itself.

the terror of the sea, assimilating his poetic product to a primal object, be it that of the actual sea or of the sea of ink into which his text dissolves. That is, Byron, like Adorno, would have the possibility for significance reduced to that of bearing witness to this primacy, to our correspondently "necessary" exile to the purgatory of "semblance." Alternately, the strain's "moral" significance may be seen as consisting precisely in that pain's sublime inscrutability itself, its sensuous ineffability. The moral significance then would consist in the orientation this basic human experience, despite its irreducible otherness, gives our moral compass, like Mount Blanc's inaccessible pinnacle. A lesson of my reading of *Childe Harold*, however, is that these two options—Adornian humility and Coleridgean sublimity—amount to the same thing: namely, what Christensen terms *sacrificial objectification*. The experience of the latter is the common beginning and end point of epic pilgrimage and lyric: the home that we come to know for the first time precisely by learning to unlearn the conceit that it has anything to teach, by learning that its enigmatic "command" is not to condition a new, autonomous practice but is to be abjectly, compulsively obeyed.

As in Adorno, our right to poetry reduces to the right to scream under torture; the strain of poetry is in the end always the strain of this pain. Memory amounts not to a means of bridging time, melding intention and execution into coherent action, historicizing the self, but to a pain that effectively removes the self out of time and into an experience of sheer objectivity, unmitigated by temporal self-consciousness, a Macbethian submission to the sublimely inexplicable yet epistemologically secure principle that "blood follows blood." Thus an aim of my reading of the role of Shakespearean allusion in *Childe Harold* has been to show how critical awareness of such allusion functions preemptively to undermine the same critical subjectivity it appears to assert, how it renders critique inconsequential or, in Christensen's terms, just another "instance" of convulsively unfitting defiance which, as such, is assimilated to the "code" or law of such defiance (*L* 16–17). Like Macbeth's, then, our knowledge becomes our undoing. Understanding this is key to avoiding the repetition of the sacrificial objectivism that Christensen identifies as characteristic of so much Byron criticism.[36] Like the supreme fit of violence with which *Macbeth* concludes, the sublime ecstasy of pain is not the self-renunci-

---

36. I would suggest that Christensen himself does not escape this charge. Christensen's very opposition between strong and weak versions of Byron is arguably in keeping with the logic of his weakness. For, according to Christensen, in its "weak" or "inconsequential" configuration Byron's text functions preemptively to commodify the same irreducibly dynamic and idiosyncratic vicissitudes of desire that his strong text would mobilize. This regulating, homogenizing process is effected in two directions simultaneously: toward the mysterious past that has left Harold so "satiated" and, by analogy, toward Byron's own mysteriously scandalous

ation it pretends to be but the final refuge of a dialectic of enlightenment—a tyrannical regulation, preemptively making all contingent, temporal developments fit back into a static code—with nothing left to sacrifice but selfhood. The will to know posits a grounding in unknowing or unconscious facticity: a bloody, inky substance, which the pulp of the pirated editions of Byron may be said perfectly to emblematize except for the fact that this pulp is also just what that will—like the severed head of Macbeth (and, I'll suggest, that of Marino Faliero)—simply, empirically, is. The point is that here only a vacuous principle of certainty distinguishes being from representing: vacuous in the sense that it cannot give but only take from the self that espouses it.

## III

For Byron's Romantic predecessors, the fall of the Venetian republic had offered itself not just as an image of social autonomy and of lost history but as one that also contrasted poignantly with the corruption and inane rivalries of recent history, in particular the humiliating way that Venice volleyed back and forth between the empires of Napoleon and Austria. For the early Romantics the image of Venice crystallized in two principal tropes. First it served the construction of elegiac selfhood, as in William Wordsworth's "On the Extinction of the Venetian Republic." Second, Gothic novelists like Anne Radcliffe used Venice as a place of supernatural spectacle upon which to project historical fantasies of auratic majesty and nightmares of political corruption and surveillance. Byron's *Childe Harold* Canto 4 virtually defined Venice for the remainder of the nineteenth century by effectively combining these two tropes, significantly refining the kind of elegiac poetics Curran identifies in Smith.

---

biography. In both cases the formal "stenographic dialectic" functions to neutralize by preemptively codifying the supposedly primordial, idiosyncratic "difference" of experience:

> The hero's nameless guilt is the zone where the general, such as familial past, the *zeitgeist,* or poetic tradition, meshes with the particular. By making the hero impossibly responsible for a past that can be neither spoken nor remembered, the nameless guilt catalyzes an impressive assertion of force that appears at once completely spontaneous and utterly destined. . . . What the reader identifies with, what he or she applies to him- or herself, is not any particular feature of the Byronic hero but the very incompatibility between code and instance that structures the Byronic hero and that, because of its instability, propels the Byronic plot—which is a self-reflexive exercise in habitual identification. . . . The mystified passage from code to instance becomes an instance that is repeated in a code called the Byronic text. (*L* 16–17)

In the first stanza Byron introduces readers to Venice as arising "As from the stroke of the Enchanter's wand" (4.1),[37] an enchantment that six stanzas later is already lost, mournfully "let go" as an "over-weening phantas[y] unsound" (lines 61–62). Byron provocatively insists that the object of his psychologically realistic grief was always already a fantasy. Adding yet another twist to this already contradictory amalgam of supernaturalism and psychological realism, Byron brings this fantastical and elegiac Venice to bear as an indictment of contemporary politics, likening it to a prisoner with "clanking chains" (102–3) and "trampled" (101) by illegitimate foreign powers. Venice's fate is "shameful to nations," Byron says (150); but when he dwells on England's share in this shame, it is clear that the fate at issue is less the city's than Byron's own. Indeed Byron finally outdoes Wordsworth in elegizing the world's failure to properly respect what he poetically imagines, appealing to the reader not just to adore his impossible dreams but to do so precisely for the sake of their impossibility. "I seek no sympathies" (87), Byron writes; instead "I bleed" (89). Byron pointedly offers readers just the bloody trace of having his imagined Venice beat out of him by the hostile world. Like a modern self-ironizing advertisement, Byron encourages us to learn masochistically to cherish this trace as a trace, a punishing reminder of how absolutely cut off we are from its source. The most Byron lets us hope for is to mix our blood with his. Thus elegiac supernaturalism sustains the beautiful soul's model of subjectivity by fostering its sense of incompatibility with the actual world. Another word for the beautiful soul is in fact the Byronic hero as defined by *Childe Harold's Pilgrimage* in passages like the following:

> [I] meditate amongst decay, and stand
> A ruin amidst ruins; there to track
> Fall'n states and buried greatness, o'er a land
> Which *was* the mightiest in its old command,
> And *is* the loveliest, and must ever be
> The master-mould of Nature's heavenly hand,
> Wherein were cast the heroic and the free
> The beautiful, the brave—the lords of earth and sea[38]

Heroism here requires being a ruin among ruins; greatness is measured by its destruction. In turn, poetic "*tracking*" of this destruction becomes a way

---

37. McGann, ed., *Lord Byron: The Major Works*.
38. Ibid., 220–27.

of reenacting it, of cultivating beautiful souls who define value by its worldly absence.

But Byron's figuration of Venetian heroism in *Child Harold's Pilgrimage* would not be his last. In between his writing of this fourth canto in 1817 and his 1820 play *Marino Faliero*, the modern watershed known as *Don Juan* marked a transformation in Byron's approach to artistic and historical heroism. Byron begins *Don Juan* in his own voice by declaring, "I want a hero." To explain this want Byron lists the obvious candidates from recent French and English political history. The list is prodigious and credible, yet Byron construes this bounty not as potentially satiating his "want" but, on the contrary, as its precipitating cause. For readers of *Childe Harold* nothing would be more expected than that Byron should scorn the public attention lavished on political leaders. But Byron's point here is in fact just the opposite. He does not reject popularly chosen heroes for being popularly chosen; he rejects them because the public itself rejects them. As Byron explains in the remainder of the stanza, the collective agent of his historical "age" nominates heroes precisely for the sake of preparing them for sacrifice:

> I want a hero: an uncommon want,
> When every year and month sends forth a new one,
> Till, after cloying the gazettes with cant,
> The age discovers he is not the true one;
> Of such as these I should not care to vaunt,
> I'll therefore take our ancient friend Don Juan,
> We all have seen him, in the pantomime,
> Sent to the Devil somewhat ere his time.
> (I.1)

Byron calls his want uncommon, but he also insists it makes him not a rebel but a follower: his want testifies to conformity, not defiance. Byron's want is the historically specific one that Shelley describes in his *Defense of Poetry*, where he writes that "we want the ability to imagine what we know; we've eaten more than we can digest."[39] Byron's want is imaginatively to inhabit his "age's" compulsively consumerist spirit. So the ineffably tragic Byronic "I" of *Childe Harold*—who does not speak so much as "bleed"—gets assimilated to the collective literary agency of gazetteers. Byron says he "should not care to vaunt" what the latter deem untrue; yet, with extreme finesse, Byron assimilates the use of "should" as a term expressing first personal preference to its

---

39. Donald H. Reiman, ed., *Shelley's Poetry and Prose*, 530.

use as a term of impersonal or third personal imperative: what he "should care to do," as a Childe Harold–like sovereign individual, gets assimilated to what he "should do" as a matter of normative convention. Where Wordsworth defined his lyric voice in opposition to that of the modern urban crowd, Byron here makes the crowd's voice his own.[40]

The final couplet of this opening stanza turns on the word *pantomime* because such assimilation effectively cancels the lyric poet's individuality. Byron is not saying the problem that his version of the Don Juan story will correct is that the earlier versions were pantomimes, or voiceless imitations. Rather, the problem is that these pantomimes "sent Juan to the Devil ere his time": they were too judgmental and too invested in preemptively tragic conclusions. In other words, Byron's point is that past versions did not pantomime enough, that they compromised the comic play of imitation to the tragic conclusiveness of definitive judgments.

This explains the enigmatic passivity that so characterizes Juan throughout the poem. The underappreciated link between Juan's passivity and his heroism is an ethical one, what Byron above terms *friendship*. The prejudicial pantomimes of the past neglect not just Juan the hero but concomitantly Juan "our ancient friend." The gazetteers undermine heroism and friendship not because they don't believe in them but because their belief is a hollow pretext for asserting consumerist freedom of choice, or rather the implicitly sacrificial freedom to choose and then choose again and again in perpetuity.[41] Hence it is fitting that Byron's hero Juan takes his name from the rhyme "new one" and "true one": the mangled anglicizing of the name evokes a new truth that transcends consumerist obsession with new truths precisely by finally "digesting" that obsession, by owning it as such. The archaic, Anglo-Saxon sound of the bisyllabic pronunciation insinuates the weight of historical iner-

---

40. The radicality of Byron's populist wager here may be underscored by noting how it contrasts with Raymond Williams's (somewhat Wordsworthian) effort to redeem the colloquial (or gazetteers') usage of the word *tragedy* by testifying to its high cultural bona fides. Byron poetically inhabits consumerist celebrity culture as autonomous, as a specifically modern phenomenon, not as a vicissitude of the normative tradition of tragic heroism. Yet Williams interestingly acknowledges in passing the possible futility of his project in a way that may give it a poignantly *and* Byronically comic cast: "It takes, I believe, many years to move from first shaping these questions, in a personal uncertainty about the implications of what is being taught to putting them at all precisely and being in any position to try to answer them. The difficulties are in any case so severe that no time is really long enough. But the moment comes when it is necessary to make a beginning" (*Modern Tragedy*, 33).

41. This concern in the interim has arguably only intensified, leading William Deresiewicz recently to contend that "in the age of the entrepreneurial self, even our closest relationships are being pressed onto this template." "Faux Friendship."

tia, what Edmund Burke characterized as the "sluggishness" of tradition.[42] In other words, the rhyme-molded mangling of Juan's name, both in virtue and in spite of its evident comic effect, enacts the form of tragedy at the level of poetic speech: the underlying truth of the reader's implication in this "age" of obsessive consumerism is betrayed by the reader's own voice. This tragic fate is proclaimed by a Burkean inertia of the English tongue which becomes like a rock within one's mouth. Yet, as this image suggests, Byron turns Burke on his head by pitching this fate in an emphatically comic register. He could not do otherwise since this is the fate precisely of consumerist inauthenticity: there is no truth to be tragically revealed but the truth of the inescapability of consumerist illusion. Modern tragedy cannot avoid becoming a comic pantomime of itself. Yet Byron's highly nuanced appeal is finally to make his age's shared implication in this tragicomic fate the basis for a new, true form of friendship.

## IV

If a characteristically modern, historicist claim of Hegel's *The Phenomenology of Spirit* is that we know who we are only by retrospectively considering what we have done, this claim is challenged by another that is equally consequential for the book but that militates against both the specificity of modernity and the philosophical value of history: namely, Aristotle's contention that poetry is more philosophical than history. J. M. Bernstein resolves the uneasy juxtaposition of these two governing principles by construing Hegel's project as a "poetics of action."[43] However, the *Phenomenology*'s modernism hinges, importantly, on a pointed subversion of this contention of Aristotle's, a subversion that produces a poetics of specifically historical action. That is, Hegel elicits a new, specifically modern poetics from the kind of historical contingency that Aristotle could conceive only in contrast to poetry.

Bernstein's elision of the historical aspect of action reflects the dehistoricizing tendency of his Hegel interpretation generally, which leads to a skewed understanding of Hegel's poetics as well. In the *Phenomenology*, poetry and history commonly hinge on the theatrical (and for Hegel, the ultimately essentially comic) aspect of acting as role-playing or, as Hegel particularly emphasizes, adopting and removing masks (or *pantomime*). Poetry and history are the two sides of the one coin that is Absolute Knowing, Hegel's name for the ethical norm that makes modern historical self-consciousness what it is:

---

42. Burke, *Reflections on the Revolution in France,* ed. Mitchell, 1993, 51.
43. Bernstein, "Confession and Forgiveness," 34–65.

namely, consciousness of the self as both the creator and recollector of action that itself comes about under irreducibly contingent conditions. In other words, Hegel casts the agent of Absolute Knowing as a cause and effect of chance. Yet the final comic surprise of the *Phenomenology* is not that such Knowing is epistemologically groundless but that this groundlessness is beside the point: its normative force is just the force of its appeal to perpetuate a certain rhythm of comic performance, of masking and unmasking, for its own sake.

As Christensen emphasizes, an echo of the "blank," radically formal individuality that characterizes Antigone's pathos continues to define the shape of our experience today. Gillian Rose finds a distinction, however, between the tragic pathos of Antigone's will to achieve the content of ethical substance in the form of contingent action, on the one hand, and the consumerist complacency modern, subjectivistic willing, which is all but indifferent to ethical aspiration and hence incapable of tragic action. The modern consumerist subject unthinkingly assumes that there is nothing more to ethical action and satisfaction than the transitory fulfillment of fickle, arbitrary desires. Thus, whereas Hegel found a compelling means of illustrating the shape of the Ethical Order in classical tragedy, Rose finds the modern experience of individualistic personhood to be essentially comic:

> Antigone stakes her life as the individuated pathos of substantial life in collision with itself; she presents part of its truth and she acknowledges the part of that truth *which exceeds her*. By contrast, modern law is that of *legal status*, where those with subjective rights and subjective ends deceive themselves and others that they act for the universal when they care only for their own interests . . . it is comic . . . in the sense of bitter and repugnant intrigue by individuals who deceive others by seeming to share their interests and whose real interest is without substance. These modern comic characters are unmasked by others and not by their own self-dissolving inwardness of humor.[44]

Does Antigone still have anything to teach Byron's modern gazetteers who are superficially her mirror image? Who have tamed and domesticated her radical will to substance precisely by making the sheer form of willing into a substance of its own, reducing the will's content to arbitrary, impotent, merely subjective preference?

J. M. Bernstein builds on the Aristotelian model to argue, in contrast to Rose, that modern action, selfhood, and recognition generally maintain an

---

44. Gilliam Rose, "The Comedy of Hegel," 109–10, italics original.

essentially tragic character. According to Bernstein, Hegel's discussion of "confession" offers an "expressivist" conception of action that preserves the essentially tragic form of action while freeing it from this implication in knowledge of necessary or probable causal relations. Like Aristotelian catharsis, confession overcomes neither our actions' subjection to contingency nor our consequent subjection to externally imposed fate, but rather offers us a means of giving that fate a recognizable, ordered place in our individual lives. But the means offered by confession is more conducive to such rationalizing reconstruction because, in contrast to the privative experience of pity and fear, confession is essentially a socially adjudicated, discursive practice: what counts as confession must be conjointly adjudicated by more than one individual, whereas what counts as pity and fear need not.

True recognition of an act of confession is nothing other than an act of forgiveness, and the mutual recognition in which confession meets forgiveness converts what had been a break in the ethical structure into a pillar of that structure itself. Bernstein writes:

> To see this identity of myself with the one who has injured me is already implicitly to have forgiven them. Until . . . I have forgiven her I cannot perceive the continuity between us. The act of forgiveness must then, like confession, have a cognitive component *in* it. The act of forgiveness is an act of recognition through which, by releasing the transgressor from her deed I release myself from my hurt. Forgiveness must express my particularity as well as renouncing it. Forgiving obeys the "unwritten law" which inscribes my originary debt to the other, my having my meaning and being through her.[45]

While Hegel uses the tragic form to show how the sacrifice of the self constituted the Ethical Order, Bernstein uses it to map the self-expressive experience of confession and forgiveness. In *Antigone* Bernstein finds the "exemplary" confession of the modern, actively self-determining self (94):[46] "Through her deed, Antigone reveals both a new meaning, an unbound claim to individuality as requiring recognition, and stakes herself on that meaning claim" (95). Whereas for Hegel, Antigone's deed was ultimately revealed to be "disunited" by its contingent pathos, Bernstein makes such disunifying contingency a constitutive condition of self-determining action. The self per se is engendered when its confession of this ineliminable condition is recognized as such, and thus forgiven; this forgiveness is the self's "originary debt." By offering such a confession, Antigone's act is distinguished as a claim to selfhood

---

45. J. M. Bernstein, "Confession and Forgiveness," 62.
46. Jay Bernstein, "Conscience and Transgression," 94.

from the "blank," selfless backdrop of the Ethical Order: "Antigone, unknown even to herself, is the first expressive subject. . . . If tragic action requires that a self stake its all, then the Greeks did not truly have a tragic conception of action or self since for them there was no such self" (96).

Here, however, the expressive, mutually recognitive structure of confession and forgiveness seems to have been lost in the shuffle. In what sense can Antigone confess if there is no one to recognize her confession as such? In fact, Antigone's supposed act of confession is not situated at a historical distance from us, according to Bernstein; it is not essentially linked with either the Ethical Order or the Religion of Art as distinct historical shapes of Spirit; instead it is in itself nothing other than what it is for us. Bernstein turns to *Antigone* not as a historical document but as a therapeutic tool for a modern self whose historical horizon has completely receded behind a psychological one. *Antigone* appeals specifically to our forgiveness and recognition; in turn, this appeal makes us alive to the "originary debt" that we who would forgive must share with the confessor. *Antigone* shows the philosophical narcissist how to mourn and forgive the otherness of the world:

> In releasing the conscientious Antigone from her deed, the hard-hearted Creon—who is also, as judge, the philosophical, transcendental "I"—releases himself from his absorption in pain and anger. Mourning the loss of purity as uncontaminated universality, as in mourning the death of that other without whom in the bliss of love I did not believe I could be without and survive, I complete my mourning by forgiving the other (for their transgression, for dying and leaving me behind, for the world being infinitely separate from me), and so forgive myself (for living and surviving and having a world); hence, the sense in which forgiving is a self-overcoming. I regain myself by allowing the other (the world) back as a presence to me in order that I may be a presence for her (and so again for myself).[47]

Bernstein extracts Antigone's act of pathos from its historical context in order to cast modern selfhood and action as paradigmatically "tragic," but he disregards the fact that, as Hegel argued, that act is tragic at all only in virtue of the blank Destiny that is externally imposed upon it, that "disunites" it, rendering it an act not of a self but of pathos. Thus Bernstein does not see that the "originary debt" that he would have us confessing disunites the expressive appeal for recognition just as inevitably as Antigone's pathos disunited her act. In the end, what the confessing self is essentially always confessing is his

---

47. Bernstein, "Confession and Forgiveness," 62–63.

inability to eliminate the same contingency of action that was also Antigone's downfall. How, in any specific case, he may fail to eliminate it is entirely his to determine expressively through his confession. But the confessing self is a self whose actions are by necessity always less than entirely his, who is perpetually subject to a fate that is, to some degree, externally imposed and, like Antigone's, a blank Destiny; it is just his actions' irreducible, "blank" subjection to contingency that compels interminable confession.

Consequently, in the passage above, Bernstein, despite his use of the first person, describes mourning as characteristic of a shape of Spirit that could not be his own: that is, for him, confession can never mean what it says because what it evidently always means is the supposed unavoidability of certain psychological and epistemological conditions, and hence the inevitability of crime and the absence of meaningfully individual responsibility. Bernstein effectively diagnoses confession not as a self-expression but as a self-preempting repetition: the compulsive, repetitious "acting out" of a self that is unable to remember and work through the obstacles to its expression. For Freud and Hegel alike, however, the point of such diagnosis is to help us to recognize such repetition for what it is by *remembering*, thereby opening the possibility for what Freud characterized as self-maintaining mourning in contrast to melancholic self-loss.[48]

Thus Bernstein's account of confession also enacts a repetition like the one it describes, because it ends up reiterating rather than overcoming the comedy of legal personhood described by Rose: the comedy of individuals perpetually misrecognizing themselves in illusions of their intrinsic purposiveness. This comedy is the inevitable result of modern repackaging of Antigone's pathos, which simply appropriates the ancient experience of blank Destiny in order to make lighter the work of explaining the distinct experience of modern selfhood. This is the experience of what we are for ourselves: what Bernstein characterizes as the tragically "originary debt" of selfhood generally, and what Jagentowicz Mills calls "the representation of difference beyond the domination of the logic of identity" (266),[49] and what Butler describes as primordial psychic and textual difference that "upsets the vocabulary of kinship that is a precondition of the human, implicitly raising the question for us of what those preconditions really must be" (82).[50] In all of these characterizations, the elusive "other" or "difference" is just the negative register of the all too easily accessible, arbitrary self-sameness of legal personhood. Directly responding to such characterizations, Rose writes that all "dualistic relations to 'the other,' to

---

48. Freud, "Mourning and Melancholia," 168.
49. Mills, "Hegel's Antigone," 266.
50. Judith Butler, *Antigone's Claim*, 82.

'the world' are attempts to quieten and deny the broken middle, the third term which arises out of misrecognition of desire, of work, of my and of your self-relation mediated by the self-relation of the other" (111). In particular, merely putting "pathos of the concept in place of its logos" results in a "mourning [that] cannot work [but] remains melancholia. . . . Instead of producing a work, this self-inhibited mourning produces a play, the *Trauerspiel*, the interminable mourning play and lament, of post-modernity" (106).

Hegel's own characterization of the missing "middle term," of the way in which the perpetual diremption of ethical substance and contingent action begins to be resolved, is Religion, and in particular the Religion of Art in the form of tragedy and comedy. Crucially, both for Hegel's theory of the Religion of Art and for the general reading of *Phenomenology* I am pursuing, the selfhood that begins emerging in the tragic art form is not confessional; quite the contrary, this artistic selfhood "self-consciously . . . asserts" its "rights and purposes," not "naturally" or "naively" but as a function of artistic "impersonation," or "mask" wearing. Mediated by the artist's self-consciousness, Antigone's pathos is no longer a personal contingency but expresses a "universal individuality" and therefore inspires emotions in the audience that are not arbitrary but "cathartic" or clarifying in the Aristotelian sense (443ff.).

The Religion of Art finally begins to realize the Notion of the substantively expressive Subject, the "Substance that is also Subject": "Through the religion of Art, Spirit has advanced from the form of *Substance* to assume that of *Subject,* for *it produces* its [outer] shape, thus making explicit in it the act, or the self-consciousness, that merely vanishes in the awful Substance, and does not apprehend its own self in its trust" (453). The Notion of this artistic subjectivity, asserting itself through the "production" of its own substance, signals what it would be to overcome what Hegel calls "the unthinking mingling of individuality and essence" (449). In tragic art, "the true union, that of the self, Fate, and substance, is not yet present"; what such a union requires is that the "self-consciousness of the hero . . . step forth from his mask and present itself as knowing itself to be the fate both of the gods of the chorus and of the absolute powers themselves, and as being no longer separated from the chorus, from the universal consciousness" (450). This, on Hegel's account, is just what comic art accomplishes.

The comic player wears a mask in order to remove that of others; in this sense the substance of his negating activity is for the player to choose, and this choice is expressive of his self. Thus, in comedy, misrecognition is not replaced, as it is in tragedy, by recognition of the subject in an act unified by external necessity; rather, it is replaced by recognition of the subject in an act unified by a self-imposed necessity, that of his own comic unmasking: to see imposters unmasked is to see that they had *needed* such unmasking all along. Yet, in contrast to tragic reversals, comic reversals are normatively binding not because their revelations are conclusive but, on the contrary, because they remain interminably subject to analogous reversals. Unlike tragedy, comic action draws none of its normative authority from epistemological payoffs but only from the autonomous appeal of its aesthetic form as such, an appeal to perpetuate the series of maskings and unmaskings for its own sake.

Yet, although comedy embodies the Subject's essential negativity, this embodiment remains dependent, Hegel writes, upon instances of "empty repose and oblivion" to which it may apply its unmasking activity. The parasitic character of comedy is its own ironically tragic flaw because the comic's self comes at the cost of potentially alienating his entire world: with nothing left to unmask, the comic is bereft of Substance and Self alike, left only "the grief which expresses itself in the hard saying that 'God is dead'" (455). Robert Pippin has diagnosed Nietzsche's unmasking of God's death in terms of melancholia,[51] and Hegel's characterization here certainly indicates that the comic type as such is susceptible to the same diagnosis. Bernstein would no doubt argue that it does; indeed, the analogy Bernstein draws between confessional mourning and tragedy might be complemented nicely by the analogy between the judgmental melancholic and comic obsessing over having unmasked a dead God.

But a striking aspect of the final section of the Religion chapter, and then the concluding chapter of *Phenomenology* as a whole, is the way in which the formal characteristics Hegel attributes to comic poetics reappear in his own characterizations of the way in which Absolute Knowing relates to all of the preceding shapes of Spirit. The medium of this relation, "*erinnern*" ("remembering" or "inwardizing") maintains the comic's resolutely negative relation to its objects. If Hegel acknowledges that the comic self is susceptible to absolutizing this negativity to the point of being consumed by it, Hegel does not, like Bernstein, respond to this susceptibility by re-anchoring the subject in the epistemological tragedy of his inescapable contingent actions.

Rather than limiting the Subject's responsibility to this naturalized reiteration of Antigone's pathos as a self-"disuniting" confession, Hegel avoids comic melancholia by radicalizing subjective responsibility. Drawing on Freud's account of melancholia as a narcissistic impasse from which the social act of mourning provides release, Rose writes that tragedy allows only for "aberrated," perpetually deferred, and thus self-undermining mourning; true mourning is only "inaugurated" with "the comedy of Absolute Spirit" (109).

---

51. Robert B. Pippin, "The Death of God and Modern Melancholy."

What this comedy unmasks is the apparent "naturalness" or "givenness" in which past moments of subjective expression are recalled in memory. Refiguring these moments as "Substance that is also Subject," such comedy resolves the melancholic experience of unmitigated alienation into a kind of mourning that accepts expressive responsibility for what is lost.

The specifically memorial shape of Absolute Knowing begins to emerge immediately following the dissolution of the Art of Religion. In the paragraph following the above reference to the comic's grieving over the death of God, Hegel writes:

> The works of the Muse now lack the power of the Spirit, for the Spirit has gained its certainty of itself from the crushing of gods and men. *They have become what they are for us now*—beautiful fruit already picked from the tree, which a friendly Fate has offered us, as a girl might set the fruit before us. It cannot give us the actual life in which they existed.... It gives not the spring and summer of the ethical life in which they blossomed and ripened, but only the veiled recollection of that actual world. (455, my emphasis)

Our experience of art per se is mediated by memory; artistic subjectivity is essentially memorial subjectivity. The "life" in which artworks are engendered is not accessible to us, but we may nonetheless express ourselves by considering such works in abstraction from the life that bore them: thus, just as the Religion of Art expressed itself by representing a shape of Spirit no longer accessible to it, *we* express ourselves by representing, in memory, the Religion of Art itself, which is no longer accessible to us. Thus expressive memory comes to constitute a distinctly modern, radically ironic shape of Spirit unto itself:

> Just as the girl who offers us the plucked fruits is more than the Nature which directly provides... *because she sums all this up in a higher mode, in the gleam of her self-conscious eye and in the gesture with which she offers them*, so, too, the Spirit of the Fate that presents us with those works of art is more than the ethical life and the actual world of that nation, for it is the *inwardizing* in us of the Spirit which in them was still [only] *outwardly* manifested; it is the Spirit of the tragic Fate which gathers all those individual gods and attributes of the [divine] substance into one pantheon, into the Spirit that is itself conscious of itself as Spirit. (456, my emphasis)

If one aspect of the irony of the modern fate is that the impossibility of tragedy should have a tragic aspect of its own, another is that "Absolute Knowing" should constitute a fate at all, since a fate is just what is not absolute but irremediably temporally contingent. But it is *as* a fate that memorial Absolute Knowing continues to constitute a temporal "experience" for us. The memorial subject escapes comic melancholia because, although the former's self-assertion is dependent upon the material provided by history, her memorial unmasking does not reveal it as definitely "empty" and "dead" but only accepts its denaturalization. While the melancholic asserts his utter independence from the dead God, the memorial Subject accepts her continued dependence upon the "givenness," the unavoidability of history per se; it is only in virtue of the "fruits" it offers that she may effect the "winks" and "gestures" that subjectivize her by denaturalizing them.

The memorial Subject is effectively sustained by the ongoing tension between the naturalness of a past that is necessarily "given" to her in memory and the comic denaturalization that attends to memorial reconstruction: this reconstruction is not out to "kill off" this givenness in the manner that left the melancholy comic empty-handed, but to "preserve it in its cancellation," to denaturalize it by way of a very specific and nuanced irony that also recognizes the ongoing dependence of denaturalization per se upon the naturalness and givenness of the past. Thus our self-expressive remembering necessarily also entails an "active forgetting." The experience of Absolute Knowing is the experience of an ironic Subject constituted not just by memory but also by acceptance of memory's inherent corruption.

If memory is constitutive of our shape of Spirit, if our expressive projects necessarily assume this retrospective character, if we become who we are in virtue of how we remember who we were, this all may seem like an odd fate, but Hegel's main point is to emphasize just that this *is* a fate. Absolute Knowing does not stand above and look down upon the various, less-than-absolutely knowing, shapes of Spirit; rather, it is just that shape constituted exclusively by the activity itself of recollection, of running through previous shapes. We assert who we are by bringing expressive negativity to bear on our manner of recollection: by denaturalizing the past in a distinctive manner, by bringing an expressive style to bear on the activity of remembering, the contours begin to emerge of the shape of our fate: it is not in the works of art themselves that we may glimpse the "Spirit of the Fate" but "in the gleam of the self-conscious eye and in the gesture with which they are offered" to us by the activity itself of remembering. Remembering is the medium through which we assert our Subjectivity, and we do so not by recalling the naturalized "fruits" of the past, and still less by resituating them in their habitat, but by way of comic, stylistic "winks" and "gestures" that undermine such naturalism and thereby register something of what it is to be a memorial, an absolutely knowing subject.

As in the Religion of the tragic and the comic art forms, the material by means of which our memorial subjectivity asserts itself is essentially anachronistic; indeed, given Hegel's characterization in the above passage, together with *Phenomenology*'s very prominent reliance upon literary references, this material is paradigmatically constituted by the products of the Religion of Art itself. We assert who we are by means of those products as products, which is to say precisely not on the basis of the "life" that produced them. As Shklar puts it, Hegel heralds "the birth of a new age" precisely by offering an "elegy" for the old: "an account of the deeds and works which reveal the meaning and purpose of the life now at an end."[52]

What does it mean, then, to recognize ourselves in such a resolutely denaturalizing activity? What is the shape of a life that is not sustained by a whole ecosystem but only by the deracinated, stranded remnants, orphaned fruits, of such systems? One thing we can say with certainty is that this would require a shift in the significance of recognition itself, that our self-recognition transpires somehow differently from how it had in the past. We can experience *anagnorisis* during a production of *Antigone*, but, for us, such recognition is neither exemplary of our experience in the way it had been for the Ethical Order, nor is it a religious experience. For Hegel, this is the ironic "reversal of fortune" definitive of modernity per se; something like: it is modernity's tragic fate to have lost the experience of tragic fate. Correspondingly, I suggest that the rift that characterized those earlier shapes of Spirit—between Subject and Substance, contingent action and lawful necessity—ultimately finds resolution through our recognition of this ironic fate of ours.

To see our entire history in Bernstein's terms, as having occurred for us, is to see that it is our fate to be radically self-accountable. But a fate of such radical self-reference is one that only comedy, not tragedy, can sustain. In the final paragraph of *Phenomenology*, Hegel emphasizes that the only way this memorial Subject of Absolute Knowing avoids the impasse of the melancholy comic is by a kind of forgetting: it "has to start afresh to bring itself to maturity *as if*, for it, all that preceded were lost and it had learned nothing" (492, my emphasis). Hegel here can avoid the false consciousness of Bernstein's ostensible confession because, Hegel insists, the work of recollection that such forgetting allows does not fall back into the binary options of full presence or full absence, natural life or natural death; rather, the memorial Subject "sums all this up in a higher mode" and "preserves the higher form of the substance" (492), restoring what Rose called the "broken middle."

---

52. Judith Shklar, "Hegel's *Phenomenology*: An Elegy for Hellas," 73.

This presents a picture of rhythmically integrated forgetting and remembering that recalls, in Hegel's preface, the characterization of speculative propositions in terms of their *"accentuated* rhythm": "The form of the proposition is the appearance of the determinate sense, or the accent that distinguishes its fulfillment; but that the predicate expresses the Substance, and that the Subject itself falls into the universal, this is the *unity* in which the accent dies away" (38). Here Hegel seems to use *accent* to refer to a proposition that conjoins subject and predicate to produce a *"determinate* sense"—this determinacy being an accomplishment of and testament to the negativity of the Subject— while meter refers to Substance, the universality that threatens to engulf this determinacy but nevertheless still depends on it in order to register *as* universal to begin with. Thus, for Absolute Knowing, the crystallization and dissolution of Subject and Substance is not the matter of unequivocal death by unmasking that it was for the Religion of comic art. Rather, it is a matter of syncopations emerging and enlivening and then dissipating within an otherwise unvarying meter.

Absolute Knowing, as historical reconstruction by means of speculative propositions, would operate something like a denaturalized Aristotelian poetics, "clarifying" the hypothetical universal to which contingent temporal manifestation of particular, remembered acts are implicitly opposed. In contrast to Aristotle, Absolute Knowing would not construe this universal as a naturally given causal necessity, nor, in contrast to Bernstein, would it construe this in terms of "originary" psychological and epistemological contours of selfhood; rather, the Absolute Subject is in a position to recognize historical necessities not as limiting her expressive memorializing but as a constitutive presupposition of that memorializing itself: only *given* the necessity and substantiality of history can the Subject of memory begin to assert itself against the grain of that same givenness.

But the result of such assertion is, as the conclusion of *Phenomenology* insists, just to "reproduce" such givenness and necessity in "new forms." Just as the comic's unmaskings retrospectively demonstrate their own necessity, so our denaturalizing memorializations demonstrate theirs; but this necessity is just what the Substance of history is. Thus, whereas the melancholic shows only the necessary emptiness of things external to the self and, ultimately, of the self, the memorial subject shows the necessary fullness and substantiality of history and of those of us who sustain it and are sustained by it.

This need not be as formalistically circular as it may seem, since the content of this experience would be the same kind of potentially very rich and specific literary "fruits" upon which *Phenomenology* itself relies so heavily.

For us, the question at stake in such works is whether we merely recycle our memorial subjectivity by reiterating received, naturalized meanings, thereby allowing the subjective "accent to die away" in the unvarying "meter" of Substance, or somehow accentuate this meter, giving it a "determinate sense" by way of the comic poetics of remembering itself. We experience our shape of Spirit as a normative demand for such determinacy.

Works such as *Antigone* are "preserved in a higher mode" in such experience precisely because what *we* want from such works is not an opportunity to clarify a "blank Destiny" but an opportunity to "accentuate," to give some "determinate sense" to a legal self for whom self-sameness is omnipresent but arbitrary, and otherness is an equally arbitrary absence. Finally, it is in this rhythmic interdependence of meter and accent brought to bear by such poetics that *Phenomenology*'s own unity of action is or is not to be found and that we will or will not recognize ourselves. The integrated "rhythm" generated by subjective accentuation of Substance is the "middle term" that, Rose says, full mutual recognition requires now, of us, even more than it did of Hegel, and that modern repackagings of Antigone's tragic pathos cannot supply. Rather, it is the task precisely of

> the comedy of Absolute Spirit . . . to work through the mourning required by the disasters of modernity, to . . . return the spirit of misrecognition to its trinity of full mutual recognition, instead of lamenting those disasters as the universal "spirit" of metaphysics, of the logocentric West. . . . Given the anxiety produced . . . by the modern evasion of mutual recognition attendant on the separation of subjective rights from the law of the modern state, intensified by the individualism of post-modernity, to rediscover politics we need to reconfigure the broken middle, not to deconstruct static dualisms. (111–12)

Dieter Henrich compellingly evokes such a reconfiguration in a discussion of the role of contingency in the institution of friendship. Friendship is ethically normative by virtue of asserting, not renouncing, the actual contingent forms it assumes:

> According to Hegel's ethical principle, it is only through the assimilation of the self into a higher, integrated, substantial relationship that the self can become itself. Likewise the fact that I have entered into a friendship with this particular person, under these particular circumstances, must be recognized to be contingent. The notion of predestination distorts the nature of the ethical achievement of *letting the contingent be,* and of realizing an ethical necessity in contingent circumstances.[53]

---

53. Dieter Henrich, *Hegel im Kontext,* 173, my translation and emphasis.

An echo of Hamlet's famous "let be" is audible in Henrich's formulation, as is Henrich's invocation of the question of predestination. This is appropriate because Hamlet's basic concern regarding the purposiveness of action is prompted by anxiety about blind contingency on the one hand and empty, mechanical, Polonius-like repetition on the other. Hamlet's affirmation of fatalism—what he, paraphrasing St. Matthew, calls the "special providence in the fall of a sparrow"—is crucially predicated upon his refusal of release from "disjointed" temporality. His injunction to Horatio to "report me and my cause aright" may be the definitive enactment of this refusal, making his cause a matter not of definitive tragic recognition and clarification but of interminable transmission. But this refusal is also pointedly suggested by Hamlet's provocative remark that "providence" may—like, of all things, physical exercise—have its appropriate place in an all-too-mechanical routine, "the breathing time."[54]

Hamlet's self-realization is explicitly and rather comically predicated upon contingent routine. (Whether this involves mocking the Gospel or extending the latter's own proper comedy is another question, although one that instructively underscores the contrast between the innate open-endedness of comedy and the tragedy's dependence on definite conclusions.) Likewise, Hamlet's act of becoming conscious of this impersonal routine or mask itself constitutes the middle term between universal and particular that, according to Hegel, sustains normative social institutions like friendship, such as that between Hamlet and Horatio and (perhaps especially) the audience member or reader, for whom Horatio clearly stands in. In other words, Hamlet's act demonstrates the dependence of ethical norms not upon tragic fate but precisely upon a contingency that is comically interminable.

I have tried to show that a pivotal point in the chapters on Religion and Absolute Knowing is that Spirit's experience of becoming self-conscious as Spirit is a specifically memorial, historicizing experience that involves a more exacting unification of self and action than Bernstein's conception of tragic action allows. As Spirit becomes self-conscious, the naturalistic experience (psychologically and epistemologically dictated) of trespass and suffering, upon which Bernstein's account relies, becomes unavailable. The self is still defined by its responsibility and indebtedness; indeed, it is precisely because the self becomes so thoroughly and radically defined by the memorial practice of self-accounting in the final chapters of *Phenomenology* that its experience can no longer be explained in terms of tragedy. Bernstein's resistance to the radical implications of the book's final chapters testifies to the daunting

---

54. Shakespeare, *The Tragedy of Hamlet*, V.ii.174, 1351.

burden that the unavailability of tragedy imposes, a burden that attempts by Bernstein and others to recover Antigone as "exemplary" of modern selfhood would reassuringly elide.

This reassurance comes at the cost of a monstrous leveling, not only of history, which is reduced to a perpetual rehearsal of the rivalry between Antigone and Creon, but also of the expressive possibilities available to us for historical remembrance, which are reduced to formal inevitabilities which, as such, forestall expressive accentuation. To recognize the inaccessibility of tragedy to the modern self is to recognize the unprecedented burden of a self whose unity consists in its complete self-accountability; but it is also to recognize the unprecedented scope of an expressive freedom unburdened by naturalism or Romanticism. The tragedy of Hamlet's indecipherable cause gives way to the comically impossible necessity of persisting, somehow, in reporting it. The dialectical rhythms mobilized by such persistence—of remembering and forgetting, recognition and misrecognition, masking and unmasking—themselves stand to "let be" the ethically accented accident, the poetry of history.

## V

I would suggest that these observations on the relation between the forms of comedy and modern ethical life help illuminate what moved Byron to interrupt his work on *Don Juan* to write a drama about the history of Venice. Byron seems to have been seriously invested in the cause of Italian independence while writing *Marino Faliero*,[55] and the question of how to define and create a republic, an autonomous social life, is the question on which the play pivots. Like *Don Juan* the play is an attempt to transcend modern consumerism by befriending a hero of a shared collective history, to become, in the play's signature line, "a friend to Venice." The play tells the story of the mid-fourteenth-century eponymous Doge who attempts to mount an ultimately unsuccessful coup when the judicial Council of Forty imposes a merely token punishment upon the nobleman Steno for making a joke questioning the elderly Faliero's virility and his young wife's fidelity. The object of Faliero's outrage is ostensibly the dishonor this does less to him and his wife than to Venetian society as a whole; it indicates a society that has lost touch with republican virtue. Faliero notes that "had Steno, instead of on the Doge's throne, stampt the same

---

55. E. D. H. Johnson writes that Byron was committed to the "revolutionary movement to establish the independence of Italy" and "in a mood of high hope for the emancipation of the Italians from the tyrannical government which was oppressing them." "A Political Interpretation of Byron's *Marino Faliero*," 418, 420.

brand upon a peasant's stool, His blood had gilt the threshold; for the [man] had stabb'd him on the instant." By contrast, the Council dispenses a debased, merely nominal justice as if it were a commodity like bread:

> The most despised, wronged, outraged, helpless wretch,
> Who begs his bread, if 'tis refused by one,
> May win it from another kinder heart;
> But he, who is denied his right by those
> Whose place it is to do no wrong, is poorer
> Than the rejected beggar—he's a slave—
> Where is our redress?[56]

Faliero defends the strictly functional, effective status of social norms like nobility or heroism: these exist, if at all, as consequences of spontaneous organic social life; either they are spontaneously upheld by practical communal consent, or they simply are not real norms. In Faliero's allegory, this is what distinguishes normative esteem from a commodity like bread.[57] The Council's judgment isn't an arbitrary property or effect of the republic but defines what the republic essentially is. Collective self-authorship applies to all aspects of the republic. Even "The sovereign is a citizen," Faliero trenchantly notes; "they made me so." Faliero is a rebel, he says, "who fain would be a citizen / Or nothing, and who as left his throne to be so. . . . when I lay / Aside the dignities which I have borne, / 'Tis not to put on others, but to be / Mate to my fellows," "a friend to Venice" (I.ii).

For this reason finding fault with a criminal sentence is not a matter of an objective disagreement but of saying one's community is not one's own; it is an act of self-exile. So Faliero despairs of actual practical remedies, hypothetically asking, "Where is our redress?" (I.ii.110). He echoes the problem that Hamlet called the "dullness" or "sickness" of any actually available means of "revenge":[58] the collective social rottenness of Venice is so consuming that it preempts any individual attempt to correct it. What is at stake is the very definition of Venetian republicanism itself: as in *Don Juan*, for Faliero the republic will prove itself either to have or lack substance according to whether it can uphold and act on some standard of "our ancient friendship": an ethical bond

---

56. "Marino Faliero, Doge of Venice," 1.2.101–10.

57. This is akin to Rousseau's distinction, in the first part of the essay "The Origin of Inequality," between the strictly physical kind of overpowering that transpires in nature and "dominion and servitude" as specifically cultural norms. Rousseau, *Basic Political Writings*.

58. William Shakespeare, *Hamlet*, IV.iv.33.

that binds us more deeply than the transient cultural currency of the gazetteers' latest opinions.

Faliero provisionally seems to find a means of redress in the existential integrity of *amor fati*, embracing contingency for contingency's sake in the manner of Byron's Manfred and, above all, of Hamlet. At this point autonomy becomes for Faliero a matter merely of seeing one's fate determined not by corrupt law but by pure chance: of, as Faliero says, "throwing the die" (III.i.55), or in Hamlet's terms "let[ting] be."[59] "My life was staked upon a mighty hazard," Faliero proclaims. "The truth is in abeyance," "the future will judge" (*M* V.i.225, 229). But of course Faliero's ultimate choice to pursue Napoleonic conquest is as far from letting be as it gets; the Hametian pose amounts to an enabling pretext. Faliero's co-conspirator Israel is closer to the truth when he suggests their common aim is death. Just as the beautiful soul logic of Childe Harold replaced sympathy per se with the traces of blood spilt in sacrifice to sympathy's impossibility, so here sympathetic "ties" (*M* II. ii.84) among friends and family are not

> For those who are called to the high destinies
> Which purify corrupted commonwealths;
> We must forget all feelings save the one,
> We must resign all passions save our purpose,
> We must behold no object save our county,
> And only look on Death as beautiful.
> (*M* II.ii.85–90)

Tragically beautiful souls, Israel and Faliero reject contingent social actuality in favor of an ideal so antithetical to reality that it allows beauty only in death.

Tellingly, Faliero and Isreal see themselves not as the same plural first person but the same singular first person: "We shall be," Faliero announces, "like the two Bruti" (*M* III.i.74). But "the one cause" (*M* I.ii.496) that Faliero lets Israel believe they share could not ever really be shared, not just because it is suicidal but, more profoundly, because the tragic hero role has become a reified commodity like bread which as such is equally indifferent to all who claim it. The beautiful soul's self-destruction buys just the *name* or certificate (or as in *Childe Harold* the red badge) of republican virtue; to paraphrase Adorno and Horkheimer, it buys not Venice itself but proof of its existence.[60]

However, by introducing the figure of "the Bruti" as a commodified token or currency of tragic heroism, Byron transforms the context in which Faliero's

---

59. Ibid., V.ii.225.
60. "What is offered is not Italy but evidence that it exists." *Dialectic of Enlightenment,* 119.

action is to be evaluated. Marino Faliero is both the same as Childe Harold and crucially different because Faliero's aim is finally *knowledge that* he is the same: like the gazetteers in *Don Juan,* Faliero's aim is not so much to be a tragic hero but to know himself to be one; he's not Childe Harold but precisely a Childe Harold wannabe, which makes all the difference. Byron situates Faliero in a consumer culture in which Childe Harold–like heroism, like that of "the Bruti," circulates like money. In other words, Byron retrojects the eighteenth-century collapse of the republic back into the fourteenth century This retrojection makes the fall of Venice no longer symbolize the contrast between the crisis of consumer modernity and the glory of history. Instead, Byron insinuates that this crisis was always already integral to the life of the historical republic itself. As James Chandler emphasizes in his account of the "case" both *in* Romantic historicism and *of* Romantic historicism, this method is one of historicizing one's own means of historicizing, so that, in Chandler's words, "'British Romanticism' was itself constituted as a practice of specifying the dated state of historical cultures in and as literary texts."[61] In a profound yet modest way Byron thus anticipates what Sartre called the progressive-regressive method of historicist critique,[62] the approach most audaciously deployed by Adorno and Horkheimer's account of how the dialectic of enlightenment and the culture industry are engaged in *The Odyssey.*[63]

To understand the significance of Byron's deployment of this approach here it is helpful to consider it in terms of the figure that has emblematized Byronic poetics since Jerome McGann returned Byron to scholarly attention in the late 1960s: "fiery dust." Byron coined the term in *Childe Harold's Pilgrimage,* not in reference to himself but to Rousseau whom he called "one, whose dust was once all fire." Byron specifically refers, he says, to "the account in [Rousseau's] 'Confessions' of his passion for the Comtesse . . . and his long walk every morning for the sake of the single kiss which was the common salutation of French acquaintance." In his poetic account of this pointed tragic passion, Byron writes that Rousseau

> . . . hallowed the memorable kiss
> Which every morn his fevered lip would greet
> From hers, who but with friendship his would meet;

---

61. *England in 1819,* 5.
62. *Search for a Method.*
63. "The antireason of totalitarian capitalism, whose technique of satisfying needs, in their objectified form determined by domination, makes the satisfaction of needs impossible and tends toward the extermination of humanity—this antireason appears prototypically in the hero [Odysseus] who escapes the sacrifice by sacrificing himself." *Dialectic of Enlightenment,* 43.

> But to that gentle touch, through brain and breast
> Flash'd the thrill'd spirit's love-devouring heat;
> In that absorbing sigh perchance more blest,
> Than vulgar minds may be with all they seek possest.[64]

For Byron, Rousseau's unrequited love is more rewarding than vulgarly requited love because, by accepting his powerlessness to physically fulfill his desire, he transforms his desire from something he's subjected to into a means of relatively autonomous self-creation, of exercising a degree of poetic sovereignty over his experience both in virtue and in spite of the compromised status of that experience. Byron thus foreshadows the fittingly Rousseauian distinction Faliero draws between ethical norms and bread: Byron valorizes poetic autonomy precisely because it can't be vulgarly "possest" but may be achieved only through the kind of implicitly ethical recognition Byron offers here: through a community—such as that created by Byron and his readers—who recognize and care about such autonomy as a criterion of poetic praiseworthiness.

However, in his note on these lines Byron reverts to the beautiful soul rhetoric of ineffability that predominates in *Childe Harold*: "Rousseau's description of his feelings on this occasion may be considered as the most passionate expression of love that ever kindled into words; which must be felt, from their very force, to be inadequate: a painting can give no sufficient idea of the ocean."[65] Byron slyly stages a performative contradiction between verse and gloss. The claim of his verse was that Rousseau's fire is admirable because it's drawn from the most unlikely material, the most impersonal, common salutation of acquaintance: the creative autonomy of Rousseau's passion is borne out by the fact that it sets *even* dust afire. But Byron proceeds in his note to claim that his words cannot do justice to Rousseau's passion, just as a painting can't do justice to the ocean. The rhetoric of sublimity here could not be more undisguised or, for that matter, more trite. But, trite or otherwise, the rhetoric of sublimity could not be less appropriate in a gloss of this verse, since what made Rousseau's fiery dust praiseworthy in the first place was precisely that it was achieved by the most commonplace means. Thus Byron finally praises Rousseau in a way that implicitly discredits what supposedly made him praiseworthy.

But this kind of rhetorical self-deconstruction is finally the basis of Byron's claim to the kind of poetic sovereignty he described in terms of fiery dust. As Bourdieu remarks, "Nothing is more distinctive, more distinguished, than the

---

64. *The Major Works*, III.79.
65. Ibid., III.79n.

capacity to confer aesthetic status on objects that are banal or even 'common.'"[66] Byron's claim depends on demonstrating that poetic conventions, like conventional aesthetics of sublimity, are things Byron stands aloof from and plays with, exposing their inadequacies in respect to their creative source. In consequence, McGann says, Byron's poetry doesn't reveal but obscures the poet who writes it, leaving him "a congeries of contradictory impulses and unfulfilled potentials."[67] This explains not only why Byron would praise Rousseau in an inappropriate way but also why he'd do so in a trite way: for Byron's point is in a sense to demonstrate the triteness of poetry per se relative to the poet.

The beautiful soul's transcendence is purchased by perpetual "recreative" performative demonstration of the tragic impossibility of even minimally effective normative communication or action. This purchase and the model of ethical agency subtending it are legible not just in Byron's text but also in the print culture in which it circulated. Due to Byron's unprecedented literary celebrity, his work was subject to widespread pirating. Arguably, this circumstance helped Byron maintain the gap between the true Byron and the Byron available for popular consumption. But this also underscores the fact that this division parallels the defining split within the commodity form itself: between, in Marx's characterization, the thing of magical charms and supernatural powers that presents itself to the mind's eye and the "trivial thing" that meets the physical eye.[68] And as a matter of fact Byron's pirates self-consciously traded not merely in the text that Byron produced but also in the fantasy of Byronic selfhood which that text evoked. It wasn't Byron's official publisher but pirates who first labeled *Don Juan* as a product of Byron, advertising its formerly anonymous author by way of illustration in 1821 and by name in 1822. One illicit publisher wrote that when he first published Byron, "Few except gentleman read his work, but in cheap form it was soon in the hand of every mechanic in the kingdom."[69] This suggests that, just as Bourdieu and Campbell describe, these mechanics paradoxically sought to buy a sense of aristocratic aloofness from commerce.

## VI

Sexual politics could not be more central to *Faliero*, and it correspondingly is a key aspect of the self-commodification we have been tracking. Rousseau called writing a degenerate substitute and supplement to true communica-

---

66. Pierre Bourdieu, *Distinction*, 5.
67. *Fiery Dust*, 83.
68. Karl Marx, *Capital*.
69. St. Claire, *Reading the Romantic Nation*, 683.

tion by voice, and Derrida finds it telling that in his *Confessions,* Rousseau uses the same terms to describe masturbation as a degenerate substitute for valid expressions of passion.[70] But, as we saw, Byron's verse praised Rousseau precisely for how, in the case of his unrequited love for the Comtesse, he heroically overturned just such an invidious distinction between authentic and inauthentic forms of passion, making a generic salutation into an exemplary expression of love. If Derrida is closer than Byron to the truth about Rousseau, he is likewise closer to the truth about the prevailing aesthetic ideology of *Childe Harold* which yields to prejudice against actual inauthentic practice and, instead of setting that dust afire, valorizes the normative ideal of a true fire beyond the dust of actuality. This is the end point of the elegiac subjectivity described by the "beautiful soul" and the "romantic ideology": the fantasy of escape from historical reality into the sublime indeterminacy of individual selfhood.

Faliero makes social prestige Napoleonically synonymous with masculine virility, and commentary on the play has arguably implicated itself in this sexism by disregarding Faliero's wife, Angiolina, completely. Yet she arguably offers a glimpse of subjective sovereignty that recalls Byron's lyrical celebration of fiery dust: that is, of a poetic autonomy that cannot be vulgarly "possest" but that exists only by being recognized as such by other agents of such autonomy. She urges Faliero to recognize that his need for vengeance could be sated if he just let the imputations against his virility stand and redefined his love in a way not beholden to that vulgar standard of authenticity.

> I am too well avenged, for you still love me,
> And trust, and honour me; and all men know
> That you are just, and I am true: what more
> Could I require, or you command?
> (II.i.281–84)

Like Juan's passive sluggishness, and especially like the Comtesse's routine salutation of acquaintance, the extremely formulaic nature of Angiolina's question foregrounds inescapable implication in convention in a way that opens the possibility for a kind of heroism beyond the tragic rebellion of beautiful souls: the opportunity autonomously to redefine marriage and nobility per se in rather postindividualist and post-tragic terms, terms rooted in perpetuating or pantomiming a formula rather than contesting judgments upon his virility and her fidelity. Angiolina recalls the Promethus of Byron and Shelley alike

---

70. "It has never been possible to desire the presence 'in person,' before this play of substitution and the symbolic experience of auto-affection." Derrida, *Of Grammatology,* 154.

when she observes that the question of Steno's sentence is immaterial, that "all acquittance" should "be left to his own shamelessness or shame" (II.i). Like Prometheus, Angiolina realizes that the most devastating punishment is forgiveness and thus comes much closer to the truth of the "letting be" to which Faliero had initially pretended. If an ethically shared cause, unlike commodities like bread, is created spontaneously by the act of sharing itself, and hence finally pursues no effect beyond the effect of that act, then a Promethean opportunity is presented to Faliero by Angiolina to transcend resentful possessive individualism and radically redefine the terms of normative debate: to create the social life they would like and thus achieve the genuine republicanism Faliero ostensibly covets.

But, unwilling to divest of this sense of his own virility, Faliero proceeds with his putsch and as a result is sentenced to death and *damnatio memoria*: he is erased from the records and his portrait in the palace is blacked out. Tellingly, Faliero takes this annihilation as a safer investment than the ambiguous kind of postindividual autonomy Angiolina offered. Faliero knows he has greater market value in a definitive absence than an ambiguous presence.

> The veil which blacken o'er this blighted name,
> And hides, or seems to hide, these lineaments,
> Shall draw more gazers than the thousand portraits
> Which glitter round it in their picture trappings.
> (V.i.501–4)

The blackened portrait is Faliero's voucher that he has officially been cashed out, that he may now circulate in the virile currency of "the Brutis'" tragic heroism. The infinite exchangeability of this currency is underscored when, on the brink of execution, Faliero issues a final apologia comparing himself to King Agis of Sparta. The very exchangeability of Faliero's tragic creditors—Hamlet, Brutus, and Agis—dissolves them all into gazetteers' commodified heroism.

Byron's big insight here is that modern hegemony doesn't inhere in the norms themselves of marriage, friendship, heroism, and for that matter art and history (all of which crystallize for Byron in the question of Venetian republicanism). Instead what's hegemonic is the complacent, gazetteer-like subordination of norms' actual efficacy to proof of such efficacy. This logic of reversal characterizes the world of Byron's play. Not only does the Doge attempt to overthrow his own state, but dialectical inversion saturates the culture down to the level of personality. For instance, once one conspirator worries that another, the plebian Bertram, exhibits perversely extravagant sensibility:

> . . . I've seen that man
> Weep like an infant o'er the misery
> Of others, heedless of his, though greater;
> And in a recent quarrel I beheld him
> Turn sick at sight of blood, although a villain's.
> (II.ii)

Isreal agrees with this characterization of Bertram but explains that this in fact attests to Bertram's bravery: "The truly brave are soft of heart and eyes" (II.ii), Isreal says.

Angiolina's unrequited appeal to Faliero is an appeal to effect an analogous reversal: to, like Juan, render heroic what appears passive. Ironically Faliero himself asks Angiolina to remember him in terms extremely evocative of Juan's inertia: as if echoing Angiolina's appeal to him, Faliero asks her to remember him in remarkably formulaic terms, not as the object of ineffable grief but on the contrary—as Byron's pointedly specifies—as *allegories of himself*: the "*shadow*" of a "*fancy*," a "*name*" on her "*lips*," a "*thing*": "When I *am* nothing, let that which I *was* / Be still sometimes a name on thy sweet lips, / A shadow in thy fancy, of a thing / Which would not have thee mourn it" (II.ii). Poignantly, instead of fulfilling each other's appeal, Faliero and Angiolina each mirror the other's hauntingly formalist mode of expressing their appeal. On the other hand it is arguably just such a *pantomime of marriage*—embracing the shadow for its own sake—that most fulfills those appeals. This would be to read the play like a radicalized version of Keats's Eve of St. Agnes: as a self-haunting story of a love that can't be narrated because it's consummated in an otherworldly intercourse of dreams. The poignancy of Faliero's and Angiolina's failure is accessible only by way of the form of comedy. It is in the form of such poignancy that Hegel says comedy "completes" tragedy because such poignancy is unmitigated by the consolation of conclusive knowledge, because it is an irreducible function of the aesthetic form itself of the actor's self-consciousness, of the interminable interplay between spectacle and spectator, never resolving into the kind of definitive recognition promised by tragedy.

## VII

As I discussed in chapter 1, a most illuminating example of (tragic) narrative development suspended by and assimilated to (implicitly comic) allegorical play is offered by the conclusion of Byron's apocalyptic lyric "Darkness." Here Byron's makes Romanticism's ultimate tragic scenario—the world's end—the occasion for a formal experiment that, without compromising the earnestly tragic content, evokes this in a quasi-comic mode that is more trenchant and bracing for resisting the consolations of the beautiful soul. Anticipating *Don Juan*'s opening vision of friendship and *Childe Harold*'s verse celebration of Rousseau's fiery dust, "Darkness" exposes ideological illusions not for the sake of pretending to transcend them but in order to weave the gap itself— between tragedy on the one hand and ideological compensations thereof on the other—into the texture of a new form of life that would supplant the Romantic ideology precisely by virtue of resisting any claims to know such ideology to be definitively supplanted. To be sure, the overt provocation of Byron's apocalyptic vision is its claim that all cultural illusions tragically cede to a proto-Darwinian, survival-of-the-fittest free-for-all that Byron would apparently have us read as barbaric. In other words, the shock value of Byron's tragic vision remains beholden to normative moralism precisely because it is so diligently offensive, because its catalog of moral collapse is so thorough. But despite this moralistic content, the subtle form itself of post-personal personification opens the possibility for a new ontological and discursive status that is irreducible to the poem's all too legible normative judgments. This is the status that Timothy Morton associates with the form of echo:

> The form of echo gets in the way of a stable concept of what is natural. Echoes are literally how poetry, as sheer writing or as sheer voice, carries on after our own, or the Poet's, or the protagonist's, voice has died away. They are the earth of poetry, the weeds of writing growing up out of the cracks of significance. Weeds are flowers in the wrong place, and in this instance, the echo is a rhetorical flower in the wrong place, making a mockery of exactly who the narrator is and exactly where she is "placed."[71]

Byron's post-personal personification similarly suggests what Frances Ferguson calls Romantic formalism, the "sense of form per se, the ability to continue a series or a pattern, in a way that ceases to rely altogether on the existence of any object. "According to Ferguson what modern criticism tends to construe as a sublime "gap" [between subject and object, norm and fact, self and other, etc.], Romantic formalism "sees an interval. . . . The interval represents the formalist discovery of the patterning of language as at least as important as its ostensible referents." This is a form of communication that is subversive for how little it pretends to mean, that communicates less referentially than by way of "the spirit animating paraphrase, an exchange of what

---

71. Timothy Morton, "The Dark Ecology of Elegy," 252.

you mean for what I would say, and in which the coordination of meaning counts neither as oppression nor as formal accident."[72]

In this doubly tragic situation, the conceits of moral agency have become unbelievable, and yet this unbelievability cannot be articulated but from an implicitly moral perspective; hence Byron's lyric would inaugurate a new language game: a new true norm of ethical and discursive exchange by way not of meanings and identities but of the act of conferring masks. Thus the formal rhythm of theatrical performance assumes the kind of ethical integrity and autonomy that makes comedy, on Hegel's view, complete tragedy. From this more complex perspective of comic self-awareness Judith Butler writes that "what seems like tragic blindness turns out to be more like . . . comic myopia," not because comedy has greater insight into any fixed truth but because the formal play itself of interminable masking and unmasking better evokes the essential performativity of self-knowledge and action as such.[73] Byron construes modernity's comic self-reification as fate in the form of the temporality of de Man's masks, Morton's echoes, and Ferguson's intervals: having one's selfhood translated into an interminable series of allegories of itself; a rhythm of masking and unmasking whose interminability attests to the self's tragic unfixability even as this unfixability itself opens the possibility for Butler's performativity or what Rose terms "work." In a manner that is also powerfully evocative of an ethical rhythm of theatricality that completes tragedy by dispensing with its claims to personal depth and epistemological insight, Leo Bersani describes the sociality and eroticism of cruising in terms of a "discipline of impersonal intimacy": a pleasure "in being 'reduced' to an impersonal rhythm" that "doesn't satisfy conscious or unconscious desires; instead, it testifies to the seductiveness of the ceaseless movement toward and away from things without which there would be no particular desire for *any* thing, a seductiveness that is the ontological ground of the desirability of all things."[74] For Bersani this discipline of impersonal intimacy heralds an "ecological ethics . . . in which the subject, having willed its own lessness, can live less invasively in the world," making it "not only imperative but natural to treat the outside as we would a home."[75]

Correspondingly, whether we judge Byron's play to move beyond *Childe Harold*'s exoticizing, elegiac, and Gothic tropes of Venice is beside the point, because the play—like Byron's late work generally—lets us rest no easier with our judgments than it does the gazetteers. The lesson of Byron's Venice is that

---

72. Frances Ferguson, *Solitude and the Sublime*, 169.
73. Judith P. Butler, *Subjects of Desire*, 21.
74. Leo Bersani, *Is the Rectum a Grave?* 47ff.
75. Ibid., 62.

in consumer society, such uneasiness is the condition of effective engagement in the "performative" "work" of art and history as such. If Plutarch introduces King Agis's story by noting that "as Phocion told Antipater, 'I cannot be both your flunky and your friend,'" [76] then Byron suggests that there is a certain flunkiness involved in even requiring this choice to be definitively decided (or cashed out). When the soft-eyed and -hearted Bertram lives up to Isreal's assessment and performs the play's single bravest act, risking his life to warn his childhood friend Lioni of the personal threat to him of the insurrection, Bertram declares, "Perish Venice rather than my friend." But Lioni cannot let this act of friendship stand without contractualizing it, reducing friend to flunky by trying to buy full disclosure and repentance: "Nobility itself I guarantee thee, / So that thou art sincere and penitent." But Bertram immediately recognizes this betrayal for what it is and reverses course, replying, "I have thought again: it must not be . . . having done my duty / By thee, I now must do it by my country!" (IV.i). This singularly heroic act of devotion, predicated as it is upon a series of maskings and unmaskings, is precisely what ends up disclosing the plot and dooming the insurrection. Precipitated by a character at once marginal and underdeveloped but also overdetermined, this doom cannot appear other than tragicomic. As the key agent of the play's tragic reversal, Bertram becomes less an empty, multimasked figure and more a *figure of* masking itself. As the soft-eyed sentimentalist who would weep for a villain as soon as a hero, Bertram is less a hero per se than a Juan-like allegory for the "want" of a hero. His heroism consists in how it, like "Darkness," forces this want to recoil upon the reader. Byron's Venice is, like modernity generally, a republic of flunkies in which friendship secured equals friendship sold out. In contrast to *Childe Harold*, *Don Juan* and *Marino Faliero* remodel friendship as a paradoxical (heroically mundane, tragically comic) capacity to haunt our flunkiness by resisting tragedy's promise definitively to escape it.

---

76. Plutarch, *Lives*, 4.496; translation modified.

CHAPTER 4

# Shelley's Viral Prophecy

*The Erotics of Chance*

I

THE FOREGOING chapter explored the argument of Hegel's *Phenomenology* that the pursuit of Enlightenment insight ends up resurrecting much of the absolutism it pretends to undermine. Anticipating Latour's critique, Hegel suggests that, in Diderot's Byronic *Rameau's Nephew*, comic unmasking of cultural hypocrisy depends upon an underlying hypostatization of natural truth that finally brooks *no* formally coherent representation. Remarkably, Jerome McGann acknowledges as much in his commentary on *Don Juan* XV, stanza 1:

> A latent cynicism and despair—the "lurking thought" behind these lines—sharpens the verse to a fine edge.... The subject is the environment which [Byron and Shelley], along with their contemporaries, were "doomed to inflict or bear" (*Childe Harold* III.71; hereafter *CH*). The grand illusion of Romantic *ideology* is that one may escape such a world through imagination and poetry. The great truth of Romantic *work* is that there is no escape, that there is only revelation (in a wholly secular sense).... Imagination and poetry do not offer a relief and escape but a permanent and self-realized condition of suffering, a Romantic Agony.[1]

---

1. *The Romantic Ideology*, 131.

As the reference to Mario Praz's book *The Romantic Agony* suggests, this ideology describes the logic of Romantic Gothicism, or "haunting" generally, as exemplified particularly by the "following figure," or *doppelgänger,* central to, among many other iconically Romantic works, *Caleb Williams, The Rime of the Ancient Mariner, Hart-Leap Well, Frankenstein,* and *The Private Memoirs and Confessions of a Justified Sinner.* The emphasis that McGann places upon the role of the "lurking thought" in *Don Juan*'s skeptical materialism perfectly characterizes a moment in Percy Shelley's creative development. Shelley began his literary career as a Voltairian pamphleteer advocating atheism and (not coincidentally) a Gothic novelist specializing in erotic gore and *doppelgänger.* Shelley's roommate at Oxford recounts that Shelley

> consulted his books, how to raise a ghost; and once, at midnight,—he was then at Eton—he stole from his Dame's house, and quitting the town, crossed the field towards a running stream. As he walked along the pathway amidst the long grass, he heard it rustle behind him; he dared not look back; he felt convinced that the devil followed him; he walked fast, and held tight the skull, the prescribed assistant of his incantations. When he had crossed the field he felt less fearful, for the grass no longer rustled, so the devil no longer followed him. (T. J. Hogg, volume 1, 36)

However, this chapter attempts to show that the distinctive literary accomplishment of the mature Shelley has to do with overcoming both Enlightenment skepticism and the regressive fantasies it can entail. The mature Shelley accomplishes a critical poetics of an emphatically urbane, nonmetaphysical and non-self-destructive kind. If *Childe Harold* (hereafter *CH*) inaugurates Byron's distinctive mode of poetics and critique, as McGann suggests, then Michael Ferber articulates the generally accepted view when he says that it is with the completion of "Alastor; or, the Spirit of Solitude" that "Shelley becomes Shelley," that "he arrives at the modes, themes, and style distinctive of his 'mature' poetry" (23). In Greek, "Alastor" names an "avenging demon," and there is certainly a Byronic perversity to the notion of coming into one's own under the aegis of vengeance. Accordingly, in his preface to the poem, Shelley suggests that the world is a fundamentally vengeful place and that it rewards those who recognize its true nature by killing them off quickly rather than subjecting them, like those who fail to do so, to "slow and poisonous decay": "that Power which strikes the luminaries of the world with sudden darkness and extinction, by awakening them to too exquisite a perception of its influence, dooms to a slow and poisonous decay those meaner spirits that dare to abjure its dominion" (73). Harold Bloom writes in his gloss of this passage:

> That Power is the Imagination, in its Wordsworthian formulation, and it brings with it a choice between two kinds of destruction: . . . The first becomes a quest for a finite and measured object of desire which shall yet encompass in itself the beauty and truth of the infinite and unmeasured conceptions of the Poet. This quest is necessarily in vain, and leads to the untimely death of the quester. Such a theme would not have been acceptable to Wordsworth or Coleridge, and yet is the legitimate offspring of their own art and imaginative theory. . . . To put it as a contrary of Wordsworth's language, Nature always will and must betray the human heart that loves her, for Nature. . . is not adequate to meet the demands made upon her by the human imagination.[2]

This conception of a kind of Manichean antagonism between Imagination and Nature, between man and the world in which he is fated to pass his life, certainly is in keeping with the idea that Shelley's poem, and through it what we have come to recognize as "*the* mature Shelley," are born under the sign of a vengeful demon. Like McGann on Byron, Bloom suggests that "Shelley becomes Shelley" by asserting his incommensurability not only with Nature but also with his own poetic progenitors, Wordsworth and Coleridge, who, by denying their incompatibility with Nature, are figured as representing not the nurturing soil of Shelleyan poetics but the "slow and poisonous decay" which this poetics spring to life by repudiating.

But this is, in a sense, to read *Alastor*'s title with insufficient attention to what Bloom instructively identifies as Shelley's distinctive "urbane irony" (283). The preface does not *only*, as Bloom claims, contrast "two kinds of destruction: the Poet's solitude and the unimaginative man's lonely gregariousness" (285); it also, crucially, contrasts the "*intercourse with an intelligence similar to himself*" which the imaginative Poet actually "thirsts for," and the "single image," the "prototype of his conception," with which he vainly tries to quench that thirst. "A Defence of Poetry" (hereafter "Defence") argues that "the great secret of morals is Love; or a going out of our own nature, and an identification of ourselves with the beautiful which exists in thought, action, or person, not our own," and that "the great instrument of moral good is the imagination; and poetry administers to the effect by acting upon the cause" (517). In this light, *Alastor*'s Poet can be seen to confuse cause and effect, devoting his love wholly to a certain "image," forgetting that the point of the imagination itself is the "requisitions" it makes "on the sympathy of corresponding powers in other human beings." In *Alastor*'s preface, Shelley hardly holds the quest for

---

2. *The Visionary Company,* 285ff.

sympathy to be vain; rather, it is precisely in contrast to that worthy end that the Poet's "vacancy of spirit makes itself felt":

> The intellectual faculties, the imagination, the functions of sense, have their respective requisitions on the sympathy of corresponding powers in other human beings. The Poet is represented as uniting these requisitions, and attaching them to a single image. He seeks in vain for a prototype of his conception. Blasted by his disappointment, he descends to an untimely grave. (73)

Put most simply, the problem Shelley describes is not the Poet's quest for human sympathy but where he looks for it, and this implies that there *is* a right place to look for it. Shelley's conception of this right place evidently has to do with a notion of the poetic imagination as (1) integrally dependent on human sympathy as its underlying purpose, but (2) unable to definitively capture or fulfill that purpose in any of its determinate products. The inherently "excessive" character of that purpose, its being always "too exquisite" for any determinate poetic product to capture, is the condition of sustaining the sympathetic imagination. This means that Shelleyan imagination doesn't presuppose repudiation of nature and that Shelley becoming Shelley doesn't presuppose repudiating Wordsworth and Coleridge. Shelley certainly did consider his precursors' triumphant reconciliationism as a significant failure. But he saw that failure, like that of *Alastor*'s Poet, not as a matter of failing to assert imaginative independence from nature but as a matter of failing to meet the imagination's *own* "requisitions of sympathy." If, as the purpose of the poetic imagination, sympathy may sustain such imagination only to the extent that it defies definitive embodiment, if it is inherently excessive, then there is an important sense in which, for Shelley, such imagination necessarily fails. But, again, this hardly makes it vain: on the contrary, the argument of the following will be that it is precisely as an attempt to reconstruct Wordsworth's, Coleridge's, the Poet's, and finally his own failures as constitutive (or "legislative") moments in the collective project of human sympathy ("the world," or what Shelley, also in "Defence," calls the "one great poem" to which all poetic efforts belong) that Shelley offers his distinctive contribution to that project, that "Shelley becomes Shelley."

## II

Thus Alastor, the vengeful demon, is precisely what the poem's subtitle calls it: "The Spirit of Solitude": the spirit that, in the words of the preface, simultaneously animates and dooms the "attempt to exist without human sympathy" (73). The prevailing theme of the poem is the way in which the quest to achieve unity with nature—to achieve, in Wordsworth's terms, coherence in oneself through the "piety" of "nature" itself—derails when the idea, the "conceptual prototype," of such unity is given precedence over its practical execution. It is just such a distinction—between the actual practical accomplishment of love and obsession with the abstract idea of loving—that the epigraph from Augustine registers: "*Nondum amabam, et amare amabam, quærebam quid amarem, amans amare.*" Augustine's less poetical contextualization makes the point most clearly:

> As yet I had never been in love and I longed to love; and from a subconscious poverty of mind I hated the thought of being less inwardly destitute. I sought an object for my love; I was in love with love. . . . My hunger was internal, deprived of inward food, that is of you yourself, my God. But that was not the kind of hunger I felt. I was without any desire for incorruptible nourishment, not because I was replete with it, but the emptier I was, the more unappetizing such food became. (III.i.1)

Interestingly, although Augustine is talking about carnal desire, he faults himself not for incontinence itself so much as for the conceptual obfuscation that underwrites it by assimilating actual love to love of the idea of loving. *Alastor*'s Poet's fundamental problem is the same. As a love-object, the Poet views the idea of loving as representative of a shrinking from the true practice of loving, an inversion of the "spirit of sweet human love" into a baleful "spirit of solitude": "The spirit of sweet human love has sent / a vision to the sleep of him who spurned / Her choicest gifts" (lines 203–5).

Moreover, Augustine, again like *Alastor,* characterizes this idea not only as false but also as part of a compulsive, strategic resistance to the truth: the false object does not merely misdirect the desire but transforms it into a positive, systematic *aversion* to its actual aim, so that "the emptier I was, the more unappetizing [that aim] became," while "inward destitution," by contrast, became cherished for its own sake. So, as the love of loving gets established as an end in itself, its pursuit progressively exacerbates the same lack it is supposed to fulfill. It is a classic Freudian neurosis insofar as an actual, but troubling, desire gives way to an untroubling, because tightly regulated, pursuit that not only neglects the real desire but positively stigmatizes it, makes it an object of "hatred." On the other hand, what is satisfying for the neurosis is detrimental to the person; one feeds off one's own hunger. In respect to its ostensible end, the love of loving is not merely vain but positively destructive.

If the Poet's "spurning the gifts" of the beneficent spirit of love makes that spirit devolve to a baleful "spirit of solitude" that generates only a "vision," or negation, of such love, then Shelley is most concerned to show how the Poet, like Augustine, practically enacts this negation in the very moment of conceiving it. Thus, in the immediately ensuing sentence:

> He eagerly pursues
> Beyond the realms of dream that fleeting shade;
> He overleaps the bounds. Alas! Alas!
> Were limbs, and breath, and being intertwined
> Thus treacherously? Lost, lost, for ever lost,
> In the wide pathless desert of dim sleep,
> That beautiful shape! Does the dark gate of death
> Conduct to thy mysterious paradise,
> O Sleep? . . .
> This doubt with sudden tide flowed on his heart,
> The insatiate hope which it awakened, stung
> His brain even like despair.
> (205–22)

The "vision" is so seductively "treacherous" that merely to bear witness to it is already to "overleap the bounds." To spurn the gifts of actual love in life is to subject oneself to "doubts" (i.e., intimations) of such gifts beyond life. This is to commit oneself to an "insatiate hope" to escape life, to live according to an insatiable desire for death. As such, this hope "stings like despair," for it is precisely a sense of the futility of life that sustains it. Shelley expands on the metaphor of the sting in the next stanza, where he likens the Poet's condition to the "Frantic . . . dizzying anguish" and "blind flight" of an eagle that is "grasped / In folds of the green serpent" and that "feels her breast / Burn with the poison" (227–29). As in Augustine's account of compulsively self-destructive love of love, the Poet's vision of love is an inversion not only of real love but of reality generally; it is a systematic upheaval of the order of the world. The Poet is described as at once "fleeing" (237) and being "driven by" (232) the "bright shadow" (233) of the dream that is at once "lovely" (233) and "distempered" (225).

A crucial lesson of Freud's account of the death drive is its constitutive elusiveness: to call death the aim of life is to say that the ostensible purposes of temporal life are subordinate to some countervailing, radically disruptive force (*Beyond the Pleasure Principle, BPP*). Yet this is, in a sense, precisely not to say that this force may be understood as an alternate version of those purposes; rather, it is the radical undoing of purposiveness generally. This is a lesson that

Freud, in his very exposition of the death drive *as a drive,* may be seen to resist. Instead of entertaining the possibility clearly posed by his own ruminations that some mental activity may *fail* to obey any purpose, Freud advances the hypothesis that such failure is itself evidence of a deeper purpose. For Freud, the repetitions of traumatic neurosis are finally not abortive attempts to install the pleasure principle by retrospectively "binding" and "disposing of" the traumatic stimulus, as Freud himself suggests they could be (33ff.), but expressions of a positive compulsion *to* repeat. The traumatized mind hasn't failed to integrate the traumatic event into the purposive economy of the pleasure principle. Rather, trauma reduces the mind to *obeying* a purpose prior to that economy: that of a drive aimed ultimately at returning to the inorganic state of being that preceded life: *"the aim of all life is death"* (46). Imputing an implicit purposiveness to the repetition compulsion that dissolves all purpose, Freud exhibits a strategic resistance analogous to Augustine's, assimilating the disruptive ambiguities of practical life to overriding conceptual dictates.

Shelley goes on to describe "the Poet's path" ("Defence" 429) as integrally involved in death's ever "accumulating" "implications" (425, 431). Shelley equivocates whether the Poet is beckoned "By love, or dream, or god, or mightier Death" (428); but it becomes clear that this question is immaterial, for, underlying each option, the ultimate beckoner is the Poet's own "thought":

> ... undulating woods, and silent well,
> And leaping rivulet, and evening gloom
> Now deepening the dark shades, for speech assuming
> Held commune with him, as if he and it
> Were all that was,—only ... when his regard
> Was raised by intense pensiveness, ... two eyes,
> Two starry eyes, hung in the gloom of thought,
> And seemed with their serene and azure smiles
> To beckon him.
> (484–92)

The eyes beckoning the Poet themselves emanate from his own thought, and the sheer, formal self-destructiveness animating this beckoning becomes apparent as Shelley shows how the Poet persists in separating the end of his pursuit from the means, even as that end is recognized as his own thought:

> Obedient to the light
> That shone within his soul, he went, pursuing

> The windings of the dell. . . .
> . . .—"O Stream!
> Whose source is inaccessibly profound,
> Whither do thy mysterious waters tend?
> Thou imagest my life. . . .
> . . . and the wide sky,
> And measureless ocean may declare as soon
> What oozy cavern or what wandering cloud
> Contains thy waters, as the universe
> Tell where these living thoughts reside, when stretched
> Upon thy flowers my bloodless limbs shall waste
> I' the passing wind!"
> (493–513)

The Poet comes to recognize Death as "king of this frail world" and possessed of "devastating omnipotence," and yet as fundamentally indifferent to the concerns of the living, a "sightless" "storm," "irresistible" yet blind, arbitrary with respect to human meanings and values (609–14). In the passage above, however, we can see the Poet perpetuating the formal negativity of the death drive even after accepting the meaninglessness of his own death. He imagines how his "bloodless limbs shall waste / I' the passing wind," thereby ceding his life, so to speak, to the "vultures," Yet the Poet nonetheless manages to perpetuate the serpents' negative, poisoning activity even after there is nothing left of him to poison, insofar as he persists in abstracting from his own processes of thought an aim, origin, or home "where these living thoughts reside." Just as the act of love gave way to its negation to become love of loving, and just as the purpose of life was revealed to be Death, now, having seen through even the latter, the Poet proceeds to negate the purposiveness of the act of "seeing through" itself, of thought per se: "Consequently," William Ulmer writes, "the poem's deferrals leave meaning, for the Poet's perspective, firmly centered on an origin left intact by the inability to represent or incarnate it. The allegory of *Alastor* trades temporal freedom and flux for an obsessional Sameness" (41).

One difficulty faced by this reading, however, is posed by the poem's narrative frame. As I noted in passing, the poem begins by invoking a natural unity implicitly continuous with poetic activity (under the aegis of Wordsworthian "natural piety"). Yet this invocation issues from the narrator's own perspective of radically isolated individuality (or "Spirit of Solitude") that knows only exchange ("recompense"), possession (what is "dear to me"), and infraction ("injury," "boast"): the narrator is a free radical that is yet to be integrated into the unity of nature and that therefore can appeal only for "forgiveness" as the means of such integration:

> Earth, ocean, air, beloved brotherhood!
> If our great Mother has imbued my soul
> With aught of natural piety to feel
> Your love, and recompense the boon with mine. . . .
> If spring's voluptuous pantings when she breathes
> Her first sweet kisses, have been dear to me;
> If no bright bird, insect, or gentle beast
> I consciously have injured, but still loved
> And cherished these my kindred; then forgive
> This boast, beloved brethren, and withdraw
> No portion of your wonted favour now!
> (1–17)

The Poet's dilemma is equally that of the narrator: for the lone individual the "mystery" of natural continuity can ultimately only mean the mystery of death; to the free radical it can only ever constitute its negation.[3] Thus it's from death itself that this individual would win "trophies," not of integration, but that merely defer, repress, or "still" inherently disruptive, "obstinate questionings":

>    Mother of this unfathomable world!
> Favour my solemn song, for I have loved
> Thee ever, and thee only . . .
> . . . I have made my bed
> In charnels and on coffins, where black death
> Keeps record of the trophies won from thee,
> Hoping to still these obstinate questionings
> Of thee and thine, by forcing some lone ghost,
> Thy messenger, to render up the tale
> Of what we are.
> (18–29)

In his pursuit of such trophies, the narrator himself exemplifies the same self-undermining pursuit that he attributes to the Poet and for which Augustine

---

3. William Keach writes that *Alastor* "is centrally about the failure of both protagonist and narrator to sustain through 'natural piety' a condition of 'beloved brotherhood' with 'Earth, ocean, air'" (37).

supplies the epigraph: for the Poet and the narrator (no less than Freud himself), the idea of Death serves as a means of resisting its actuality.

At the same time, however, the narrator's quotation of Wordsworth's "obstinate questionings" suggests that what he is doing is not *only* resisting but also reflecting upon, or at least rehearsing or performing, resistance in a way that cannot be reduced to the sheer resistance of a Byron or Macbeth. This would open the possibility that the lesson we have been drawing from the poem—that, in Ulmer's words, "death is the last refuge of a linguistic idealism that insists on meaning as the closure of tenor and vehicle, soul and body" (43)—is a judgment rendered not only *upon* the poem but also *by* the poem upon itself. This distinction becomes more pronounced in the final stanza of the narrator's prologue. Following the narrator's initial, Wordsworthian claim to continuity with the "stillness" and the "moveless" "serenity" of nature, the narrator addresses nature from a markedly indeterminate, equivocal perspective:

> . . . though ne'er yet
> Thou hast unveil'd thy inmost sanctuary,
> Enough from incommunicable dream,
> And twilight phantasms, and deep noonday thought,
> Has shone within me, that serenely now
> And moveless, as a long-forgotten lyre
> Suspended in the solitary dome
> Of some mysterious and deserted fane,
> I wait thy breath, Great Parent . . .
> (37–45)

What is striking about this passage is the way in which it shows the narrator *resituating* himself, and his narrative and poetic *activity*, with respect to the natural mystery which he would have that activity uncover. No longer a possessive individual that addresses nature from without, that could "injure" nature but that pledges to "recompense" what of nature is "dear to me," now the narrator (anticipating a principal figure of the "Defence") likens himself to a lyre and his narrative and poetic production to the sound that nature's own winds produce as they flow through it. This is hardly to resolve the fundamentally self-contradictory way in which the narrator has defined his, like the Poet's, quest. Indeed, the abrupt, blithe claim the narrator makes to having achieved the same stillness that the prior stanza had figured as absolutely elusive testifies to how remote such a resolution still is. Yet I'd like to suggest that it does at least evoke the form that such a resolution might eventually take. For even as the narrator makes cheap claims to success that only testify to how remote success actually is, by construing the activity itself of such claim-making as an activity of nature itself, he makes his readers alive to the possibility that the kind of failure the narrator and Poet alike exhibit need not preclude reunification with nature but may constitute a means of such reunification.

This possibility is most precisely registered by the dual senses of "strain" that are in play in the following lines; Shelley suggests that if the "strain" or compulsion undermining the quest of the Poet and narrator alike is the poem's dominant topos, then such compulsion may itself provide the material for a reconciliation with nature, a "strain" of a harmony that is genuinely new:

> I wait thy breath, Great Parent, that my strain
> May modulate with murmurs of the air,
> And motions of the forests and the sea,
> And voice of living beings, and woven hymns
> Of night and day, and the deep heart of man.
> (45–49)

If, as Shelley argues in the "Defence," the "great instrument" of sympathy is the poetic imagination, then this instrument may be properly played only independently, or in defiance, of determinate "purposes" and "aims." For the latter are merely sympathy's "effects," not its "cause," and "poetry administers to the effect by acting upon the cause." But it does this precisely by creating a "void," or lack of aim; hence poetry presupposes, rather than vanquishes, compulsive feeding off one's own hunger:

> Those in whom the poetical faculty, though great, is less intense . . . have frequently affected a moral aim, and the effect of their poetry is diminished in exact proportion to the degree in which they compel us to advert to this purpose. . . . Poetry enlarges the circumference of the imagination by replenishing it with thoughts of ever new delight, which have the power of attracting and assimilating to their own nature all other thoughts, and which form new internals and interstices whose void for ever craves fresh food. (517ff.)

## III

If Shelley's account looks forward to Freud's account of death, it simultaneously looks back to Plato's account of love. Indeed, aside from Shelley's well-known interest in the *Symposium,* the central role played by the problem of compulsive repetition in Plato's account of love makes it, along with Wordsworth's "Ode: Intimations of Immortality" (hereafter "Ode") an unavoidable referent of *Alastor*. In the dialogue, Socrates casts his eulogy to Eros as an absolute repudiation of those of his forerunners and can in this respect be compared to Bloom's casting of Shelley as repudiating his forebears, Wordsworth and Coleridge. Socrates chastises his companions for taking the goal of their competition to be that one "should be thought to eulogize Eros, and not just eulogize him," and consequently for "attribut[ing] to the matter at hand . . . the greatest and fairest things possible regardless of whether this was so or not" (198e). Like the ritual of Agathon's "victory sacrifice," they take eulogy to involve a ritual of homage and thanksgiving, invoking what is greatest and fairest in praise and thanks for gifts whose particular character they do not pretend to understand. This characterization of his competitors doesn't appear altogether fair, but in any event it makes Socrates intention for *his* eulogy clear: it will not be a mere obeisance that maintains an absolute separation between divine and mortal but (to frontload the key term of Plato's account) an *ascent* toward the divine, an approach toward truth which narrows that separation.

The comparison of Shelley's "Mont Blanc" with Coleridge's "Hymn before sunrise, in the vale of Chamouni" (hereafter "Hymn") shows Shelley analogously setting out to correct a misguided concept of "paying tribute" or "praise": the practice that Coleridge's "Hymn" ostensibly embodies and that Shelley figures in the first section of "Mont Blanc." Both poems may be seen as responding to the question posed in the middle of the "Hymn":

> And you, ye five wild torrents fiercely glad!
> Who called you forth from night and utter death . . .
> Who gave you your invulnerable life,
> Your strength, your speed, your fury, and your joy,
> Unceasing thunder and eternal foam?
> And who commanded (and the silence came),
> Here let the billows stiffen, and have rest?
> (39–48)

For Coleridge and Shelley alike, the origin is sublime, inherently ineffable, and thus merely negatively indexed as, variously, the invisible, the silent, the secret. The spectacle of the mountain opens the poet's mind to the prospect of something beyond all spatial and temporal bounds: the finite, empirical object provides access to a sense of the infinite, unconditioned order of being. On this point the two characterizations overlap remarkably. Coleridge writes: "O dread and silent Mount! I gazed upon thee, / Till thou, still present to the bodily sense, / Didst vanish from my thought: entranced in prayer / I worshipped the Invisible alone" (13–16); Shelley's version attempts to evoke more fully this paradoxical vision of invisibility, sound of silence:

> . . . the snows descend
> Upon that Mountain; none beholds them there,
> Nor when the flakes burn in the sinking sun,
> Or the star-beams dart through them;—Winds contend
> Silently there, and heap the snow with breath
> Rapid and strong, but silently! Its home
> The voiceless lightning in these solitudes
> Keeps innocently, and like vapour broods
> Over the snow. The secret strength of things
> Which governs thought, and to the infinite dome
> Of heaven is as a law, inhabits thee!
> (131–41)

In Coleridge and Shelley alike there is a tension between two conceptions of this sublime origin: first as a kind of ontological absolute, a condition of the possibility of the world as we know it, and of which certain, particularly striking features of the world (such as the mountain) serve to remind us; but second, not merely as a precondition of reality, of which we may be ignorant or cognizant but in neither case do we thereby *change* reality but, on the contrary, as a means of actually bringing ourselves and the origin into closer proximity, of positively reconstituting (or, for Shelley, "legislating" anew) our mutual relation. This distinction parallels that which Socrates draws between his colleagues' indeterminate praise, which affirms an absolute separation between the object of praise and the subject uttering it, and Socrates' own which pretends to participate in, or "ascend" toward, Eros *by means of* praising it. Arguably, it is precisely the tension between these two conceptions that the conclusion of the "Hymn," despite its emphatic identification of "praising" God with "uttering forth God," is designed to suppress. After appealing to the "flowers," "goats," "eagles," "lightnings," and other "wonders of the element" to "Utter forth God, and fill the hills with praise!" the poet appeals to the mountain as well:

> Thou too again, stupendous Mountain! Thou
> That as I raise my head, awhile bowed low
> In adoration, upward from thy base
> Slow traveling with dim eyes suffused with tears,

Solemnly seemest, like a vapoury cloud,
To rise before me—Rise, O ever rise,
Rise like a cloud of incense, from the Earth!
Thou kingly Spirit throned among the hills,
Thou dread ambassador from Earth to Heaven,
Great hierarch! Tell thou the silent sky,
And tell the stars, and tell yon rising sun,
Earth, with her thousand voices, praises God.
(74–85)

The capacity to "utter forth God" by the very act of praising him, which Coleridge expressly affirms in all of life's multifarious forms (Earth's "thousand voices") and likens to the perpetual "rise" of the mountain, making the latter an "ambassador from Earth to Heaven," he also simultaneously implicitly denies insofar as all of those voices are assimilated to that of the "Great hierarch." Like Socrates' competitors, Coleridge allows only *one* form of praise and, by this practical restriction, implicitly preempts the expressive specificity that the act of praise is supposed to promise: rather than giving voice to what is specific about the experience of seeing the invisible, hearing the silent, unlocking the secret of an unconditioned order of being, Coleridge, like Socrates' colleagues, compels praise to assume the form of conventional, ritualistic exercise, a perfunctory bow to the "Great hierarch" whose primacy among "the Earth's thousand voices" is to be accepted on faith. Ultimately, the "Hymn" promotes not expression but hegemony and thus does not overcome the tension between praising and "uttering forth God" so much as it reinforces it.[4]

It will help illuminate Shelley's response to this hegemonic maneuver of Coleridge's to consider Socrates' response to that of his competitors. Socrates intends his eulogy to demystify and secularize Eros, emphasizing that it is "about this very word" (199d). Thus Socrates begins by pointing out its peculiar logical structure: Eros requires a genitive object; it is always *of* a particular object. The implication of this logical structure is that "the desirous thing desires what it is in need of, and does not desire unless it is in need" (200b) and, consequently, that "Eros is in need of and does not have beauty

---

4. David Lloyd and Paul Thomas critique Coleridge in terms of such a hegemonic function: "The oppositional relation between culture and society can only be maintained ideally; in practice, the very formulation of the space of culture demands . . . its actualization in pedagogical institutions whose function is to transform the individual of civil society into the subject of the state. . . . And it is not that Coleridge programmatically influences these struggles . . . but that he grasps and articulates the very process through which the new citizen-subjects must come into being, be "educed," and the corresponding institutional forms that their education requires" (*Culture and the State,* 67ff.).

". . . is neither beautiful . . . nor good" (201b). Eros represents the negative aspect of human desire, the fact that we want what we do not have, that we want to make ours only what is not ours. The fact that Eros functions in this negative way opens up an intermediary space between complete knowing and ignorance, beauty and ugliness: a middle ground of practical ambiguity that Socrates' competitors' hegemonic appeal to conventional religious authority, like Coleridge's, tends to suppress. In turn, as a practical consequence unto himself of the logical principle he represents, Eros is not, in fact, a god at all but a demon, an intermediary between the human and the divine. Indeed, the practical consequence of Eros's logical negativity, his constitutive dependence upon what he lacks, is to make his fundamental function that of *mediation*: "'Interpreting and ferrying to gods things from human beings and to human beings things from gods'" (202e). By recognizing rather than suppressing the irreducible element of ambiguity in practical life, this doctrine of *Eros* can, ironically, be seen as attesting more faithfully to the strictly functional disruptiveness of death than Freud's doctrine of the death drive. By the same token, however, whereas Socrates claimed that his account would be distinguished from his companions' by determining Eros's specific truth, he does so only to reveal that Eros's defining function is to inject a generalized indeterminacy or ambiguity into human practical life, and thus to preclude such conclusive determination.

Thus there is a profound and characteristically Socratic irony to this account, an irony that tends to push the account from the exclusively theoretical onto the practical plane, such that we come to see Socrates' claim to state a singular truth also, and perhaps more importantly, as an exemplary instance unto itself of the ubiquitous "interpreting and ferrying" that truth entails. This irony is, I think, the key to understanding Diotima's famous and odd formulation: "eros is not of the beautiful," but of "bringing to birth in the beautiful" (206b). Diotima claims that the activity of "ferrying and interpreting" "shares" in immortality without actually *being* "the immortal," which itself does not share in this activity but "has a different way" (208b). As Diotima characterizes it, "the pregnant draws near to beauty, . . . becomes glad and in its rejoicing dissolves and then gives birth and produces offspring" (206d). This reproductive activity manages to share in the divine, Diotima suggests, not in virtue of successfully seducing or capturing it and "ferrying" it home, nor of arriving at an interpretation so correct that it goes beyond interpretation and becomes simple truth; on the contrary, it comes to participate in the divine precisely in virtue of its own, eminently temporal and concrete *self-propagation*. Hence the ultimate object of desire is always the regenerative activity itself to which desiring gives rise: eros is "*of* engendering," Diotima says, "because engendering is born forever and is immortal as far as that can happen to a mortal being" (207a). The activity of bringing to birth is itself "born forever": birthing gives birth to birthing in perpetuity. Consequently, we approach the beautiful object of our desire only to discover that it ultimately devolves to, or, in Diotima's term, "dissolves" into, the activity itself of our approaching. This is just what Shelley is getting at when he writes in the "Defence" that "man in society, with all his passions and his pleasures, . . . becomes the object of the passions and pleasure of man; and additional class of emotions produces an augmented treasure of expressions; and language, gesture and the imitative arts, become at once the representation and the medium, the pencil and the picture, the chisel and the statue, the chord and the harmony" (511). It is evident, however, that Shelley's and Diotima's characterizations of erotic practice bring us perilously close to Augustine's "love of loving," and thus require us to return to the problem of repetition.

Socrates' famous last words in the dialogue, according to Aristodemus's hazy memory, are to the effect that "the same man should know how to make comedy and tragedy; and that he who is by art a tragic poet is also a comic poet" (223d). The problem with Alcibiades's love for Socrates can be characterized along these lines: he only knows how to love tragically, which leads him hubristically to, in Shelley's term, "overleap" beyond his erotic means and, falling far short of his aim, to confuse compulsive suffering, which he likens to a viper's "burning poison," with meaningful tragedy (218a). Hence Socrates' advice to Alcibiades is to "consider better: without your being aware of it—I may be nothing. Thought, you know, begins to have keen eyesight when the sight of the eyes starts to decline from its peak; and you are still far from that" (219a); how far is measured according to Diotima's account of erotic ascent:

> From one to two, and from two to all beautiful bodies; and from beautiful bodies to beautiful pursuits; and from pursuits to beautiful lessons; and from lessons to end at the lesson, which is the lesson of nothing else than the beautiful itself; and at last to know what is beauty itself. . . . Only here, in seeing in the way the beautiful is seeable, will [a human being] get to engender not phantom images of virtue . . . but true. . . . Once he has given birth to and cherished true virtue, it lies within him to become dear to god, and, if it is possible for any human being, to become immortal as well. (211c–212a)

Sustaining the "pregnancy" of desire is not a matter of disavowing the "phantom images" in which beauty may appear to us; on the contrary, the example of Alcibiades demonstrates the "deflating" or "evacuating" effect of such overweening pretense. Alcibiades needs to acknowledge that he sees *too well*,

Socrates says, to bear witness to the higher-order beauty of thought he claims to love in Socrates. Alcibiades thinks higher-order beauty may be captured in the tangible physical forms of lower-order beauty; in effect, he makes a fetish of Socrates' body, attributing to it qualities that it is not in the nature of a body to have. In doing so, he emblematizes what Nietzsche criticized as philosophical *Bedürftigkeit* (indigence or neediness) (*Beyond Good and Evil* 90), and Diotima as a "calculating" and "enslaving" "contentment with the beauty in one" (210d): Alcibiades needs to *know* he's possessing the object of his desire in the same compulsive way a child needs to know he's got his favorite toy in his hands or an adolescent needs to know his love is reciprocated.

To be sure, in the cases of the child and the adolescent such neediness is not necessarily inappropriate: for them the "tragedy" that results when the love-object resists that neediness can be *productive*; it can meaningfully inform the lover about herself and the world by bringing into better relief the subtle limits upon what she may realistically demand of the world. The child or adolescent may *grow,* or advance his or her character development, as a result of such tragic disappointment, becoming new persons in the sense that they would no longer be prone to repeat precisely the same tragedy. But it is a regressive—and as Coleridge and Socrates' colleagues exemplify, also oppressive, hegemonic—fantasy to believe that the love of wisdom is propelled by the same need for discrete love-objects.

In Plato's account, it is an indication of growth or "ascent" that what was formally exclusively tragic comes to assume a comic aspect as well: part of tragic *anagnorisis,* of genuinely *learning* something from my tragic fate, is to become incapable of repeating the same disappointment in precisely the same terms. The effect of such learning is to "bring to birth" a new person for whom the prospect of repeating the same disappointment in the same terms would involve a comic misrecognition on my part, both of my self and my world. Shelley likewise would have us understand the defining moment of sympathy in terms of the imaginative "distention" it requires: "The imagination is enlarged by a sympathy with pains and passions so mighty that they distend in their conception the capacity of that by which they are conceived"; thus sympathy inspiring poetry "multiplies all that it reflects, and endows it with the power of propagating its like wherever it may fall" (520). This is also the way to understand that view of Shelley's with which we began, according to which the power of truth "strikes the luminaries with extinction by awakening them to too exquisite a perception of its influence": to penetrate to truth is by definition to fall out of the practical "interpreting and ferrying" devoted to pursuing it; falling short of such penetration does not undermine this pursuit but sustains it; this is its inherently double-edged or "vengeful" nature. Thus

Ulmer writes that "Shelleyan desire continually reinstates the forces threatening it through its structural dependence on them" (28).[5]

If the meaningfulness of our practical projects depends in some sense on their failure, then Plato suggests that tragedy and comedy are simply the forms in which the significance of our practical failures crystallizes for us. To be sure, there is no denying that in her account of the ascent, Diotima appears to hold out the possibility of achieving immortality despite her claim that the immortal itself "has a different way" from, and is not implicated in, erotic ascending. Socrates' impassive response to Alcibiades erotic advances clearly lends itself to the inference that Socrates is supposed to represent the actualization of this possibility. Socrates may thus be seen as a version of Coleridge's "Great hierarch," hegemonically assimilating all diffuse erotic striving to one, bluntly hypostatized ideal. What is remarkable about the dialogue's ending, however, is the emphatic way in which Plato nonetheless insists on Socrates' abiding implication in the inexorable corporeal repetitions of temporal existence: Plato's provocative concluding sentence evokes precisely the *inertia* of Socrates' sleeping body, its intransigent, mechanical "order." Socrates' evidently extreme bodily discipline only accentuates the fact that the compulsion to sleep is no less involuntarily imposed upon him than Aristophanes's hiccups: in a sense, we may see Socrates' sleep as merely the final iteration in the series of corporeal compulsions that proceeded through hiccups, sneezing, and laughing. If we chose to see Socrates as pregnant with immortality, Plato insists that we understand that he is *only* pregnant with it, that he is pressing up against the limits of earthly existence, perhaps, but not pushing beyond them. Thus Plato suggests that even the final stage of Diotima's ascent is inexorably tragic insofar as immortality or beauty itself may be temporally "realized" only at the cost of reducing it to an "image." The comic aspect of this scenario, then, is the flip side of the tragedy: Socrates' "loss" of immortality simultaneously "brings birth to" new possibilities not for immortality itself but for temporally "interpreting and ferrying" immortality. If the tragedy is the way in which his

---

5. It is just this double-edged character of erotic practice that, I've suggested, Coleridge's homogenization of erotic striving, under the aegis of the "Great hierarch," functions to suppress. Yet such suppression is also integral to David Towsey's deconstructive reading of Platonic Eros, insofar as it equally supposes that such striving is sustained by *successful* sublimation of erotic excess rather than, as we have seen in the *Symposium* and *Alastor*'s preface alike, by precisely the *failure* of such sublimation: "The 'excess' of the exchange between art and nature 'breeds' and 'engenders' its own version of the sublime, which is also its entry into the "divine" at the moment of its alienation from itself. . . . Inescapably antinomic, [procreation] locates immortality, reason and the transcendental within mortality, sexual merging and exchange. . . . An excess of relationship, self entwined with other to the extent that self is other, is a destructive violence, the most intense and affirmative form of love" (521ff.).

seeming actualization of immortality was revealed as only an actualization of *seeming* immortality, then the fruit of this tragedy is a new perspective that is capable of retrospectively reconstruing it as a comedy of misrecognition and that, consequently, may no longer be tragically enchanted by quite the same image of the one true immortality. This is not to say that it cannot subsequently be tragically enchanted by *another* such image, but, having watched the prior tragic enchantment "dissolve" into a comedy of misrecognition, this perspective has "ascended" in the sense that it no longer sees quite so much distance between the object of desire and the activity of desiring, between the immortal itself and the mortal activity that merely "shares" in it. By the same token, it no longer sees quite so much distance between tragedy and comedy.

It is precisely such a retrospective rewriting that Shelley gives to Coleridge's "Hymn," transforming the relation to the "Great hierarch," which, as determined by the "Hymn," is bound to lead only to inanely tragic repetition of formulaic submission before an inaccessible authority, into a case of essentially comic misrecognition by articulating a more refined conception of what "paying tribute" means, and thereby rendering obsolete, no longer properly inhabitable, the simple relation of religious supplication. Shelley concludes "Mont Blanc" by asking, of the same "thousand voices" of the Earth that Coleridge had bowing before the "Great hierarch": "And what were thou, and earth, and stars, and sea, / If to the human mind's imaginings / Silence and solitude were vacancy?" (143–45). Coleridge's vision of "the Invisible" is made to testify, no longer to an inscrutable, higher power but to the power immanent to the poetic imagination that defines it as such to begin with. In the same terms, the opening section of the poem figures the reconciliation of the contending senses of praise—that of merely paying tribute to God and that of actually contributing thereby to God's constitution ("uttering forth God")—where the "Hymn," as we saw, hegemonically assimilated the latter for the former:

> The everlasting universe of things
> Flows through the mind, and rolls its rapid waves,
> Now dark—now glittering—now reflecting gloom—
> Now lending splendour, where from secret springs
> The source of human thought its tribute brings
> Of waters,—with a sound but half its own,
> Such as a feeble brook will oft assume
> In the wild woods, among the mountains lone,
> Where waterfalls around it leap for ever,
> Where woods and winds contend, and a vast river
> Over its rocks ceaselessly bursts and raves.
> (1–11)

The universe flows through the mind yet is nurtured from a "feeble brook" to a "vast river" by the mind's own "tributes" to it: the falls, contending winds, and woods—the universe is ultimately nothing other than the sum of those tributes so that in the sublime spectacle of its "raving" and "bursting," the mind finds precisely itself reflected. Shelley takes advantage of the dual senses of "tribute"—as the source itself (the tributary) and the expression of debt to the source[6]—not to surreptitiously assimilate one to the other but to evoke an overriding "unity of the flow": of mind and its object (the universe), of source and derivative, of sound and echo, and of the object and its sublimation. Thus "Mont Blanc" undertakes two projects simultaneously: (1) to show the unity of imagination and nature in the eternal process of imaginative "interpreting and ferrying," and (2) to "bring to birth" the pregnant promise implicit to, albeit suppressed by, Coleridge's "Hymn."[7] While the first project may, no less than the "Hymn"'s claim to articulate a definitive unity of imagination and nature, be destined to end in tragedy, the second has the effect of rehabilitating the "Hymn"'s tragedy as a case of essentially comic misrecognition, and, thereby, of mitigating the tragedy of the first project by practically exemplifying a moment within the same eternal process it cannot but fail to definitively articulate.

## IV

Socrates' account of Eros reveals the discursive poverty it repudiates and would overcome, the beautiful ideal it would seduce in order to achieve this overcoming, and, finally, the tragic upshot that the seduction succeeds only to disclose that it could not and can never succeed and hence was also a case of comic misrecognition all along. But the offspring of Socrates' failed seduction is not his speech itself (this is the *attempt* at seduction) but what his auditors, and finally we, Plato's readers, make of his speech. That the speech bears some kind of fruit is indicated by the fact that, in its wake, we cannot return to Socrates' competitors' speeches and read them as we had before; we are *called upon* to recognize the possibility for a less impoverished, more resourceful

---

6. Analogously, in *Prometheus Unbound* reference is made to "Indus and its tribute rivers" (III.iii). With respect to water flows, the *OED* defines "tributary" as a "stream contributing its flow to a larger stream or lake; an affluent, feeder."

7. Whereas Earl Wasserman argues that in "Mont Blanc," "in an effort to make coherent sense of mortal existence, [Shelley] envisions a transcendent constant behind these apparent cessations and vacancies" (6; cf. 223ff.), I am suggesting that Shelley pursues such sense not in a "transcendental constant" but, on the one hand, in reconstituting Coleridge's postulation of such a constant as a pregnant "interpreting and ferrying," which inspired his own production of "Mont Blanc," and, on the other hand, in a vision of and endless chain of such transmission, which may inspire, in turn, further poetic production.

discourse than we had before: to learn from rather than repeat this tragedy, to *grow* or bring birth to something new. This is an eminently "pregnant" result, one could say, yet it is left to us to bring this pregnancy to birth. Only the concrete attempt to actualize this promise will determine the precise measure and quality of the fruit the speech bears.

It is precisely in these terms of a pregnancy which has yet to be delivered that the enigmatic conclusion of *Alastor* should be understood and, in turn, that the narrator's initially apparently vain quest, his compulsive "strain," to reconcile himself to nature promises, precisely by *not* producing, the harmonious "strain" of just such reconciliation. Just as Plato closes the *Symposium* with Socrates' inert body, the poem ends with the narrator addressing the Poet's corpse directly; the lesson the narrator draws from this death, like that which I am suggesting we draw from the *Symposium,* is the tragic ineliminability of compulsive repetition (or, for Freud, "death") in life generally. Yet this is a tragedy, the narrator insists, that makes itself felt *in practice,* not theoretical insight: it is not by elegizing the Poet, pretending to *contain* death in expressions of grief, but precisely by renouncing such containment, that we will properly recognize the implications of this tragedy:

> . . . Art and eloquence,
> And all the shews o' the world are frail and vain
> To weep a loss that turns their lights to shade.
> It is a woe too "deep for tears," when all
> Is reft at once, when some surpassing Spirit,
> Whose light adorned the world around it, leaves
> Those who remain behind, not sobs or groans,
> The passionate tumult of a clinging hope;
> But pale despair and cold tranquility,
> Nature's vast form, the web of human things,
> Birth and the grave, that are not as they were.
> (710–20)

If all is no longer as it was, from nature to the human experience that, as represented by the Poet and the narrator, stood in perpetual opposition to nature, then this is emphatically not a matter of a loss that we should grieve, since grieving is in its own way still a "clinging hope" that what's lost may be retrieved; as such, this hope necessarily remains implicated in the same antithesis of individual and nature, and compulsive struggle to overcome that antithesis, that precipitated the loss to begin with. Grieving death, whether affectively or artistically, whether by way of "tears" or "thoughts," actually propagates death insofar as it perpetuates the repetition compulsion that brought it about. To show this, however, is not to point out the *inherent* vanity of erotic striving but to precipitate the opening of new possibilities for undertaking it, to "bring to birth" a new self incapable of experiencing precisely the same tragedy.[8] If, as I argued, the Macbethian lyric subject of *CH* is so absolutely destructive that it is finally inconsequential—that it finally serves a will not to act but to know at the expense of acting—then *Alastor* offers a reflection upon such destruction that dispels, not repetition per se, but the dream of a "Roman Death" by which Horatio would rationalize repetition, the prototypically Romantic fantasy that repetition is somehow demonically prescribed. In other words, Shelley offers us a historical consciousness *of* Byron's historical consciousness that gives the latter's contradiction significant form rather than, on Bloom's own rather Byronic model, pretending to debunk them only to repeat them. Such poetry embodies a norm for a self-historicizing, as opposed to a resentfully, defensively self-certifying kind of reflection: a reflection that moves beyond "Romantic Ideology" not by pretending simply to debunk and ostracize it but by using the material it offers to shape itself a past and to engender an emphatically belated, memorial modernity through the act of such shaping.

Such a revolutionary promise clearly figures in the resolution of Wordsworth's "Ode," which Shelley cites:

> The Clouds that gather round the setting sun
> Do take a sober colouring from an eye
> That hath kept watch o'er man's mortality;
> Another race hath been, and other palms are won.
> Thanks to the human heart by which we live,
> Thanks to its tenderness, its joys, and fears,
> To me the meanest flower that blows can give
> Thoughts that do often lie too deep for tears.
> (197–204)

---

8. Thus *Alastor* can be seen to prefigure the kind of "cleansing of the ontological situation" that, according to D. J. Hughes, characterizes *Prometheus Unbound* in particular and Shelley's poetic method generally: "[*Prometheus*] contains two . . . large dramatic operations, 1. the events leading to the unchaining of Prometheus, and 2. the building of another process by which Prometheus, in his symbolic role, can find a fresh hypostasis, not in the actuality which Shelley is anxious to spiritualize in the poem, but in the Potentiality where the poem finally leaves us. Paul Valéry speaks of the poet as cleansing the verbal situation. Shelley, in his most ambitious poem, can be seen as cleansing the ontological situation, restoring our sense of the potential, turning, through a series of verbal strategies, the actual back upon itself. The world at the end of the poem is a virtual one, with the seeds of decline checked, themselves remaining in potency" (107–8).

If, for Wordsworth, to "grieve not" means to ". . . find / Strength in what remains behind," then the conclusion of the "Ode" goes so far as to show how such "grieving" does not merely "clingingly hope" for the return of the lost object but *constitutes* that object by the very act of mourning its loss: the "tear" originates conjointly with the "thought" that negates it, that has a depth it cannot match. In section X, the "thought" provoked by birdsong, which in section III had thrown the poet into a tailspin of self-doubt, is now embraced precisely *for* its negating effects; hence "We will grieve not, rather find / Strength in what remains behind . . . In the soothing thoughts that spring / Out of human suffering; / In the faith that looks through death" (180–86). Thus at the conclusion of the "Ode" the Poet acknowledges that nature does "take a sober colouring from an eye" that looks out from the experience of keeping "watch o'er man's mortality." In contrast to Coleridge's "Hymn," the "Ode" here acknowledges that "colouring" nature with the same "mortality" that cuts man off from it offers the sole means of exercising a "faith that looks through death." What Wordsworth evokes here is the experience not of the fragmenting negativity of thought *as opposed to* the positive unity of nature, but of such negativity *by means of* that unity. If the "might" of nature remains uncompromised, it is only so that it may thereby register the "sober colouring" with which that negativity infuses it. Instead of trying to see negativity or "mortality" or "death" itself reflected in what it negates, thought attempts to capture a "faith that looks through death," that recognizes living nature not only as the antithesis of such negation but also, and indeed consequently, as *practically* inextricable from it: as united in an overarching practical unity or what Wordsworth's 1802 preface terms a "habit of mind" (598). By recognizing the sunset as "taking" its very coloring from the poet's own negativity, and that negativity, in turn, as infusing the natural spectacle of that sunset itself, the poet dissolves the rift between negative thought and positive nature, integrating both in the unified act of poetic "interpreting and ferrying" itself.

According to Geoffrey Hartman, Wordsworth's "*credo* is that integration—or reintegration will triumph. . . . The poems written between 1797 and 1807 reflect [that] triumph. . . . Often they are that triumph itself" (*The Fateful Question of Culture* 6ff.). Thus the mind's disruptive negativity is finally tamed within a memorial poetics of what Hartman calls "elation," drawing on Hegel's concept of reconciliation or "sublation." It is only the "first part" of this poetics that registers the inextricability of whole and fragment, of natural unity and disruptive imagination:

> The burden of the second part of Wordsworth's *Er-innerung* [is] tranquil recollection [which] preserves the experience of yesterday . . . so inwardly

that it seems to be forgotten; not a part of *us* but of a *substance* in which we participate.... The form of dealing with death is now drawn as if directly from language rather than from the epitaph tradition. There is a new immediacy.... Since the subject is a death, we can also talk of purification; though as a spiritual and verbal, not a ritual process. Through purified words we glimpse the nature of all words. Words ... are the elated monument. (189)

Hartman's contrast of a progressive, "spiritual and verbal purification," on the one hand, with rather inert and repetitious "ritual" and "epitaph," on the other, is in keeping with the Platonic contrast between pregnant and nonpregnant desire. On Hartman's reading, the "Ode" offers a determinately embodied "immediacy," "tranquility," "purity," "substantiality" and "monumentality," and hence transitions from "intimations of immortality" to achieved immortality itself. But it is just such reconciliation that *Alastor*'s conclusion resists by revealing the Poet's pretense to immortality to conceal a void that defies grieving: a *radically* inert body analogous to the one Plato revealed beneath the "phantom image" of Socrates' immortality. That the reader's attempts to unite with nature need not succumb to self-destructive compulsion in just the same way as the Poet's and narrator's, that erotic striving per se need not be vain, is not "triumphantly" attested by a poetic "monument" that the reader is given to revere in the manner of Coleridge's "Great hierarch" but is held out as a *promise* which is left to the reader to realize. It is only as a result of such realization that the "strain" of erotic negativity, which exhausts *Alastor*'s actual content, may, retrospectively, be made one with the "strain" of a poetic harmonization achieved in the wake of, or inspired by, that negativity. Thus Shelley's characterization of the way in which *Alastor*'s narrator's premature claim to a conciliatory "serenity" belies the actual remoteness of reconciliation finally applies to *all* claims to achieved "tranquility." In keeping with Socrates' account of Eros's integral negativity, *Alastor,* contra Hartman's Wordsworth, suggests that continuity with nature is sustained only by its absence, as a promise yet to be realized, a "phantom image of beauty" that, precisely as a mere phantom rather than achieved "monument," inspires erotic striving rather than putting it to rest.

Paralleling the account I'm offering, Hartman offers an account of Wordsworth's pivotal historical importance in terms of the struggle between Eros and Death. The kind of repetition compulsion, or death, that we have been considering throughout—"loving loving" as opposed to doing it—Hartman suggestively explores in terms of what he calls the distinctively modern "abstract life." To this he opposes the singular capacity of *culture*—and by *culture* he "mean[s] the ring and function of the word, its emotional and conceptual resonance"—to "keep hope in *embodiment* alive" in the modern context (26); "*to redeem imagination from abstraction,* to achieve, with or without the state, a more embodied and less alienated way of life" (180). Pushing us to accept a concretely practical, creative responsibility for the constitution of the world we inhabit is, according to Hartman, the signal contribution of Wordsworth's poetics to the idea of culture in the modern context. Wordsworth does so by shifting experience from the realm of the "found" to that of the "made," thereby implicating us inexorably in what Hartman calls an "*imaginaire*" of which our *own* active, creative contribution is the very condition of possibility. What a poem like the "Ode" transmits is simply the *occasion* or "potentiality" for such an *imaginaire* which it is up to its readers to actualize: "the *imaginaire* created is not so much a heightened picture of forces within a specific historical moment as the *transmission* of a *potentiality* whose realism and idealism can no longer be distinguished and that we reclaim, whether it actually existed or not" (16n13). If the "faith that sees through death" is itself a product of "interpreting and ferrying," then to become possessed of this faith is necessarily already to be implicated in the same creative activity to which it bears witness. A hard lesson of Shelley's rewriting of the "Ode" in *Alastor,* however, is that such a creative onus is finally incommensurable both with the "tranquilly" "triumphant" poetics of memorial elation and, in turn, with the determinate political implications that Hartman would draw from such poetics:

> Wordsworth's poetry does not reflect in any simple way an existing situation; it surrounds it, rather, with an imaginative aura . . . that helped to create the sense of a particularly *English* culture. I speculate that this saved English politics from the virulence of a nostalgic political ideal centering on rural virtue, which led to serious ravages on the continent. (7)

The "potentiality" that Wordsworth's poetry "transmits" is, according Hartman, that of shedding subjection to the "given," whether this be conceived in terms of natural immediacy, cultural or ethnic positivism, metaphysics of tradition, or even democratic procedures. But, by linking Wordsworthian imagination to certain determinate realities, to a supposed "beneficial political influence" (16n13), to "a sense of particularly *English* culture," and even to the "specific gravity of his words" (190), Hartman runs the risks of undermining such "potentiality" and of bestowing upon political realities a distractingly if not balefully imaginary sanction. Indeed, as if to renounce such linkages, Hartman goes on to say:

Today there are those who see the "general culture" as hegemonic. If we acknowledge, however, the antinomy between "a culture" and "culture," then the right conclusion would be that it is "a culture" that tends toward hegemony, while "culture," understood as the development of a public sphere, a "republic of letters" in which ideas can be freely exchanged, is what is fragile. (41)

Hartman construes "general culture" as a universally available alternative or remedy for nostalgic cultural politics—which one can either take or leave and which "English culture" has had the good fortune to, in some degree, have taken. What *Alastor*, by contrast, promises is not merely one option among others for inhabiting the world, but rather the potential of an *utterly* changed world, a world "legislated" anew. In this comparison, Hartman's construal appears to veer from an actually embodied practice to an abstracted practice of such practice analogous to Augustine's love of loving. As Shelley shows, the "potentiality" Hartman would propagate is too exacting for "serene," "moveless" embodiment; the imagination is "distended" by what it lacks, not by what it has, whether this be embodied in "English culture," "general culture," or even the "Great Ode."

In this respect Hartman can be seen insufficiently to heed his own apt observation that "for a critical perspective on culture to establish itself creatively—that is, in a way that is involved with art, *even becoming art*—might mean ... an exilic perspective, a language disturbance that goes back to cultural displacement" (227). But Hartman's suggestion that genuinely embodied cultural practice might necessarily be marginal, "exiled" from "general culture," points up a sense in which, at least in the case of Shelley's reception of Wordsworth, Coleridge, and also Plato, such practice is not in fact properly characterizable as *culture* to begin with, for what it embodies is not a collectivity so much as an idiosyncratic tradition of "interpreting and ferrying" so exacting in its practical demands as to effectively defy objective conceptualization *as* a "tradition": it's an "exiled" practice which one either propagates or not but which defies adequate, general-purpose characterization from without. Putting it in these terms makes Shelley sound like a kind of proto-Pynchon; and, in fact, the kind of apocalyptic aesthetic and praxis that gives Shelley's Romanticism a postmodern edge is precisely what Robert Kaufman's compelling reading of the "Defence" most emphasizes: "Working from materials at hand, poetry must reinvent itself and society; a new poetic must do to capitalism what Milton's poetic did to feudalism: namely, supersede it, through the immanent, imaginative projection of something new and previously inconceivable" (718). Shelley would mobilize the practical opportunities contingently availed by the present to reconstruct the past in ways that open an unforeseeable future "potentiality": what Kaufman calls a "post-everything world."

What Shelley in fact *embodies*, then, and retrospectively shows Wordsworth, Coleridge, and Plato respectively to embody, is nothing as objectively determinate as a "general culture" or "a culture" or even a "monument" to their absence, but (to introduce a third usage of the term) a *strain*, a lineage of singular instances of erotic striving, or, as Shelley puts it in the "Defence," "episodes to that great poem, which all poets . . . have built up since the beginning of the world" (522): a series of tragic and comic poetic efforts so intimately linked that each is inconceivable without all the rest. Each is thus in a sense a rewriting or "bringing to birth" of all the rest, in the sense in which Diotima says that the ultimate erotic object—the image of immortality and beauty that inspires erotic striving, what Shelley here calls the "one great poem"—is not in fact an object at all but the practice of erotic striving itself, pregnant "interpreting and ferrying," or for Wordsworth the immanently purposive yet "blind" "mechanisms of thought." Combining its active objective senses, this "strain" may at most be construed as a practice of cultivation that is sustained not by producing but by resisting positive culture. The abstracting, hegemonic function prevails for Coleridge, like for Augustine, the Poet of *Alastor* and Alcibiades, because they, as Shelley says of the Poet, "overleap," making a fetish out of the sublime object itself rather than recognizing it as merely the "phantom image of beauty" which our erotic tragedies and comedies presuppose. So Coleridge may be seen to implicate himself in the same self-undermining "death spiral" that ensnares the poet of *Alastor*.

## V

There is much mutual illumination to be gained by applying the above considerations to the question of the politics of Shelley's poetry. *Alastor*'s ambivalence regarding equality and inequality raises this question implicitly, while Shelley's subsequent does so explicitly by its frequent references to contemporary political events and figures, by the preeminence of the theme of liberty, and by a critical virulence that puts that liberty into practice, if often only within the relatively safe confines of private correspondence. The topical and inflammatory features of *The Mask of Anarchy*, for instance, could not be more pronounced, but they contrast markedly with the ironically reserved manner in which Shelley, in a letter to Leigh Hunt, broaches the question of the poem's eventual publication: "I wish to ask you if you know of any bookseller who would like to publish a little volume of *popular songs* wholly political, & destined to awaken & direct the imagination of the reformers. I see you smile but answer my question" (May 1, 1820). Presumably the latter sentence indicates the author's awareness that the wish expressed by the former sentence is, due to the threat of persecution for treason, futile. The latter sentence acknowledges not only that the former is an exercise in futility, then, but that the whole effort Shelley has evidently already undertaken to create lyrics at once political and "popular" is futile as well.

According to Susan Wolfson, the unpublishability of Shelley's political poetry is not a disappointing afterthought but the enabling condition of its creation, the fundamentally *a*political, complacent, and deeply self-indulgent fantasy of political activism animating that work (*Formal Charges* 196ff.). This is, in a sense, analogous to reading the formal idiosyncrasies of Burke's *Reflections*—as I suggested in chapter 1—as a kind of alibi protecting Burke from the charge of engaging in the same kind of social theorizing for which he attacks the revolutionaries. Like the "winking" gesture to Hunt, which functions to dismiss with an emphatically intimate smile not just the volume Shelley is ostensibly proposing but the very idea of a poetry both political and popular, the most notable idiosyncrasy of Burke's *Reflections* is the manner in which it disguises them as private correspondence. In Wittgenstein's terms, Shelley's letter nicely illustrates something about the somewhat hypocritical "language game" of private correspondence among self-consciously radical-chic Romantics. The emphatic intimacy of Shelley's wink allows Shelley and Hunt alike to see themselves clearly reflected in their personal roles as radical literati, which is to say that it is an interpolating gesture, confirming the two men in familiar conventional identities all the more powerfully for the conceit that such confirmation cannot be clearly and explicitly articulated as such. Yet the alias for that interpolation is markedly un- or even anti-Romantic: a conventional pleasantry, a polite "smile." The gesture is exactly as conventional as the identity it would confirm, which is to say that it functions not to disguise but to expose the conventionality of the interpolation it encodes.

Wolfson argues that the rhetoric and formal maneuvers of *The Mask* fulfill an analogous function, bolstering the conceit that politics may inhere in, and be sustained by, nothing more than the self-involvement of purely formal poetic imagination. She finds it damning that the poem narrates a dream from which the poet himself never awakes, while the only stanza repeated in the poem, the second iteration of which also concludes the poem, is a call to England's oppressed precisely to *awaken*.

> As I lay asleep in Italy
> There came a voice from over the Sea,
> And with great power it forth led me
> To walk in the visions of Poesy. (1–4)
>
> . . . .
>
> Rise like Lions after slumber
> In unvanquishable number—
> Shake your chains to Earth like dew
> Which in sleep had fallen on you—
> Ye are many—they are few. (155–55; 368–72)

Wolfson writes that "the close of the poem, in which the internal oratory becomes the stirring drama, all but effaces the opening tableau, of a poet's quiescence and self-imposed isolation from the distant political scene" (197). So *The Mask of Anarchy*, which Shelley pointedly identifies with Castlereagh, in fact has no right to such a topical reference, since *The Mask* as a whole is merely an exercise in dream-weaving, signifying nothing beyond the pleasures *intrinsic* to that exercise itself, a doubly vain self-pleasuring. Like poetry according to Plato, Shelleyan poetry according to Wolfson prompts readers to eschew the burden of real political deliberation in favor of a contagious, pathological delusion, a lawless masquerade, or, precisely, a *Mask of Anarchy*.

But the pun of Shelley's title, like the syntactical ambiguity that troubles Shelley's definition of Poesy in the poem's first stanza—in short, Shelley's *poetic form*—cannot be contained by this account. Wolfson justly notes that "*The Mask* never really unmasks [its] dreamy origin" (197) but fails to consider the poem's arguably most remarkable formal feature, the provocative manner in which it engages, without resolving, the issue of mimesis, the question of what it is to imitate, reflect, mask or unmask, in the first place. Shelley not only refuses to unmask his poem's dream status but extravagantly embellishes it, making *The Mask* the poem of a dream which itself issues in a second dream that then gives rise, somehow, to a poem. Such implicitly interminable digression is in keeping with Shelley's surprising, Burkean suggestion that liberty is not something that admits of unproblematic, definitive realization or "unmasking" but may only be "echoed" through a return to or, precisely, reiteration of, "the old laws of England" (335; 331). Wolfson notes that the poem within the poem is presented not as reality but as conjecture—a new iteration, then, of the dream within the dream within the poem. But she overlooks how Shelley uses repetition to reinforce, or literally "echo," this conjectural origin: introducing it with not one but two iterations of "as if." Correspondingly, the poem's climactic call to arms is in fact not a climax at all but, precisely, a *refrain,* the only one of the poem. Wolfson fails to consider the possibility that it is precisely the dream of *definitive* unmasking that the poem's form would question. This resistance may betray a fear of masks analogous to Plato's and a concomitant fear of political *action,* of attempts to imitate ideals in practice, uninsured by any reliably "unmasked" epistemological guarantees.

Shelley's implicit insistence on masks' inescapability provokingly questions the distinction itself between politics and poetics, suggesting that one inevitably masks the other. In turn, this suggests that the contemporaneous antithesis to Shelley's "popular song," the notoriously dense and allusive *Prometheus Unbound,* would be at least as political as *The Mask*. Most crucially, this suggests that what makes *The Mask* political is fundamentally not its ostensibly political content, its overt reference to actual political personages and events, but rather its deployment of the kind of formal patterning or masking we've evoked. Indeed *Prometheus* construes its political themes entirely in terms of poetic form. Questions of different types of political relationship, legitimacy, and agency are all thoroughly integrated with, or masked by, issues of poetic form and allusion. The backstory of *Prometheus* is the classical myth of the loss of the Golden Age when Saturn was displaced by Jupiter. And, like Keats in *Hyperion* and *The Fall of Hyperion,* Shelley links this pagan myth with the biblical design of a fall, redemption, and millennial return to a lost felicity. A formal parallel or allegory is thus established between the redemption narrative itself—the particular story of Prometheus's retrieval of lost happiness—and Shelley's formal integration of these distinct pagan and biblical materials. Moreover, as in *The Mask,* Shelley culminates this narrative by extravagantly detailing the celebration of another allegory, Prometheus's wedding with his returned from exile bride, Asia.

Prometheus represents the familiar tragic figure who was once whole but has fallen into division and now seeks to redeem his lost integrity. The Golden Age was a time of bliss but ignorance, and after Jupiter replaced Saturn, Prometheus tried to give mankind knowledge that they might resist Jupiter's tyranny. As the play begins, we already see Prometheus tormented by Jupiter's punishment for his transgression, but more importantly Prometheus is *self-conflicted* by his own lust for vengeance: "eyeless in hate," his is "the wreck of his own will." This suggests that all of Jupiter's power is vested in him by his victim. The implication is very Blakean: that Jupiter is mankind's own worst potentiality—the corruption of love into self-love and obsession with domination—which has been projected by the mind of man in the fantasy of a cruel tyrant-god. The play is about how Prometheus overcomes his hate through love, but it's crucial that the resolution is built upon and retains the trace of disunity: the reunion of Prometheus and Asia is represented not as a reintegration of the primal, blissfully ignorant Golden Age but as a marriage that, according to Demogorgon's concluding lyric, continues to demand "Gentleness, Virtue, Wisdom and Endurance." The key dramatic transformation of Prometheus's character from hate to love has transpired already by the end of his opening monologue. Taking Christ-like pity on his tormentor liberates Prometheus from him: "I wish no living thing to suffer pain" (I.305). Unbeknownst to Prometheus, this act of forgiveness sets Asia free from her exile, and the bulk of the play will focus on her return journey to Prometheus. Just as in *The Mask of Anarchy*, then, confusion of dream and reality is a constitutive condition of the poem as such: what appeared as the story of Prometheus's and Jupiter's political agon turned out *also* to be his and Asia's love story. *Prometheus Unbound*'s representation of Asia's exiled dream of love for and with the embattled Prometheus perfectly parallels Shelley's exiled dream of love for and with the embattled reformists of England.

The stories that both poems tell likewise foreground the role of chance (or anarchy) in a way that underscores why poetic imagination rather than narrative explication is the most appropriate and accurate means of political representation. Shelley's "Preface" to *Prometheus* indicate that this apparently "merely" formal literary alternative was motivated by considerable reflection on the history of ethical and political ontology, reflection that throws the individualistic, moral focus of Wolfson's contrast between political committed action and poetic dreaming into question.

> The only imaginary being, resembling in any degree Prometheus, is Satan; and Prometheus is, in my judgment, a more poetical character than Satan, because, in addition to courage, and majesty, and firm and patient opposition to omnipotent force, he is susceptible of being described as exempt from the taints of ambition, envy, revenge, and a desire for personal aggrandizement, which, in the hero of *Paradise Lost,* interfere with the interest. The character of Satan engenders in the mind a pernicious casuistry which leads us to weigh his faults with his wrongs, and to excuse the former because the latter exceed all measure. (133)

The one phrase in the whole preface that is most revealing of how Shelley conceives of Prometheus and what he wants his character to represent is "pernicious casuistry." Casuistry has two main meanings, both of which are in play: (1) ethical argument applying to particular cases and (2) specious, overly subtle reasoning. Shelley's misgiving about Milton's Satan is that he is *too much like a rational (Cartesian) individual.* Politically, such individualism was progressive in Milton's time, but Shelley believes that in his own it has become a limitation. We weigh what Satan does against what he suffers on the basis of certain assumptions about what can be expected of individuals: Satan remains governed by what Shelley in the "Defence" calls "the selfish and calculating principle." Casuistry reduces people to facts, and actions to calculations. This was not at all pernicious but a liberating revelation when the idea of republicanism was new, but Shelley sees it as an obstacle to the thinking of his own time. So a key part of Shelley's intention for Prometheus is that he will show us how to transcend this "selfish and calculating principle": Prometheus's behavior would defy casuistry or any kind of rational balancing of what he does or could do against what he has suffered.

This sort of transcending historically imposed limits is connected to what Shelley thinks the role of imagination and poetry has always been, but *especially now* in the Romantic period:

> The great writers of our own age are, we have reason to suppose, the companions and forerunners of some unimagined change in our social condition or the opinions which cement it. The cloud of mind is discharging its collected lightning, and the equilibrium between institutions and opinions is now restoring or is about to be restored. (134)

To help catalyze this "collected lightning," artists must take incalculable risks. Shelley claims that artists transcend calculating individuality only by submitting themselves somewhat to chance, letting their art take them in directions they don't necessarily understand and can't be sure will succeed: "Whatever talents a person may possess to amuse and instruct others, be they ever so inconsiderable, he is yet bound to exert them." We can't know what powers we have until we undertake experiments to test them; hence whatever powers we have are discovered and defined only in their actual application. "Poets, not otherwise than philosophers, painters, sculptors and musicians, are, in one sense, the creators, and, in another, the creations, of their age." This is what Shelley means by calling poets "the unacknowledged legislators of the world": that through their imaginative inventions they recreate the world. So it's clear that what Shelley is after is too radical for casuistry. Shelley overarching point here, what made Satan politically progressive in Milton's time and what stands to make Prometheus progressive in Shelley's is that they just occupy their historical context—embellishing it, enriching our knowledge of it—but should reframe that context, reconceive it in fresh terms, terms that represent "shadows cast by futurity upon the present," that reflect the as yet unknowable political norms and values still to come.

We create our age in the sense that any historical age is defined by the sum of the acts it comprises; but if our acts give expression to a collective dream of freedom or love, then that dream can be said to create us, to be *our cause*. Shelley finds something godlike in this regenerative power, but, he insists, poetry doesn't represent god as something apart from people but instead ignites the spark of divinity within people themselves, "redeems from decay the visitations of the divinity in man." This divinity is just the capacity to create ourselves through how we express ourselves. Hence Asia's journey to wed Prometheus culminates in ritual sanctioning and celebrating—ultimately in the form of a *masquerade*—of the redemption of Prometheus from Alastor's model of avenging subjectivity to a model of subjectivity built on love.[9] This redemptive process is catalyzed by an interview with Demogorgon, "the mighty darkness," who represents the random temporal succession of events, the indeterminate power that keeps all nature and history happening. Like Kant's "thing in itself," Demogorgon avails no knowledge or value but is rather the formless energy that propels the formation of knowledge and value: his "deep truth is imageless," inscrutable. He represents *chance*, the anarchic way in which events happen to happen, the sheer inexplicable thereness of the world as it unfolds: the "it" that like the ancient mariner or Hamlet might command our attention but won't allow us to know why. The lesson Asia learns from Demogorgon is negative rather than positive, namely, that she knows all she can know of love but that this is much less than what she thought she knew. Demogorgon says that "to Fate, Time, Occasion, Chance, and Change . . . / All things are subject but eternal Love," but this is just to absorb love into Demogorgon's own "darkness," assimilate it to that inscrutable "imageless truth." Hence Asia's profound response: "*of such truths / Each to itself must be the oracle*" (II.iv.119–23). It's only by accepting how little we can know of love that we might act as its oracle.

Asia's insistence that love must become its own oracle defies Demogorgon's seemingly clear and easy distinction between immortal love and time, mortality, and so on. What keeps love from becoming otherworldly is its continual engagement with the "chance, and death, and mutability" it overcomes, for these are, Shelley says, "The clogs of that which else might oversoar / The loftiest star of unascended heaven, / Pinnacled dim in the intense inane" (III.iv.205–8). Likewise, it is crucial to note that Prometheus's liberation is not unequivocally gratifying and empowering: "I speak in grief, / not exultation, for I hate no more, / As then ere misery made me wise" (I.i.53–58). As in the mariner's "sad wisdom," Prometheus's tutelage in love is not pleasant: get-

---

9. Ibid.

ting over himself, learning to connect with others in a unselfish way, entails immense "grief": as in the Daughters of Albion, a new kind of love created only by way of mourning the loss of the cherished old model of perfect unity. Hence the most beautiful famous lines with which the play ends: "to suffer woes which Hope thinks infinite . . . till Hope creates / From its own wreck the thing it contemplates." The true power of love isn't a matter of actually realizing what it hopes for; it's about how it always survives and exceeds its apparent disappointment and destruction.

Hope comes into its own posthumously, so to speak, because it is only in the wake of its own destruction that its status as simultaneously necessary and impossible becomes apparent and effective. Only as the necessity of *masking* its own impossibility is the functional truth of hope manifest, only as what Nietzsche termed the "will to mere appearance."[10] This casts *Prometheus Unbound*'s most famous lines—which more often than not are read independently of the play, at face value, as a summation of the work's and its author's actually governing principle or message—in a crucially *ironic* frame. In fact, giving definitive articulation to ultimate truths or messages is absurdly out of character for Demogorgon. As we have seen, all that he has had to do and say up to these concluding lines of the play underscores his stance of radical resistance to revelation, the conceit that truths are available for verbal articulation. It could be said that Demogorgon is given the most "revealing" line of the play, "behold!" (II.128), when he directs our attention to Asia's transfiguration (into something like the god of love, Aphrodite [or Venus]) and return to Prometheus. But this is also clearly highly redundant and ironic: Demogorgon directs us only to observe the main narrative action of the play we're already hypothetically following. His command is an empty form without content and then an essentially theatrical extravagance, calling on us to do something that we could not hear his call if we were not already doing. Thus Demogorgon implicitly mocks the very notion of revelation in the act of performing it.

To be clear, this irony does not function to deny or cancel the act of beholding; on the contrary, it is predicated on that act: only in the midst of beholding can the irony be felt of redundant appeals to behold. The lesson of this irony is not that beholding is vain or impossible but that it is impossible to do otherwise than behold, and hence it is vain to pretend that appearances conceal underlying essences whose definitive revelation would bring the act of beholding to an end. The provocation of Demogorgon's "behold" is to reveal that there is nothing to be revealed beyond or behind the play itself, the world of appearances we were, *ipso facto,* already beholding. To look behind

---

10. Nietzsche, *Beyond Good and Evil,* §230.

is always only to behold more masks (of Aphrodite, Venus, etc.): there is no going deeper toward the kind of empirical reality or natural law sought by Locke and Freud, or ascending higher on Plato's hierarchy of love or truth; the only progress is that of enriching the formal complexity, nuance, and effective eroticism (or, inversely and perhaps more to the point: mitigating the formal bluntness and effective violence) of our stagings of just this recognition. Demogorgon's articulate (albeit radically paradoxical) proposition that "hope creates from its own wreck the thing it contemplates" is no less a mask than the revelation of Asia he just tells us to behold. So the question of mask or reality is replaced by that of the relative formal richness of the communication, the organizational patterning of sympathetic and imaginative interplay, enabled by different regimes of mask-play or language games. Poets' legislation of the world is unacknowledged, according to Shelley, for the simple reason that our communication with each other is richest when we are not pretending to monitor and manipulate it from without, when we involve ourselves in patters larger and more complex than we can grasp in the course of our involvement.

At issue finally is the relative social or erotic appeal and power of different forms of reading or literacy. The paradoxical form of the proposition with which Demogorgon closes the play lends, assumes, or transmits a degree of sympathetic imagination that nonparadoxical proposition would not. But the very articulateness of the proposition, its promise if not delivery of conceptual transparency, makes it inert if not positively obstructive as a vehicle of the kind of sympathetic imagination to which Demogorgon merely points and says "behold," if only because he is pointing "behind the veil" of the world of conscious reality and knowledge. This is precisely why he offers no guidance beyond pointing and why even this pointing itself is provokingly riddled with irony: what we behold is Asia beginning her approach to reality but still in her exile in the separate reality of dreams and mythology. At the beginning of Act II we are not given merely to understand that hope is a paradox; instead, we are prompted to feel the exquisitely ambivalent melancholy of a dreamer anticipating daybreak. Crucially, Asia is not sad because she expects reality will live up to her dream but because she expects that it *will*. Consider these lines she addresses to Spring: "As suddenly / Thou comest as the memory of a dream, / Which now is sad because it hath been sweet." The paradoxical combination of sadness and sweetness recalls her sister Panthea's line from Act I: "Tis something sadder, sweeter far than all" (671), but Asia here is not characterizing an emotional content itself so much as she is delineating the specific form of a sadness that a dream can't last, the form of our affective attachment to dreams *as such* rather than as prospective realities, test runs, or wish lists. Asia's sadness is that Spring comes not as a disappointment but as a *realization* of her dream. Asia's soliloquy proceeds gorgeously to liken the passing of the dream to the fading of the morning star reflected in the lake. Asia then recalls Panthea and says that she too should come like Spring, which Panthea promptly does. Thus the pattern repeats itself of dream *fulfilled* by reality, but Asia concludes her soliloquy by categorizing "hope" generally as "sick." It's a scene of dreams realized, Spring returning, sisters reuniting, and yet sadness and sickness pervade everywhere. But later, when Panthea and Iona meld into each other's dream, and then Asia enters it too, this social sharing of dreams suggests an alternative to the sickness and sadness of dreams fulfilled. The repeated injunction to "follow, follow" pervades the dream like a heartbeat, a kind of dreaming is that is directed not toward real fulfillment but toward the will to dream for dreaming's sake. The repetitions of the injunction "to follow, follow" elaborate and give a formal rhythm to the redundancy implicit to Demogorgon's injunction "behold." Such poetic patterning was obscured by the latter injunction's promise of definitive revelation, and Demogorgon's relative conceptual transparency in the play's concluding lines holds out the same obstructive promise. How the dawning light absorbs a star, and how this absorption is reflected in a lake, can organize existential categories like subject and object, scene and event, reality and representation, and self and other in ways that can effectively integrate mental, discursive, and social life but not by virtue of adequate correspondence or knowledge of any independent reality. Like Kant's thing in itself, the inscrutability of Demogorgon's designs exposes discursive action to irreducible contingency and uncertainty, but rather than undermining communication and collaboration, this exposure stands to enhance to an extent that mere objective certainty could not. An important implication of this is that Demogorgon's concluding lines, despite their remarkable conceptual clarity, should be read not as Shelley's best approximation of a summation—his ultimate admission, albeit paradoxical, that there is some underlying propositional meaning the poem's forms are there to transmit—but as a parody of our "calculating principle's" obsolete but persistent demand for such meaning: a parody that, as such, is, no less that Asia's vision of the morning star's reflection, also an invitation to "follow, follow" the rhythm of its inversions.

In Act III, scene iii, Prometheus articulates Shelley's view of how this works: how love and art inspire each other to ever richer, more inclusive forms, thereby effecting historical progress. Initially Prometheus seems to claim that the love he and Asia share allows them simply to transcend time:

> A simple dwelling, which shall be our own;
> Where we will sit and talk of time and change,
> As the world ebbs and flows, ourselves unchanged.
> (22–24)

Yet read on:

> What can hide man from mutability?
> And if ye sigh, then I will smile; and thou,
> Ione, shalt chant fragments of sea-music,
> Until I weep, when ye shall smile away
> The tears she brought, which yet were sweet to shed.
> We will entangle buds and flowers and beams
> Which twinkle on the fountain's brim, and make
> Strange combinations out of common things
> (25–32)

So they don't transcend mutability so much as assimilate it into their loving art/artistic love: their art doesn't allow them to escape sadness and change but instead allows them to engage these "common things" more intensively, weaving "strange combinations" out of the experience of sadness and transience itself. Prometheus proceeds to name the art forms such strange combining actually produces and might yet produce:

> . . . Painting, Sculpture, and rapt Poesy,
> And arts, though unimagined, yet to be;
> The wandering voices and the shadows these
> Of all that man becomes, the mediators
> Of that best worship, love, by him and us
> Given and returned; swift shapes and sounds, which grow
> More fair and soft as man grows wise and kind,
> And, veil by veil, evil and error fall.

Since we're all alike subject to these "common things"—the impermanence, suffering, and randomness—of temporal life, art is progressive because it liberates our compassion for one another, just as Asia was liberated by Prometheus's act of forgiveness. Artistic production is linked for Shelley to the eradication of, or "falling" from, the world of "evil and error," "veil by veil." (Shelley's falling veils seem akin to Blake's opening doors of perception.) Shelley's idea is that as art progresses, we become progressively liberated from and able to dispense with "veils" to the extent that we use these to shield ourselves from one another's suffering, just as Prometheus dispensed with his rivalry with Jupiter, with his pride, his sense of what he "deserved," and so forth. So, for instance, while the calculating individualism of Milton's Satan liberated the minds of his contemporaries from the crutches of institutional church and monarch, Shelley's Prometheus aims to liberate his contemporaries from the crutch of individualism itself. All such veils/crutches, to the extent we rely on them to tell us what life means, actually drain value from life (referring to such crutches, the Earth says that "Death is the veil which those who live call life" [iii.115]). The Spirit of the Hour concludes Act 3, describing what liberation from such veils/crutches means:

> The painted veil, by those who were, called life,
> Which mimicked, as with colors idly spread,
> All men believed and hoped, is torn aside;
> The loathsome mask has fallen, the man remains
> Sceptreless, free, uncircumscribed, but man
> Equal, unclassed, tribeless, and nationless,
> Exempt from awe, worship, degree, the king
> Over himself; just, gentle, wise . . .

But Shelley crucially emphasizes that this liberation from false idols doesn't extend to liberation from "chance, death, and mutability"; such a liberation would be unthinkably, inhumanly empty, a state Shelley wonderfully terms the "intense inane":

> . . . man
> Passionless—no, yet free from guilt or pain,
> Which were, for his will made or suffered them;
> Nor yet exempt, though ruling them like slaves,
> From chance, and death, and mutability,
> The clogs of that which else might oversoar
> The loftiest star of unascended heaven,
> Pinnacled dim in the intense inane.

Act IV is like a masque play in celebration of the wedding of Prometheus and Asia. The Earth and Moon have a particularly remarkable, sexualized but mostly just wildly ecstatic exchange. The Earth concludes by observing the Moon's loving reflection in the sea, recalling Asia's image of the star reflected in the lake.

> Leave Man, who was a many-sided mirror
> Which could distort to many a shape of error
> This true fair world of things, a sea reflecting love;
> Which over all his kind, as the sun's heaven
> Gliding o'er ocean, smooth, serene, and even,
> Darting from starry depths radiance and life doth move:
> Leave Man even as a leprous child is left,
> Who follows a sick beast to some warm cleft
> Of rocks, through which the might of healing springs is poured;
> Then when it wanders home with rosy smile,
> Unconscious, and its mother fears awhile
> It is a spirit, then weeps on her child restored:
> Man, oh, not men! a chain of linkèd thought,
> Of love and might to be divided not,
> Compelling the elements with adamantine stress;

It is telling how for Shelley "man undivided" consists, on the one hand, of terrible vulnerability, misery, and fragility (a leprous child following a sick beast only surprisingly restored to its mother who'd almost lost hope), while on the other hand this fragile restoration forges links of "adamantine" strength. The social strength of discursive forms is cultivated from submission to the irreducible contingency of temporal life. When we arrive, finally, at Demogorgon's concluding lyric, then, Shelley has prepared us to read its images of triumph in just this sense of strength born of intense and interminable vulnerability. Such strength animates these most famous final lines of the play just to the extent that they are read as a parody no less radical than *The Mask*'s inversions of "Law" and "Anarchy," "Hope" and despair, and so forth. This lyric can thus be read as continuous with Demogorgon's injunction to "behold," insofar as both utterances draw their "strength" from the rhythm of formal patterns they invite us to "follow." If, in Act II, Demogorgon's "behold!" ushered in the narrative of Asia's transfiguration, then the ultimate meaning of these lines is left to readers to determine by the actions with which they follow up reading them, actions that somehow make the irreducible role of suffering and chance in "Joy, Empire and Victory" newly legible:

> To suffer woes which Hope thinks infinite;
> To forgive wrongs darker than death or night;
> To defy Power, which seems omnipotent;
> To love, and bear; to hope till Hope creates
> From its own wreck the thing it contemplates;

Neither to change, nor falter, nor repent;
This, like thy glory, Titan, is to be
Good, great and joyous, beautiful and free;
This is alone Life; Joy, Empire, and Victory!

To return again to the question of *The Mask* relation to real politics, that poem refers to both "Castlereagh" and the "Massacre at Manchester" by name, but hardly pretends to unmask the final meaning of either. On the contrary, it seems precisely to indict such pretense. Not only would Anarchy, masked as Castlereagh, pretend to unmask himself as a representative of "GOD, AND KING, AND LAW," but Shelley insists that this pretense is itself only another mask, pointedly calling the *claim* to representativeness a "*mark*" in its own right, a mere signifier or text, a point that Shelley's capitalization further accentuates (36ff.). In turn, the henchmen that would serve Anarchy likewise articulate their allegiance in terms of a discovery, disclosure, or unmasking: a revelation or "coming" of the "One" from the midst of the "motley crowd" to redeem them from the burdens of time and loneliness:

'We have waited weak and lone
For they coming, Mighty One!
Our purses are empty, our swords are cold,
Give us glory, and blood, and gold.'

Lawyers and priests a motley crowd,
To the earth their pale brows bowed;
Like a bad prayer not over loud,
Whispering—'Thou are Law and God.'
(61–69)

Anarchy's henchmen *repeat* the poet's observation from lines 36ff., but with a crucial difference: they mistake Anarchy's "mark" for his truth, the signifier for the signified, which is to say that they mistake *reading* for *revelation*. The problem Shelley raises here then is not one of insufficient skepticism, of neglecting the task of unmasking, but one of excessive dogmatism, excessive confidence that truth has been revealed once and for all, and now stands in plain sight, unmasked for direct, unmediated consumption: that the need to read masks *as* masks may conclusively be put behind us.

In *Formal Charges,* Wolfson takes Shelley to task for attaching a political sanction to the masturbatory dream of formalist poetics. But she ignores the alternative account and critique of inanition that Shelley himself offers. This critique is directed at the "slumber" Kant associated with *dogmatism,* to which Kant, and, I wish to suggest, Shelley, opposes, not the historically uprooted *liberté* which Burke impugned, but the *"free-lawfulness"* of the practical exercise of indeterminate "cognition in general" or, most precisely, *"reflection."* For all of the acuity of Wolfson's readings of the formal features of Shelley's poem, she perverts the *function* not only of those features but also, thereby, of the very experience of *reading* that the poem offers. She notes that defenders of Shelley's political poetics may stake their claims only by way of an "awkward finesse" (196), and, again, in a sense the description is apt. But, despite the sensitivity to practical issues that the phrase signals, Wolfson fails to consider that that finesse, like Shelley's formalism itself, might exhibit a practical logic of its own, and instead simply equates it with being *wrong.* Nietzsche describes an alternative way of understanding this finesse: "Judgments of value, concerning life, for it or against it, can, in the end, never be true. . . . One must by all means stretch out one's fingers and make the attempt to grasp this amazing finesse, that the value of life cannot be estimated" (*Twilight of the Idols,* §2). Kantian insistence upon the disinterested character of aesthetic judgments makes the same point: such judgments express an appreciation *that* life is purposive, without giving that appreciation any determinate conceptual content. In such judgments we express feelings of love for our fellow human beings and for nature, and of respect for moral freedom, but these feelings may not be discursively unmasked, and made to issue in determinate knowledge, without draining them of the distinctive sense of purposiveness that they mediate. Insofar that Kant accounts for aesthetic judgments as mediating feelings of love and respect, letting us know *that* life is worth living, without revealing more specifically why or how it should be lived, Kant, like Nietzsche, requires the same "finesse" of which Wolfson accuses Shelley's defenders. In keeping with what I am characterizing as the misguided accuracy of Wolfson's reading, she treats this "finesse" as the sign simply of error, and hence as something that it is the critic's job to unmask or, as she frequently says, "expose," whereas, as Kant, Nietzsche, and, I wish to suggest, Shelley, commonly maintain, it constitutes an expression or practical assertion of autonomy: the condition of the possibility of freedom and hence politics, not a retreat from the latter. Rather than neglecting to unmask itself as dream, to awake finally and definitively, or scurrying to conceal that neglect from critical "exposure," *The Mask* positively flaunts its formalist finesse.

On the grandest scale this finesse is manifest in the elaborate four-part layering Shelley gives to the poem within a dream within a dream within a poem. This topsy-turvy pattern—what begins as the poem about a dream, ends as a dream about a poem—suggests a formal routine that extends beyond the determinate confines of the actual poem. Equally significant, the points of transition—from poem to dream, from dream to dream, from dream to poem—are not signaled as moments of revelation or unmasking; quite the contrary, they are provocatively presented, in proto-Nietzschean fashion, as emphatically *lateral* movements from one mask to the next, as if negotiating Nietzsche's *"shifting sea of metaphors,"* mobilizing what Shelley in the "Defence" characterizes as the "vitality" of "metaphor" as such (512). As we saw above, Wolfson accurately identifies a syntactical ambiguity in Shelley's definition of "Poesy" in the first stanza. This ambiguity, she notes, throws into question whether poetic "vision" has any properly representational function beyond the function intrinsic to the activity of visionary seeing itself. Wolfson construes this as imposing a sedating, ideological closure. But Shelley proceeds to recount a dream within that dream, and to do so in an elusive manner that makes it difficult to grasp *what* the second dream is, in the most expansive sense, *about*. While the first dream blurred the boundary between poem and dream, the second leaves it completely unclear who or what the subject or object of the dream is and why and how the dream happens. As in Kant's aesthetic judgment, all we can know is *that* it happens: "an image rose."

> . . . one fled past, a maniac maid,
> And her name was Hope, she said:
> But she looked more like Despair,
> And she cried out in the air:
>
> 'My father Time is weak and gray
> With waiting for a better day;
> See how idiot-like he stands,
> Fumbling with his palsied hands!'
>
> 'He has had child after child,
> And the dust of death is piled
> Over every one but me—
> Misery, oh, Misery!'
>
> 'Then she lay down in the street,
> Right before the horses feet,
> Expecting, with a patient eye,
> Murder, Fraud, and Anarchy.

When between her and her foes
A mist, a light, an image rose.
Small at first, and weak, and frail
Like the vapour of a vale:
(86–105)

In Baudelaire's "À une passante," a woman appears amidst an urban crowd in mourning dress, and thus she may be seen implicitly to claim a transcendent, or as the poet says "noble," devotion and fidelity to an individual: a claim not only to transcend the *actual* death of that individual but also, and more to the point of Baudelaire's portrait, to preserve her own "statuesque" individuality from the overwhelming, de-individuating pressures of the urban scene forcing itself upon her, not least by the desires of the poet himself. Indeed, the *passante* does not merely claim this fidelity but positively *pro*claims it, displaying her dress like a kind of banner: "with fastidious hand / Raising and swaying her skirt-border and hem." Analogously in *The Mask*, the maid does not merely represent Hope but *proclaims that* she does so. Also like the *passante,* she emerges from an urban crowd and is not perceived by the poet to represent what she pretends to represent. Thus the poet's perception of her contrasts clearly with Anarchy's followers' perception of Anarchy as "Law and God," definitively absolving them of the burden of "loneliness and waiting." In fact, to the poet the maid represents the opposite of what she pretends: "Despair." She *acts* more like Despair too, preparing to commit suicide.

Shelley suggests of Anarchy that although he wears a mark that announces "I am King, and God and Law," his followers are wrong to take this at face value and suppose that he is the "Mighty One." This is akin to what I characterized as the overhasty—or, in Nietzsche's terms, "clumsy" or "overbearing"—unification entailed by Wordsworth's "Ode"'s concluding account of natural "might" as an achieved Hartmanian "elation." Baudelaire's "À une passante" raises the same formal issue. The dress of the *passante* announces "I am faithful to *one*," and the thrust of Baudelaire's poet's taunt is likewise that her knowledge of his love shows that that dress is *just* a sign or mask. But, crucially, the point here is not that the *passante* knows that the poet, as a particular individual, or "*one,*" is "*in love*" with her." On the contrary, the knowledge that the poet attributes to her would consist in an apprehension that the crowd effects a formal reconfiguration of love, a new dispensation of erotic possibility: one that precludes the individualistic fidelity that she proclaims and *requires* the kind of radical, but always only virtual, promiscuity that she pretends to defy. Like the exclusively practical normativity of Kantian aesthetic judgment, the knowledge that the poet ascribes to her is a knowledge without determinate content, and this—what Kant would call "disinterestedness"—is what makes it so provoking. The poet's love, the erotic dispensation of the crowd, is an insane love, an unfulfillable, objectless, sublime love; as Benjamin notes about Baudelaire's *passante,* the poet's desire is not so much denied as spared fulfillment. The poet is not able, and need not claim to be able, to be 'in love' with an anonymous *passante* in order for her and him commonly to recognize that both have glimpsed a kind of potential, virtual love in their moment of passing. A new *form* of love has rendered its old *content* obsolete. The urban crowd's new erotic dispensation entails that the individualistic fidelity that the mourning dress would represent is no longer there *to be* represented: it has been dissolved, on the one hand, by the radical promiscuity and, on the other, by the inexorable virtuality of the crowd's distinctive new form of eroticism.

To ask whether this new dispensation and its implications are merely a projection of the poet, as opposed to an "objectively" valid description of the world around him, is to miss the point. For the provocation that the poet would issue to the *passante* and the reader alike consists precisely in the possibility that questions of representational adequacy, or "fidelity," may not obtain in this new urban context. Baudelaire is proposing that we misconstrue not only the experience of love but also that of communication generally, poetic or otherwise, if we persist in evaluating it in terms of adequation or *fidelity* between two individuals. The ontologically unique and indivisible, what Anarchy's followers see as the "Mighty One," is simply no longer available—either to be to be loved or represented, on the one hand or, on the other hand, to do the loving and representing.

Yet Baudelaire's poem finally does nothing so much as to offer what one must call a *shocking* reassertion of the abiding normative power of love and poetry alike. Thus the poet's provocation to the reader overlaps perfectly with that to the *passante.* The poem acknowledges that we are free to persist in claims of fidelity—to the mightiness of indivisibility—in love or communication generally; but it also insinuates that we know we have no proper right to such claims, and our very recognition of this insinuation betrays us. Hence such claims become, like the *passante*'s dress, disclosed as masks that we use to hide from that knowledge. As was the case with Anarchy's eager henchmen, the belief in the "Mighty One," "God, and King, and Law," is revealed to be a compensatory illusion suppressing the actual burdens—the loneliness and waiting—of modern urban life, of navigating crowds and Nietzsche's "shifting sea of metaphors." To question the "objectivity" of that knowledge, the *passante* insinuates, is a defensive, self-condemning gesture, betraying that one *does in fact* recognize the normative force of the insinuation, even while one exercises oneself over the superfluous question of whether it *must* be recognized. Nothing is unmasked here but another mask. *The Mask* constructs a series of masks upon masks, with the result that the sheer form of overlapping repetition manages, like that of a *Matryoshka* doll, to predominate over the ostensible content. In such cases, form and content exchange roles; the content, what the doll itself is supposed to represent, becomes a mere occasion or vehicle for the formal repetition that it is the doll's primary function to represent or, better, to *reenact,* since that form is never wholly, synchronously present.

The *Matryoshka* doll analogy is seminally important to the most widely read works associated with Shelley's name, the sonnet "Ozymandias" and Mary Shelley's novel *Frankenstein, or the Modern Prometheus.* The latter's elaborately embedded narrative structure functions to effect a counterintuitive view of what it means to be a narrator to begin with: what it means to have a voice or a story to tell. Instead of independently representing a distinct personal experience or point of view, a narrator, like one in a series of *Matryoshka* dolls, is essentially a means of perpetuating and transmitting other narrators. This is to detach the purpose of representation from any particular *object* of representation. Instead, re-presenting other narratives is an end unto itself. So, in this view, there is no essential "kernel" to either the narrative or the doll. It's not as if the smallest doll at the center is the true one and others are mere packaging. Likewise it's a mistake to think the core narrative reveals the secret point or meaning of which the outer layers are like disposable wrapping. The outer layers have details that the smaller ones don't but that importantly inform them. In this sense the innermost one reflects its containers: indeed, isn't part of the point of the innermost doll that it invites us to *imagine* it containing even smaller versions of itself? Thus in a certain sense the doll reverses our intuitive understanding of the relation between form and content. Instead of form serving to "package" content, the content we see when we look at any given layer actually serves to evoke the form itself of this infinite series: of the ever smaller layers that might be contained within what we see and the ever larger layers that might contain it. This would encourage us to *resist* seeing the dolls as a hierarchically arranged, with every one being packaged either for or by the one true doll. Instead, we are encouraged to see this *apparent* hierarchy as *the image of an infinite series.* The appearance of hierarchy serves to evoke the form of this endless, nonhierarchical *Matryoshka* doll iterations of individual perspective, none prioritized over the other. The appearance of hierarchy serves to evoke *perspective*; that is, from *any particular perspective* the endless series will appear to vanish into the distance in both directions, but this is not truer of any one perspective than any other. We are actually encouraged to read the nested narratives of *Frankenstein* in this manner by the fact that Shelley's central narrator, like the central doll, is drained of individualizing detail, becomes schematic. She is less an individual than a representative of the *principle* of motherhood, the regeneration of individuals, or in other words *nesting*. The figure of Safie's mother, the principle of maternity, functions as a kind of vanishing point of individuality, where what individuality means, its supposed content, gets reflected back to us as the form of its nesting, the form of re-presenting the stories it contains and is contained by, of other individuals who are past and yet to come. Correspondingly, the only layer of the embedded narratives less individualized than that of the mother is that of Margaret, the reader surrogate: to recognize the figure of the mother as reflecting the form of nesting is likewise to add our own layer to that form.

Percy Shelley's sonnet "Ozymandias" has an embedded form similar to *Frankenstein*'s and gives this regenerative nesting function to the sculptor:

> I MET a Traveler from an antique land,
> Who said, "Two vast and trunkless legs of stone
> Stand in the desert. Near them, on the sand,
> Half sunk, a shattered visage lies, whose frown,
> And wrinkled lip, and sneer of cold command,
> Tell that its sculptor well those passions read,
> Which yet survive, stamped on these lifeless things,
> The hand that mocked them and the heart that fed:
> And on the pedestal these words appear:
> "My name is OZYMANDIAS, King of Kings.
> Look on my works ye Mighty, and despair!"
> No thing beside remains. Round the decay
> Of that Colossal Wreck, boundless and bare,
> The lone and level sands stretch far away.

The form of nesting in the sonnet does not just happen to resist hierarchy. Instead, for Percy such resistance is synonymous with the principle of artistic or social regeneration. As *The Mask* and *Prometheus Unbound* likewise emphasize, for Shelley expressions of love or hope become fruitful only in the wake of the defeat or "wreck" of the individual who would pretend to author or "own" them. This holds for the sculptor no less than Ozymandias himself: both yield to the "leveling" sands of time; both disappear in that vanishing point of individuality. What survives is the *act itself of seeing*—"reading" and "mocking": that is, not individual passion per se but the act of artistically re-presenting it. This act subverts tyrannical claims to ownership and authority, but only by exposing itself to an infinite regress that will also wreck it. It's just the inevitability of reduction to dust that the poet, without comment, leaves to us readers to respond to as we will. For Shelley, history doesn't progress hierarchically toward some goal but just endlessly repeats this cycle. Without any positive meaning or purpose, historical progress becomes a matter of forming ever richer (i.e., less tyrannical and defensive, more inclusive and nuanced) ways of bearing witness to our own essential transience. Likewise, *Frankenstein* leaves us with the wasteland of the North Pole, juxtaposed to the wreckage of would-be tyrants. In the sonnet and novel alike, the regenerative promise of an enriched human "nest" is made conditional on exposing ourselves to such wreckage, whether in the form of the monster's ugliness or the fearsome wastes of time. Our capacity not to be defeated by such wreckage but to 'contain' it somehow, to undertake another iteration of the cycle without assurance of progress toward any goal but just out of compassion or love for the act itself of bearing witness, is just what nesting is.

Thus the figure of Hope in Shelley's *The Mask* is, like Baudelaire's poet's desire, that of a hope that defies definitive fulfillment: consistent with Benjamin's emphasis on the intrinsic insanity of the Baudelaire's poet, Shelley makes Hope a suicidal "maniac." She does not in fact evoke hope at all but is, Shelley writes, "more like Despair," akin to a prophet of apocalypse raving through the streets. As in Baudelaire's "À une passante," fulfillment of an emphatically deranged desire promises only to extend and exacerbate the wreck it would overcome. Yet, also as in Baudelaire, in *The Mask,* Hope's mania is presented not as an aberration but as exemplary of or normative for a particular historical predicament. That is, the name "Hope" is not an *empty* mask, not merely arbitrarily nominal, but constitutive of a socially normative attitude. If Baudelaire's *passante*'s claim to represent fidelity is belied by the crowd that surrounds her, Shelley makes his maid's Despair a reflection of the idea that history itself has lost any purpose, has given way to something like what Kant termed "the dismal reign of chance":

'My father Time is weak and gray
With waiting for a better day;
See how idiot-like he stands,
Fumbling with his palsied hands!

'He has had child after child,
And the dust of death is piled
Over every one but me—
Misery, oh, Misery!'

No less than Anarchy's henchmen, Hope would have herself absolved of the burdens of "waiting weak and lone." The prospect of suicide, and the hysterical leap before the horses by which she would realize it, grants her, like them, the direct unmediated accession to or "vision" of truth; accordingly she "expect[s] . . . Murder, Fraud, and Anarchy" precisely "with a patient eye." But, as Kant insists, and as Shelley's account of the maid's hysteria suggests, viewing history as reduced to a "dismal reign of chance" is a priori impossible for the same reason that one can't *will* oneself into insanity or make self-loss an aim of self-assertion. As *King Lear*'s Edgar puts it, "the worst is not / So long as we can say 'This is the worst'" (IV.i).

What distinguishes Hope from Anarchy's henchmen, then, is that, by virtue of the very *legibility* of her hysteria *as such,* Hope is never fully absolved of the burdens of loneliness and waiting. The maid's hysteria continues to attest to those burdens, even as it attempts to suppress them: as per Freud, her hysteria absorbs those burdens, transforms the conflict between herself and the outside world into a conflict wholly internal to herself; but it also thereby makes the latter *legible,* makes this internal, personal conflict an impersonal, linguistic artifact. Hope's attempted suicide would prove that Time is in fact hopelessly idiotic. Definitively to *unmask* Time as idiotic, she must unmask herself as Despair, and so to this end she tries to get "the dust of death piled over" herself like the rest of Time's children. But this is only to indulge the hysterical dream that her dust-bedecked corpse would *prove* or *unmask* anything about the world, time, or anything else.[11] What would this unmasking prove exactly? To whom would the proof be offered? Kant invokes the idea of a "dismal reign of chance" in order to underscore that there is something about the very concept of history that makes it *impossible* to think of as a random process. The "rising" of the "image" in the place where the maid's corpse would unmask Time's idiocy testifies to the same point. What the maid finally proves, then, is the very opposite of what she intends: namely, the impossibility of the radical perversity and hopelessness she envisions. Thus a plausible way of understanding the emergence of the dream within the dream, the "image" that inexplicably "rises" in the closing gap "between her and her foes"—in particular, of understanding the *emphatically* unexplained, abstract, and indeterminate character of this image—is as formal testimony to the same impossibility. Like Baudelaire, Shelley does not offer this testimony in support of any proposition *about* the world but rather as exemplary of a normative rule governing how we "go on" in such a world.

Shelley does proceed to give this "image" a lot of conventionally "sublime" ornamentation, but he culminates his description in the formal, functionalist

---

11. The "hope that stings like despair" (221ff.) from which *Alastor*'s Poet suffers illustrates essentially the same point: in each case despair is prepared not by externally imposed obstacles to hope but by a self-destructive orientation of hope itself, aimed not at practical but epistemological satisfaction.

manner that Kant's account emphasizes. The image merely reflects the intrinsic purposiveness of being minded; it has no discrete meaning but attests to the formal purposiveness of thinking and meaning as such:

> With step as soft as wind it passed
> O'er the heads of men—so fast
> That they knew the presence there,
> And looked,—but all was empty air.
>
> As flowers beneath May's footstep waken,
> As stars from Night's loose hair are shaken,
> As waves arise when loud winds call,
> Thoughts sprung where'er that step did fall.
> (118–25)

Hope, as a principle of indeterminate purposiveness, does in fact receive a kind of final confirmation precisely by virtue of falling prey to desperation. But, in contrast to the confirmation she sought—confirmation that history was senseless—the confirmation she receives is not only to the opposite effect but also, and not coincidentally, communicated in the opposite manner: not as a revelatory unmasking but as a performative demonstration of the inescapability of masks.

In contrast to Hope, Anarchy and his followers do not internalize but externalize the violent cost of their certitude. In a world of "waiting weak and lone," propping up belief in *any* "Mighty One" incarnate, "King, and God, and Law" revealed, requires much destruction, "trampling," and "desolation." Trampling others becomes the "intoxicating" means of propping up the effect of the "Mighty One":

> With a pace stately and fast,
> Over English land he passed,
> Trampling to a mire of blood
> The adoring multitude.
>
> And with a mighty troop around
> With their trampling shook the ground,
> Waving each a bloody sword,
> For the service of their Lord.
>
> And with glorious triumph they
> Rode through England proud and gay,

> Drunk as with intoxication
> Of the wine of desolation.
>
> O'er fields and towns, from sea to sea,
> Passed the Pageant swift and free,
> Tearing up, and trampling down;
> Till they came to London town.
> (38–53)

Only by virtue of seeing the "One" apply its "Might" to tearing others apart can they assure themselves that the "One" has in fact been revealed to them and has absolved them of "waiting weak and lone."

This formal interdependence of unity and violence likewise lies at the root of Adorno and Horkheimer's dialectic of enlightenment. "The distance between subject and object, a presupposition of abstraction, is grounded in the distance from the thing itself which the master achieved *through the mastered*" (13, my emphasis). Adorno and Horkheimer distinguish the dialectic of enlightenment from the magic rituals in which that dialectic was only incipiently operative by virtue of the fact that the latter preserve a certain representational *specificity*.

> In magic there is specific representation. . . . Substitution in the course of sacrifice marks a step toward discursive logic. Even though the hind offered up for the daughter, and the lamb for the first-born, still had to have specific qualities, they already represented the species. They already exhibited the non-specificity of the example. But the holiness of the *hic et nunc*, the uniqueness of the chosen one into which the representative enters, radically marks it off, and makes it unfit for exchange. . . . In science there is no specific representation. . . . Representation is exchanged for the fungible—universal interchangeability. . . . The multitudinous affinities between existents are suppressed by the single relation between the subject who bestows meaning and the meaningless object, between rational significance and the chance vehicle of significance. On the magical plane, dream and image were not mere signs for the thing in question, but were bound up with it. (10ff)

A primal "mimesis" (11) is still partially operative in the "images and dreams" mobilized in magic ritual. This is crucial because it allows the ritual to preserve precisely what Kant characterized as aesthetic judgment's basis in *singularity*. Both the specificity that Adorno and Horkheimer recognize in magic rituals, and the singularity that Kant recognizes in aesthetic judgments, are rooted in what Kant calls the "primacy of the practical," while it is just this primacy that Adorno and Horkheimer say the dialectic of enlightenment functions to cancel by subordinating the variety of the actual to the unity of the *logos*. But, because "abstraction is grounded in the distance from the thing itself which the master achieve[s] *through the mastered*," it is only by virtue of exercising violence upon reality that the henchmen can assure themselves that the "Mighty One" has been revealed to them; only as the inverse reflection of that violence is that unity tangible. Hence, in the process of enlightenment, as we come to know, understand, and unify more and more of the world around us, our criterion of unity *must* become more and more elusive, intangible, or "invisible." This perpetual retreat from the *hic et nunc* is finally what Anarchy's "mask" amounts to: a mask of "impenetrable invisibility" or, precisely, of masklessness:

> The magician never interprets himself as the image of the invisible power; yet this is the very image in which man attains to the identity of self that cannot disappear through identification with another, but takes possession of itself once and for all as an impenetrable mask. It is the identity of the spirit and its correlate, the unity of nature, to which the multiplicity of qualities falls victim. Disqualified nature becomes the chaotic matter of mere classification, and the all-powerful self becomes mere possession—abstract identity. (10)

This distinction between the practical specificity preserved by primal mimesis and the dialectic of enlightenment is the proper basis from which to approach *The Mask*'s concluding refrain: "Ye are many—they are few." This has been typically if not exclusively read as expressing a crude populism. If it did express nothing more than this, it would indeed make Shelley liable to charges, such as Wolfson's, that he is merely indulging a self-pleasuring fantasy of political activism. But the foregoing has hopefully suggested that significantly more is at stake in the poem's formal distinction between many and few—multiplicity and singularity—than in populist oppositions of the people and the powerful. Shelley's poem suggests that masking anarchy actually effects violence, and if hope presupposes violence, this is only in response to this effect, an *alternative* response to just the kind of inane violence for violence's sake, or anarchy, upon which the illusion of a "Mighty One" depends.

*The Mask* thus appears to break with the contemporaneous *Prometheus Unbound* in respect to the ontological status of hope's object. Whereas in the latter Shelley claims that "Hope creates / From its own wreck the thing it contemplates" (573ff.), in the former, the emphatic hysteria of the maid's desire manages to attest to "wreckage" or "Despair" without pretending definitely to overcome it, to "create" any reality beyond it. Like Baudelaire's poet's love, the "image" to which that desperation gives rise "signifies" no more than does the "idiot's tale" to which Macbeth believes history reduced. The difference between the maid and Macbeth is that the maid's desire to have that idiocy certified is "*spared,*" while Macbeth's is not. To be spared is precisely for an "image" to "rise" between oneself and the hysterical project of self-sacrifice. As in Kant's account of the role of self-sacrifice in the sublime, this requires getting some reflective distance from this self-sacrifice, *recognizing,* reflectively processing, its insanity and morbidity rather than, like Macbeth, compulsively externalizing and unreflectively propagating that violence. Baudelaire's poet only imaginatively taunts the passer-by; he does not rape her.

In the light of this strictly formal, functionalist account of the aesthetic image, we can see how Wolfson's account of the syntactical ambiguity involved in *The Mask*'s opening construal of Poesy implicates itself in a violence analogous to that of Anarchy's henchmen. In the name of a truth that would be definitively revealed, she tears apart what Shelley offers to hold together (albeit not in the definitive manner Wolfson demands). Shelley constructs a similar syntactical ambiguity when Freedom is defined in the concluding poem within the dream:

'What are thou, Freedom? O! could slaves
Answer from their living graves
This demand—tyrants would flee
Like a dream's imagery.'
(209–12)

Just as Shelley previously made it ambiguous whether Poesy is the cause or the object of "visions," here he makes it ambiguous what is being likened, the subject fleeing or the object fled: Is it suggested that tyrants would flee as quickly as a "fleeting" dream image does, or that tyrants would flee in fright *from* such an image as it if were a ghost? This question is left unresolved, but the ambiguity itself tells us something important about the function of freedom, just as the former ambiguity did about the function of poetry. In Kant's terms, freedom is an idea of reason and as such is aesthetically accessible only negatively, as a feeling of "respect" for something we inevitably fail adequately to represent. Hence, as per Shelley, freedom flees *us* just as much as tyrants flee *it*, and to pretend otherwise is effectively to become a tyrant oneself: to pretend determinately to grasp what freedom is is effectively to *flee* freedom's defining elusiveness. Here Shelley uses poetic form to offer a compelling and rigorous portrait of a central conundrum of modern progressive politics. But these formal ambiguities also pose a practical challenge akin to those posed by Kant: the challenge to offer a singular exemplification of freedom that would be simultaneously both validated and invalidated as such an exemplification by that singularity. To presume that "the political" per se does not admit of such ambiguity, or that merely to "expose" such ambiguity as such is to act in the name of political freedom, is to expose oneself to a practically much more compelling indictment from the poetry itself. If the latter fails thereby to unmask sociopolitical "reality," the only reason is that such failure is the enabling condition of modern communication and hence sociopolitical agency.

## VI

Harold Bloom presents Wallace Stevens as Romanticism's exemplary twentieth-century "heir" by virtue of the "natural passion opposed to supernatural religion [Stevens] so eloquently expressed" (1): "The greatest poverty is not to live / In a physical world, to feel that one's desire / Is too difficult to tell from despair" (xxv). But Bloom's dichotomy arguably misreads Stevens in a manner analogous to Wolfson's misreading of *The Mask*. Stevens appears less invested in the opposition between physical reality and its abstract corruption than in characterizing an experience of "poverty" that escapes that opposition. The very indistinguishability itself of desire and despair defies Bloom's opposition, and, I have argued, heralds new norms of sympathetic and erotic imagination, a new poetics, and a new way of conceiving humanity's destiny. Such norms derive not from nature or religion but from Keatsian "wild surmises": from the practical assertion of formal imagination in a newly dehumanizing modern context of wars and crowds that render epistemological and ontological sanction beside the point. Positing human destiny upon postnatural rather than supernatural grounds, modern poetry realizes what Shelley calls its "world-legislating" potential, engendering and advancing the "social body" by virtue, not in spite, of actively masking its constitutive despair.

CHAPTER 5

# Keats's Lame Flock

*The Erotics of Waste*

I

THIS BOOK began by suggesting that the provocation the Peterloo massacre aimed to suppress was at least as much the crowd form as the reformist agenda. In turn, this final chapter suggests that the rivalry between two of England's most celebrated poets may also be grasped in terms of attempts to assert and to suppress the crowd form. This might seem like an odd claim to make about Byron and Keats because there are arguably few writers more invested in individuality. Whereas Byron's work is riddled with references to the poet's singular biography, Keats's is obsessed with the sensuous intensities of individual experience. However, as Pierre Bourdieu has shown, no modern cultural form is as deeply implicated in class politics as that of the solitary individual. The notion of individual distinction, of exercising an aristocratic taste that is justified only by its own distinctiveness, is according to Bourdieu the basic ideological conceit that legitimizes class difference in consumer society. In consumer society, in other words, individuality is the fiction most responsible for enabling the reproduction of social reality.[1]

Both Byron and Keats use enactments of poetic failure in order to critique prevailing literary conventions, but they do so to opposed effects. Byron's vir-

---

1. "Art and cultural consumption are predisposed, consciously and deliberately or not, to fulfill a social function of legitimating social differences." *Distinction*, 7.

tuoso displays of poetic self-deconstruction ultimately function to underscore the transcendent, inimitable authenticity of the *poet* who performs them. As Byron's unprecedented celebrity attests, the effect of this is not to undermine but to reinforce the logic of consumer desire. By contrast, the middle-class Keats makes an insight that becomes crucial for critical modernism: the insight that because bourgeois fantasies of individuality bear the marks of the specific class experience that gives rise to them, they need not only serve to legitimize the status quo but can also provide a basis for new, critically empowering forms of class consciousness. It is one of modernity's signature paradoxes, in other words, that the price of critical self-consciousness is recognition and acceptance of inauthenticity as its constitutive condition. As thus baldly characterized, this contrast between Byron and Keats is also gendered in a way that is retraceable to Edmund Burke's contrast between the sublime and beautiful. The sublime affirms transcendent ideals of God, reason, and selfhood by the threat that its evocation of infinite power poses to the mortal and finitely sensuous body: about the latter Burke writes that when he is faced with a "just idea of the deity," it feels "annihilated before *him*."[2] Whereas the sublime threat to the body sustains this masculine ideal, Frances Ferguson suggests that Burke's feminized notion of beauty threatens this ideal by virtue of its insidious aesthetic accessibility: "Beauty recurs throughout the Enquiry in the form of a seductive and indirect assault on the reason."[3]

Adam Smith arguably inaugurated the reified bourgeois subject by casting social sympathy as a remediating, complementary currency to capital. Smith assumed that the two currencies were mutually correcting, that sympathy modulated capitalist self-interest to the benefit of all rather than a few. In Smith's famous example, sympathizing with a lunatic is essentially a matter of a viable consumer sympathizing with an unviable or failed one:[4] the consumerist model of individuality isn't troubled but instead fortified by this ability to rehabilitating what it constitutively excludes, to define itself not just in contrast to failed consumers but *as a function of* assimilating those failures. So sympathy becomes nothing other than the oppositional positing and then assimilating of nonconsumers. Far from a remediating or an ameliorating counterpart to the logic of commoditized "distinction," then, sympathy becomes a direct extension of it. The pathos of one of Keats's best-known

---

2. *A Philosophical Enquiry*, 68, my emphasis.
3. *Solitude and the Sublime*, 50.
4. "The anguish which humanity feels . . . at the sight of such an object cannot be the reflection of any sentiment of the sufferer. . . . The compassion of the spectator must arise altogether from the consideration of what he himself would feel if he was reduced to the same unhappy situation, and, what perhaps is impossible, was at the same time able to regard it with his present reason and judgment." *The Theory of Moral Sentiments*, 8.

letters hinges on the precariousness of Smith's conception of sympathy as an alternative capital. Although Keats demolishes any ground for optimism about sympathy's redemptive power, he, consistent with Lukács's insistence on totality, does so without pretending to renounce or escape Smith's basic formal model. Keats describes the experience of being at a party and sympathetically inhabiting people in a compulsive, serial way, moving insatiably from one individual to the next: "the identity of everyone in the room begins so to press upon me," Keats writes, "that I am in a very little time annihilated."[5] Keats anticipates Baudelaire's great portraits of the self-dissolving erotic life of urban crowds, and in both cases the critique of consumerist imagination is doubled-edged: on the one hand, the poets deny that the sympathetic imagination stands to repair social disunity (on the contrary, the sympathetic imagination that was supposed to connect the poet with others ends up alienating him from himself); on the other hand, though, Keats and Baudelaire alike recognize this defeat as inescapable: it is the structural condition upon which their respective poetic efforts build. Individualist consumerism is the condition of its own critique.

Thus there's a partial truth to Smith's account that haunts subsequent modernity both in spite and in virtue of its partialness. Like his poetic successors, Smith has the implicit good faith to acknowledge that the commodity form is total and consequently that the critique of consumerism must be immanent, must follow a consumerist logic of its own. The difficulty of such acknowledgment is that it makes critique difficult to distinguish from complacency. Whatever alternative Keatsian and Baudelairian sympathy offers to capital, this alternative cannot be simply an alternative but must instead somehow constitute a second-order alternative, an alternative to the consumerist way of experiencing alternatives described by Bourdieu. Even stating the problem this way just reposes it, since the commodity's constitutive "magic" is to promise the consumer escape from the limitations of actual, consumerist social life.

The following suggests that Keats's poetry builds on his letter's insight that overcoming this paradox requires resisting claims to overcome it and learning instead to accept and embrace it in poetically novel ways.[6] Like Baudelaire,

---

5. John Strachan, ed., "To Richard Woodhouse, October 27, 1818," *The Poems of John Keats*, 17ff.

6. This position is arguably antithetical to the pervasive view expressed in James O'Rourke's remarks about teaching "Ode on a Grecian Urn": "the primary challenge ... seems to be, at every level, to find a way of conveying the poem's resistance to being reduced to a consumable meaning or a predictable narrative." When O'Rourke goes on to write that "our contributors suggest that many students do, eventually, appreciate the idea that Keats's 'beauty' and 'truth' are neither ideological effects nor transcendent truths, but markers of a strange, elusive desire. In the best of cases, they discover that desire within themselves, and they recognize

Keats suggests that if exposing the otherness that capitalism seems to exclude just reinforces the ultimate unquestionability of consumer desire, then questioning capitalism must go in the opposite direction, toward not distinction but conformity, toward an alternative experience of the *un*questionable, of involuntary submission and devotion, of compulsion akin to that described in Keats's letter. Keats and Baudelaire commonly address the paradox of consumerism by positing radically ironized yet ultimately unquestionable, robustly normative aesthetics of beauty that subsume without cancelling the consumerist aesthetics of sublime otherness. In Baudelaire's *À une passante* the deranged poet's desire for a beautiful woman passing by is a limited case of consumer desire because, as Benjamin says, her refusal to reciprocate doesn't "deny" the poet what he wants but "spares" him this:[7] fulfillment of the poet's desire could happen only by way of radical violence, either that of his own psychosis or of her rape. But Baudelaire thus manages to present us with a refracted glimpse of the costs of the distortion of the social fabric—Baudelaire exposes monstrous violence as the structural condition of modern beauty and hence confronts us with a truth about our shared situation that the aesthetic of sublime otherness suppresses. This lesson is perhaps more urgent today than ever: at a time when things that long seemed constant, like the climate and the immorality of torture, have proven all too variable, what we arguably need most from art is guidance about how to reengage an experience not of questionability but unquestionability.[8]

II

As noted in chapter 3, Byron used the same term to disparage Keats's poetry that Rousseau used to distinguish substitute passion from the real thing. Keats practiced a "masturbatory" poetics, Byron remarked.[9] But, not unlike Rous-

---

its difference from the simpler, utilitarian desires of their everyday lives," he describes nothing other than the interpellation of consumers of Bourdieuian "distinction." O'Rourke, §6.

7. *Charles Baudelaire*, 125.

8. Thus my account somewhat resists a prevailing critical consensus regarding the value of questionability not just in Keats but in Romanticism generally, a view best expressed by Wolfson's account of the "questioning presence": "If Negative Capability is defined by what it excites and declines . . . Keats's odes strengthen that capacity in their readers by requiring us to negotiate a poetic language that fixes and unfixes, forms and transforms a texture of signification. Their originating 'uncertainties, Mysteries, doubts' are sustained by the interrogative processes of the poetry itself. . . . Keats's poetry retains a mystery of signs and situation that requires negotiation through the questioning presence of a reader and achieves its fullest imaginative value in the poetics of cooperation so engendered." *The Questioning Presence*, 331ff.

9. Strachan, ed., "To John Murry, September 9, 1820," *The Poems of John Keats*, 39.

seau's, Byron's disparagement of masturbation aimed ultimately to buttress the conceit that a completely *non*-masturbatory way of doing poetry was still possible, that a legitimate and effective voice (or lyric virility) was something that a poet like Byron still really *achieved* rather than just impotently dreamed about; Susan Wolfson remarks, "To name what is unnatural and monstrous is, by reflex, to relay what wise and decent men revere."[10] But the fact that Byron felt the need defensively to distinguish himself from impotent dreamer poets perhaps signals Byron's awareness that his image of himself as standing heroically apart overlapped uncomfortably well with every mechanic's image of him. Hence, in Rene Girard's terms, Byron's claim to poetic sovereignty is arguably rooted in rivalrous, triangular desire.[11] The intensity of Byron's derision of an unpopular poet like Keats suggests that Byron seeks out rivalry *as an end in itself* even in the most unlikely places, like in middle-class Keats's and Byron's lower-class fans, in the manner Eve Sedgwick characterizes as homophobic terror.[12]

In his essay "Edmund Burke, Gilles Deleuze, and the Subversive Masochism of the Image," Peter Cosgrove elaborates how the aesthetic image and fantasy might undermine such patriarchal structures by way of Deleuze's distinction between masochism and sadism as modes of relating to hegemonic power: whereas the sadist, like the sublime consumer and subject of Romantic ideology, inflicts pain for the sake of imaginatively identifying with the powers that be, masochism has a quite different logic, principally due to its investment in the aesthetic image as such which Deleuze associates not just with femininity but with effeminacy, that is, with what has no place in heteronormative erotic and social agency. In displaying powerlessness before the woman, Deleuze writes, the masochist invests "the totality of the law . . . upon the mother who expels the father from the symbolic realm."[13] Masochism, then, resists patriarchal symbolic identity, yet it is the *theatricalization* of the submission to pain, not the submission itself, that is the crucial affront to patriarchal law. Theodor Reik writes that instead of shrinking from the coercion of pain, "the masochist *runs to meet* the dreaded event, undertakes that flight forward by *anticipating* instead of expecting the punishment."[14] As Cosgrove comments, "this 'flight forward' to embrace punishment as pleasure mocks the superego's attempts at discipline."[15] In modernity's disciplin-

---

10. *Borderlines*, 8.
11. *Deceit, Desire, and the Novel*.
12. *Between Men*.
13. Gilles Deleuze and Leopold Sacher-Masoch, *Masochism*, 78.
14. *Masochism in Modern Man*, 160.
15. "Edmund Burke, Gilles Deleuze, and the Subversive Masochism of the Image," 411.

ary regime of sublimity, of consumer enjoyment, pain is just the condition of reengaging the "action" of fantasy, of re-accessing the aesthetic as such in a way that allows us to achieve a degree of imaginative autonomy.

The crucial prototype of theatrical fantasy in Keats appears in one of Reik's case studies of masochistic fantasies. This is the story of the satyr Marsyas who challenged Apollo to a musical duel and who outplayed Apollo on his flute until Apollo turned Marsyas upside down, such that he could no longer blow his flute, whereupon Apollo declared himself the victor and hacked Marsyas to death in punishment for his audacity. Keats's aesthetics is devoted to creative reenactment of this defeat and torment by the god of poetry—or, in other words, by prevailing norms of poetic legitimacy. As early as the 1817 sonnet "On First Looking into Chapman's Homer"—in which the figure of cultural authority is directly correlated with Apollo—Keats maps out the form his masochistic aesthetic will assume in his works of 1819. The sonnet celebrates the literary epiphany catalyzed by what Keats calls Chapman's "loud and bold speech," saying the translation's rhetorical vigor makes Keats feel like Cortez gazing at the Pacific from a peak in Darien: Keats is transported to the signature sublime stance of the "stout" aristocrat triumphant upon the mountaintop. Yet Keats doesn't allow his reader or himself to thrill in this sublimity without problematizing it, juxtaposing this individual reveling in literary loudness and boldness with the emphatic silence of a crew who stand behind Cortez and don't even look at him but at each other with, Keats says, "a wild surmise." The sublimity that Keats accesses via Chapman's loud and bold speech and that Keats would reproduce via the loud and bold speech of his own sonnet is finally not offered as an actually inhabitable position but bracketed as the surmise of a silent crowd, a crowd constitutively disconnected no less from the singularity of the figure on the mountaintop than from the loud and bold literary discourse that would transport one to that sublime position. Keats's sonnet doesn't invite us to inhabit the consciousness of sublime individuality itself so much as it invites to inhabit the consciousness of *desire for* such sublimity. Keats makes the sublime no longer an actual inhabitable subjective position but a *surmise,* a theatrical spectacle projected onto the stage by a crew of spectators:[16] a surmise that attests no less to the crew's

---

16. This establishes a signature form of Keats's mature poetry, anticipating the way in which, as Chandler remarks, "the poem stages within its narrative an account of its own reception by a reviewing public" ("Hallam, Tennyson, and the Poetry of Sensation," 531). Correspondingly, Alan Bewell argues that "the depiction in *Hyperion* of Apollo's coming into power" is "coincident both with Keats's emergence from epigone to epic poet—shaping rather than being shaped by circumstance—and with his assumption of a political voice" (222). This conception of the function of aesthetics (and the mythological aesthetic of Apollo in particular) eschews the commonplace dualism of history and poetry underlying Daniel Watkins's assess-

desire for such sublimity than to their constitutive incapacity for it. I would suggest that the theatrical trope Keats deploys in this early sonnet pervades his best mature poetry as well, and serves among other things to articulate an enjoyment of fantasy for fantasy's sake, both in virtue and in spite of the fact that it also, rather masochistically, presupposes poetic failure. This represents Keats's upside-down poetics of torment by Apollo: savoring the failure itself of surmises of poetic authority to become the real thing, but thereby sustaining the relative autonomy that such surmising allows. It is a remarkable testament to Byron's acuity that the terms he chooses to elaborate his mockery of Keats register precisely this aesthetics of hanging, of passively tarrying with the negativity of failure, submission to abject compulsion.

> The *Edinburgh* praises Jack Keats or Ketch, or whatever his names are: why, his is the *Onanism* of Poetry—something like the pleasure an Italian fiddler extracted out of being suspended daily by a Street Walker in Drury Lane. This went on for some weeks: at last the Girl went to get a pint of Gin— met another, chatted too long, and Cornelli was *hanged outright before she returned.* Such like is the trash they praise, and such will be the end of the *outstretched* poesy of this miserable Self-polluter of the human mind.[17]

Perhaps Keats's most vivid exploration of masochistic erotics is the following passage from the romance "Lamia," in which Lamia rapturously describes her lover Lyscius:

> His passion, cruel grown, took on a hue
> Fierce and sanguineous as 'twas possible
> In one whose brow had no dark veins to swell.
> Fine was the mitigated fury, like
> Apollo's presence when in act to strike
> The serpent—Ha, the serpent! Certes, she
> Was none. She burnt, she loved the tyranny.
> (II, 75–81)

Lamia is enraptured by Lyscius's finely mitigated fury, his lack of swelling veins, and so on, and she elaborates this rapture by drawing the comparison to

---

ment of the conclusion of "Lamia" that "Lycius dies as the historical struggles, which give rise to myths intended to pacify those struggles, push to the foreground and overwhelm myth" (*Keats's Poetry and the Politics of the Imagination*, 154).

17. Strachan, ed., "Lord Byron to John Murray, September 4, 1820," *The Poems of John Keats*, 39.

Apollo in act to strike the serpent. The eroticism of the scene depends utterly upon the actor's double consciousness, a consciousness that reaps pleasure from torment *only to the extent that* it can also simultaneously imagine being *merely* tormented: Lamia may burn with a pleasure that attests to *not* being a snake only and precisely to the extent that she also simultaneously sees herself as merely a snake. Lamia imaginatively plays out the scene of Apollo striking down the serpent as one of mechanical violence against a dumb beast in order to relish all the more acutely the incongruity of her burning passion.

One of the pillars of contemporary Keats criticism remains Marjorie Levinson's 1988 critique. Levinson ventriloquizes Byron's disparagement of Keats's masturbatory poetics when she writes that his poetry amounts to a "reproduction of the social restriction that marked [him] as *wanting*: unequipped, ineffectual, and deeply fraudulent," and hence "an artifact in an overwrought cabinet: framed, spotlighted, exhibited as possessions that are also signs *of* possession." Taking as her own Byron's preeminent concern for sovereign authority and authorship, Levinson observes that Keats's poetry expresses its deepest "want" and "possession," that it is not he but social codes—that is, exclusive norms of poetic authorship; membership in the *crowd*—that "mark him as wanting."[18] This formulation implies that the question of Keats's poetic power admits only one of two diametrically opposed answers: one is either the marker or the one marked, and one either speaks with absolute autonomy and sovereignty or is spoken of with equally absolutely abject, servile passivity. The example of Lamia, however, demonstrates how imaginatively or poetically reconfiguring the experience of being so marked can function to subvert or expropriate that authority. Lamia's fantasy articulates her pleasure here in a way that implicitly functions to usurp Lyscius's Apollonian power, making it a vehicle of her pleasure. If she, on the one hand, imagines Lyscius's domination of her as a finely mitigated fury, a mechanical violence against a thinglike beast which she, on the other hand, knows she is not, then Lamia is the author and hence owner of his power. In short, this seems an importantly subversive but underappreciated way of representing and relating to the patriarchal sublime.

Overwhelming female figures form the bulk of the muses of Keats's greatest hits—Moneta, La Belle Dame sans Mercy, Lamia, St. Agnes, and Psyche, and the closely related figures of the nightingale, the Grecian urn, and the personifications of Melancholy and Autumn. Lamia has been called Keats's ultimate metapoetic statement, and I think part of the reason this characterization is justified is that the poem attempts to show why the monstrous femi-

---

18. *Keats's Life of Allegory*, 6, 19.

nine figure must supplant Apollo as poetry's presiding authority, and hence why in most of his best-known work female figures assume the Apollonian role of coldly cruel domination. As Byron and Levinson emphasize, Keats's desire is not just "ineffective" but "deeply fraudulent": he doesn't merely fail to meet Apollonian (implicitly masculine and sublime) norms of poetic legitimacy but fails properly even to desire them, instead positing and worshipping these fraudulently maternal cultural authorities, scandalous in their emasculating aesthetic accessibility, their mere beauty. The fact that Keats makes this transposition signals his apprehension of the threat that the Siren-like, monstrously feminine poses to sublime subjectivity. Thus the great poetry Keats writes after "Lamia" aligns the genders in the manner that, according to clinicians, is more typical of masochism, casting the tormenter as female and the victim as male, and this alignment constitutes an act of masochist subversion unto itself. Anne Mellor describes this alignment when she writes that "what is ultimately for Keats the appropriate relationship between female and male in poetic discourse [is] that of goddess/mother/muse to human/son/poet, a relationship that sustains the role of humble submission and dependency";[19] but, as Wolfson notes, this configuration effectively accepts the ridicule of Keats's Tory critics but subversively inverts its valuation: "sifting into a finer feminist tone Z's abuse of 'The Muses' son of promise; and what feats / He may yet do.'"[20]

In the *Fall of Hyperion* Keats creates a patroness precisely of *failed* poets—of those whose fate it is to be categorized as fanatic dreamers *as opposed to* legitimate poets—in the demigoddess Moneta. Moneta doesn't promise to reintegrate these lost souls into a larger organic totality; rather she appears more like a symptom of the *un*integrated condition of modernity per se, its inherent disposition to impotent fanatasism. Moneta's name means *money,* her brain is hollow, and her eyes, like the eyes Benjamin analyzes in Baudelaire,[21]

---

19. *Romanticism & Gender*, 185.
20. *Borderlines*, 283.
21. Whereas accounts of Keatsian normative sensation such as those of Christopher Ricks and Levinson are traditionally opposed to formalist accounts such as Helen Vendler's, a correlation of sensation and action with seriality, such as I am espousing, seems fundamental to Vendler's account of the crucial role of Baudelairean "astonishment" in the social function of poetry: "The bizarre new . . . gives that shock of pleasure which Barthes calls, borrowing the word from Baudelaire, *jouissance*. It is caused, says Baudelaire, by astonishment. . . . The temperaments which seek astonishment are not the temperaments that seek the comfort of the received forms of the past" (19). Vendler suggests that the formalist aesthetics she espouses is not historically transcendent but dependent upon actual sociohistorical mobilization of an astonishingly new sensation, upon the temporally specific *effect* of affective astonishment. In Robert Kaufman's account of the political potency of Vendler's Keats, such mobilization opens the possibility for the free reconfiguration of poetic language, the retooling of expressive subjec-

are gazeless and glassy. Moneta exemplifies both the commodity fetish and Keats's anticipation of Baudelaire's poetics of commodification. If modernity conduces not to art but to fanaticism, then for precisely this reason fantasism provides the basis for an utterly new kind of art. Just like the dream of Cortez, Keats correlates Moneta's reification with her *nonexclusivity*: her thinglike status, what makes her brain hollow and her eyes "blank," is also what allows her to "beam splendid comfort" to the multitudes: "[her eyes seem'd] visionless entire . . . / Of all external things—they saw me not / But in blank splendour beam'd like the mild moon, / Who comforts those she sees not, / who knows not / What eyes are upward cast" (I, 266–71). However, whatever "comfort" Moneta offers is predicated upon a painful tearing apart and reconstituting of the subject who feels it: the sublime poet is dismembered, reduced to "most unpoetic thing[s]," in order that his parts may be used Frankenstein-like to reconstruct a new larger and somewhat monstrous collective subject of fanatic dreamers: hence the negativity of "negative capability." The fragment "This living hand" makes such capability synonymous with literacy itself by compelling readers to imagine the poet's hand, the very instrument of the poem's creation, "drained of life."

This radical mortification is the foundation of Keats's signature aesthetic. For instance, it is precisely the deadness of the Grecian urn, its resistance to our attempts to attach living meaning and purpose to it, that makes it a vehicle of temporal transcendence and human "friendship." Likewise, in "The Eve of St. Agnes," the lovers' bliss is simply incompatible with temporal life: Porphyro's and Madeline's desire for each other carries on Psyche's legacy by being scopophilic verging on scopofanatic, transfixed by visions of the other: the legend of the "Eve of St. Agnes" is precisely that maidens get vision of their future husbands, which Madeline achieves precisely because Porphyro is, Psyche-like, so intent on getting a look at her in bed. Yet when the two move beyond staring at each other's images, they don't finally physically acquire what they see but, Keats says, "melt into each other's dream, as the rose Blendeth its odour with the violet." They fall into each other's dream and fall out of time. Hence the poem ends with a scene of very concrete mortal decay out of which the blissful lovers "glide" and "flee" like "phantoms." "Lamia" is commonly read as a more or less straightforward critique of "cold

---

tivity, which, in turn, enables political agency: "Vendler contends that for Keats, poetic thinking goes far beyond chestnuts in Keats criticism about synaesthesia and/or 'thinking in images.' Rather, poetic thinking will ultimately mean the *construction* of an *architectonics* of sensation in language, which in turn will be coordinated with an extremely complex structural polyphony, practically symphonic in its generation of simultaneous, multiple, often contradictory effects. Meanwhile this intricate yet monumentalizing constructionism is said to dissolve a previously foregrounded sense of expressive selfhood" (363ff.).

philosophy" which "clips angels' wings," "unweaves the rainbow," and reduces what was a source of "awe" to one among the "dull catalog of common things." This critique is doubtless central to the poem, but we can't let it eclipse Keats's larger point that respecting the strangeness and awesomeness of the divine means respecting its status as a dream. So just as St. Agnes's concluding scene of mortal decay functions to preserve the "phantom" form of the lovers' rapture, so too there is a sense in which by "clipping the angels' wings" Apollonius also implicitly (and unwittingly) sets them free to fly again. He releases Lamia back to the realm of fantasy. Thus by making Lamia "melt into a shade" (II, 229–39), Apollonius despite himself arguably restores her to her properly divine place outside time.

Concomitantly, the late works' transposition of the Apollo figure unto that of monstrous females is a function of the fact that these works don't just schematize but aesthetically inhabit the experience of poetic defeat. They don't merely register defeat, or even just mark themselves as wanting, but take the next step of exploring the consequences of this defeat. In the modern context of the disciplinary sublime this means exploring what is entailed by loving emasculating beauty, not just as a mark of poetic defeat but as an aesthetic experience. This means not just getting turned upside down by the poet god but undertaking the futile effort itself to play the flute while upside down.

Such effort is nicely showcased by the "Ode on Melancholy." The poem issues an argument that relishing despair is the condition of relishing joy, but the poem ultimately enacts despair by way of its very failure to contain despair in such an argument. The poem concludes:

> Ay, in the very temple of Delight
> Veil'd Melancholy has her sovran shrine,
> Though seen of none save him whose strenuous tongue
> Can burst Joy's grape against his palate fine;
> His soul shall taste the sadness of her might,
> And be among her cloudy trophies hung.
> (25–30)

Ostensibly the message here is that an economic exchange must be made: that one may purchase bursting rights to joy's grape only by giving one's soul as a trophy to melancholy. But in fact there is no bargain to make; the two sides of the equation here are dialectically inextricable: what the poem says is refuted by what it shows. Just as Lamia's burning passion depends upon her fantasy of Apollo in act to strike the serpent, the Sovran shrine is not sovereignty itself but a fantasy of sovereignty's cold cruelty. Like Lyscius's bloodless mitigated fury, Moneta's blank face and the cold pastoral, the shrine is pallid in its emphatic idealization: its trophies are cloudy, and, tellingly, its might has taste only for the soul. All this Apollonian abstraction serves to throw into relief the sensuousness of the tongue's strenuous effort to burst the grape. But it also serves to explode the poem's whole ostensible argument that sacrifice can be economized: that I could sacrifice myself to beauty and still retain the form of an autonomous, rationally choosing, individual consumer.

This reading applies especially well to the image of the tongue strenuously working to burst the grape, since that image, as evocative as it is, is also in fact rather difficult to conjure: a grape is rather too dense and rubbery to easily imagine bursting, and although the tongue is powerfully muscular, its power is diffuse rather than penetrating. A remarkable thing about the image of the tongue, however, is that in addition to being the emblem of receptive taste on the one hand and poetic voice on the other, the tongue is also a preeminent image of corporal compulsion: its muscle is naked and free-floating, unhinged from the skeletal mechanism. The tongue represents aesthetic purposiveness without purpose in terms both of aesthetic receptivity and of autonomous poetic agency, but also precisely the opposite of this; that is, insatiable exertion, wild convulsions in the void, a terrifying rather than edifying, monstrous rather than beautiful, disconnection from use, purpose, or effect. What the two aspects of Keats's image finally do then is point out the dialectical inextricability of beauty and monstrosity.

By evoking the monstrosity of the tongue's unhinged muscle and the brute animality of the snake, Keats is also figuring the humiliation of the phallus. What I've said about the perversity of the tongue's unhinged muscle clearly also applies to the penis, which is precisely to say that it does not apply to the phallus and that it functions to belie the latter's claim to sovereignty. Keats's evocation of the wildly frustrated tongue is equally an evocation of the erotics of penis abuse, exposing and relishing the vulnerability hidden by the phallic pretense to penetrating power. As in Lamia's identification with the snake, the erotics of phallic vulnerability is a matter of putting a coherent model of normative power into dialectical tension with the body's abject excess, its unhinged sensuality. It is an image that activates a specifically perverse aesthetics, like trying to play a flute upside down; yet the activity of this perversion, the impact of Marysean aesthetics as such, presupposes the conceit of aesthetic purposiveness.

What is finally most crucial to note is that reading the image this way also makes it, as an image, *self*-frustrating, since the image *does* something at odds with what it's supposedly saying. Thus this masochistic aesthetic is not just communicated by the poem's rhetoric but is integral to the operation of that rhetoric as such, an operation in which we as readers necessarily become implicated.

By staging this self-consumption as a spectacle that we can, if not escape, then at least stand somewhat apart from and contemplate rather than just blindly and compulsively enact, Keats opens the way for the return of something like aura, because, in Adorno's lingo, this functions to "de-identify" the power to whom we submit: the goddesses to whom Keats's late poems are devoted aren't representatives of a unified power but fantasy objects of such overwhelming stature that Keats can do justice to them only by way of, as Adorno and Horkheimer put it, magical mimesis: "changeable masks . . . directed to the wind and the rain, the serpent and the demon."[22] Keats makes strenuously servicing the fantasy of a supernaturalism that both overpowers and excludes him the basis of a poetics whose sensuous rewards are ancillary effects of the effort of this service itself. Re-accessing sensuality by reframing it as magic is just another way of describing the aesthetic per se, another ancillary effect of which is a new model of social sympathy: a queer or supernatural, paradoxically non-normative, currency of sociality.

## III

As the "Ode on Melancholy"' proliferating frustrations suggest, Keats's masochism issues in a discipline of serial imitation—making copies of copies for copying's sake. Correspondingly, Deleuze says that masochistic fantasies draw on painting and the theater, just as much as figures *of figuration itself* as for the content of their scenes of torment. Deleuze could be describing a Keatsian goddess when he says of Wanda in *Venus in Furs* that she "looms with her furs and her whip, adopting a suspended posture, like a tableau vivant: 'I want to show you another portrait of me, one I painted myself. You shall copy it.'" Wanda's "coldness and cruelty" is expressed through and inseparable

---

22. Adorno and Horkheimer's dialectic of enlightenment describes how the disciplinary sublime eviscerates phenomenal experience, reduces it to abstractions in a way that primitive strategies of magical mimesis do not: "The enlightenment of the self is, they say, "paid for by the acknowledgement of power as the principle of all relations. [By contrast,] the shaman's rites were directed to the wind, the rain, the serpent without, or the demon in the sick man. . . . Magic was not ordered by one, identical spirit: it changed like the cultic masks which were supposed to accord with the various spirits. [But once] disqualified nature becomes the chaotic matter of mere classification . . . [then] the all-powerful self becomes mere possession—abstract identity" (*Dialectic of Enlightenment*, 9ff.) Odysseus inaugurates this abstract identity by "acting as sacrifice and priest at one and the same time. By calculating his own sacrifice, he effectively negates the power to whom the sacrifice is made"; thus "the self loses itself in order to preserve itself" (ibid., 48ff.).

from her demand to be copied. The way in which her coldness is enjoyed has a completely different erotic logic from that which aims for definitive climax and conquest; *there's no definitive experience of her coldness*; to enjoy it is just to recopy it over and over; Wanda's coldness can't be contained as knowledge or objective property because it was always already a copy to begin with. Like Baudelaire's anonymous passerby, she is finally more an ethical imperative than an actual person or object. In other words she is Lacan's radically opaque "Real" manifest as an ethical imperative.[23]

This ethical potential is what most distinguishes the aesthetics of beauty I'm advocating from that of sublimity. Whether on the Burkean or Kantian model, aesthetic figuration of the other as sublime is implicitly exclusive, sustained by a dialectic with the nonsublime otherness it excludes. Keatsian projection of normative beauty—the goddesses commanding his self-sacrificing displays of impotence—is *inconducive* to such binaries: it defies exclusive possession. Since they're framed as social fantasies, Keats's goddesses are like Girard's Christ ejected from the arena of triangular desire:[24] like Whitman's fantasy of himself, they may "contain multitudes." Moneta's blank face opens the possibility for effective collective agency precisely because it reflects the annihilation we all share. That blank face is precisely what Jameson termed ideology's implicitly utopian *form*, the form of a promise of universality that its content inevitably distorts.[25]

Christopher Rovee offers a compelling reading of Keats that, like mine, draws a connection between Byronic disparagement of his "shabby genteel" and "masturbatory" trashiness to the radical critical formalism that Adorno described as "*museal.*" Rovee writes that Keats deploys "a museal poetics—in Adorno's double sense of museum-like and deathlike," that "teasingly insinuate[s] a subversive correspondence—beauty is trash, trash beauty—and simultaneously find[s] in that predicament a glimmer of future promise."[26] Yet Rovee's readings, focused on the Elgin marbles sonnet and the fragment, "This living hand . . . ," rather than pressing ideological form for its implicitly

---

23. Paraphrased in Žižek, *The Sublime Object of Ideology,* 162.

24. "The Gospels and the New Testament do not preach a morality of spontaneous action. They do not claim that human must get rid of imitation; they recommend imitating the sole model who never runs the danger—if we really imitate in the way that children imitate—of being transformed into a fascinating rival." Girard, *Things Hidden since the Foundation of the World,* 430.

25. "Even hegeomonic or ruling-class culture and ideology are Utopian, not in spite of their instrumental function to secure and perpetuate class privilege and power, but rather precisely because that function is also in and of itself the affirmation of collective solidarity." *The Political Unconscious,* 291.

26. "Trashing Keats," 997.

utopian broken promise of universality,[27] remain unduly wedded to the literal content of Byron's disparagements, focusing on Keats's individual, affective stance, whether of "lachrymose" self-indulgence in the sonnet or resentment in the fragment. These poems' readers "are inevitably left . . . to contemplate the ruin of museal art. 'This living hand' doesn't passively bear the mark of its non-instrumentality so much as it flaunts its neglect, and ultimately its status as historical debris. The bitterness of the speaker, his nearly accusatory stance vis-à-vis readers by whom he feels abandoned, finds its corollary in that colorless, outstretched hand."[28] Rovee correlates spectral museal waste with the overwrought affect Byron disparaged as masturbatory trash. But this is to take Byron and Adorno alike too literally. Adorno is not interested in waste as any determinate kind of content but only in its potential to dismantle the form of bourgeois subjectivity, but this is just the form that Rovee sustains by focusing on the poet's individual affective or accusatory "stance." Likewise, it is revealing to note that Byron writes not of Keats's trashiness per se; instead he says, "There is *such a trash* of Keats *and the like* upon my tables."[29] "Such a trash" names a collectivity; what makes Keats a belong to it is nothing particular about him but precisely that he is so unparticular, that he is merely "like" an indeterminate crowd of others. The problem Keats represents to Byron is not any property specific to him but his general and opposed to singular form. In turn, by saying that "such writing is a sort of mental masturbation—he is always f-gg-g his *Imagination*," Byron emphatically does *not* "mean he is *indecent*, but viciously soliciting his own idea into a state, which is neither poetry nor any thing else but a Bedlam vision produced by raw pork and opium."[30] The problem again is not Keats's personal indecency but precisely the impersonal form of the crowd, in this case the crowd of the insane, the addicted, the hungry masses. The problem with masturbatory poetics is not its trashy content but its crowd form, a point made most vividly and penetratingly by the passage from Byron's letter that I've taken as my epigraph, which remarkably recalls the scenario of Marsyas's hanging. Just as I have attempted to do, Byron correlates the experience of reveling in punishment by the authorities as the occasion of Keats's masochistic poetics. Also here the problem for Byron is that Keats's trash is "such like" that of so many else. What Byron

---

27. "The secret of aesthetic sublimation is its representation of fulfillment as a broken promise." *Dialectic of Enlightenment*, trans. Cumming, 140.
28. "Trashing Keats," 1013. Rovee's reading of the sonnet concludes: "far from repudiating luxury as an embarrassing, guilty pleasure, Keats's sonnet ultimately embraces it. . . . The lachrymose pleasure of viewing and composition trump "god-like hardship" and elemental nature" (1010).
29. Strachan, ed., August 12, 1820, *The Poems of John Keats*, 39, my emphasis.
30. Ibid., 39, September 9, 1820.

fails to acknowledge, despite his astounding insight into Keats's poetics, is the threat this form poses to Apollonian authorities such as himself (although, again, the intensity of his attack suggests that he is also not altogether insensitive to this threat).

My reading of the sensuous intensities of the "Ode of Melancholy" is meant to emphasize that the ethical imperative of the Real can be registered only in the aesthetic dimension of the "flesh" that such authority repudiates. Trash may best be grasped as a form of collectivity, but such form, in turn, is most acutely registered in such sensuous intensities that stand to crack open the solitude of hegemonic, sublime individualism. The discipline of perpetual mimesis enables a new access of the aesthetic in a way that is suggestively illuminated by the fascinating revision of Foucault's critique of the Panopticon that Frances Ferguson accomplishes in her *Pornography, the Theory: What Utilitarianism Did to Action*. Ferguson suggests that Benthamite pedagogical structures, compelling continual comparison of students' performances, need not, as Foucault claimed, compel servitude to an inscrutable, abstract omniscience but can, on the contrary, prepare what Ferguson calls a "extreme perceptibility," which I'd suggest represents the modern secular corollary of Adorno's magical mimesis. Besides the work of the Marquis de Sade, Ferguson's most recognizable example of this is athletic competition in which the value of athleticism is illuminated not by defining it abstractly but strictly by comparing and ranking discrete performances. Attending to the particular in this way means that defining athleticism finally requires availing oneself to the aesthetic, rendering an aesthetic judgment—even if all the sports analysts and statisticians will resist this out of devotion to Foucauldian abstraction. Ferguson writes, "The action that a sports team performs in winning a game is not, in the utilitarian view, a matter of their spirit or heart, because attitude disappears in the score, which makes their victory as much a matter of their opponents as themselves."[31] Ferguson's Benthamite model offers complete release neither from compulsory disciplinary exercise of sublime subjectivity nor from invidious gendering of the aesthetic image as effeminate; but it suggests a way of accepting the inescapability of modernity's disciplinary regime while nonetheless managing to exercise the relative autonomy, and to access the modicum of pleasure, afforded by aesthetic judgment. In particular, I'd suggest that the inexorable role of defeat in the image of victory opens the way for a specifically masochistic form of creatively and pleasurably re-accessing aura: in modernity's rat race we can still access some freedom and pleasure in the enactment of our defeats.[32]

---

31. *Pornography, the Theory*, xiv.

32. If the relative autonomy of masochism is a matter not of escaping this disciplinary regime but of creatively "anticipating" its effects, then Jacques Khalip's account of romantic

## IV

The presiding goddesses in Keats's best-known works represent masochistic oversubmission to ideological authority, subversively excessive ideological investment that opens up a utopian experience of unregulated sensuality and sociality from within the form of ideology itself. Whatever friendship the Grecian urn offers to man, and whatever blooming music is to be heard in autumn's dying day, both are alike due to the projected, imperious indifference to us of urn and autumn alike. The urn is a "cold pastoral" not just because its melodies are unheard or because its ultimate lesson is the arid, abstract conceptual correlation of beauty and truth, but above all because of the stern way in which the urn almost scolds us that its lesson is not only all we know but also all we *need* to know. Not the austerity of the lesson itself but the chastising way it's delivered represents a coldness within coldness. The deepest significance of the ode's final lines is not any philosophical doctrine but their theatrical enactment of draconian domination. Keats here appropriates for theater the claim to sublime omniscience—to know all we need to know—but Keats's ventriloquizing of the urn's admonishments is so emphatically theatrical that it has the effect not of valorizing such omniscience but of mocking it. For Keats the imagination is always inadequate, but Keats's deeper message is that imagination shouldn't be judged by what it can and can't acquire; it's ultimately not about knowing or possessing objects. Rather, its purpose is the discipline itself of submitting our inadequate imaginative efforts to an inscrutable and unsatisfiable judge: *conjuring an exquisitely cold and cruel dominatrix perpetually unconvinced that we've learned our lesson*. The payoff is not an illusion of identifying with erotic and poetic sovereignty but the pleasure of illusion-making freed from the compulsion continually to shore up such identification. Impotence appears not as a lack but as a *liberation* from the compulsion to identify, and license to enjoy, the marginal but radically unregulated pleasures of magical mimesis. Reading the ode on the urn in this way makes it not the

---

anonymity and dispossession seems instead to espouse the rather familiar sublime subjectivity of Wolfson's "questionability." Khalip describes romantic texts "as the site of abstentions that evoke 'identity' as always an unmade and undone 'thing,'" reconfiguring subjectivity as an "anonymous saturation in the world." Yet in contrast to the radically subversively transformative self-reifications we've traced in Keats, for Khalip this "anonymous saturation" remains signally partial and optional, preserving for the subject some "breathing space" in the midst of this supposed saturation and thereby restoring (the romantic ideology of) familiarly sublime, liberal, consumerist, questioning selfhood: "the breathing space afforded the anonymous subject between the social and political actually helps to situate it in time and place"; situatedness and saturation in the real are correlated with an implicitly transcendent "breathing" detachment so that, finally, "nonidentity promises (at least ideally) a suspension from" just the sort of "prescriptive *doing*" that is integral to the subversions described by Keats, Deleuze, and Ferguson alike. *Anonymous Life: Romanticism and Dispossession,* 14.

final word it pretends to be, but just a gambit in an ongoing masochistic game devoted not to securing triumphant, revelatory climaxes but to deferring them as long as possible.

Keats subsequent master ode, "To Autumn," zeros in on the paradox that animates all of Keats's serial reenactments of submission to cold goddesses: the paradox of wanting the sheer conclusiveness of their judgments to never end, wanting to be told more and more about how there's nothing more to be told, wanting to sustain the game of finality. What animates "To Autumn" on the deepest level is the indifference with which this desire is at once indulged and rebuffed. The poem is plainly an ode to the transience of sensuous pleasures; less plain, though, is that the pleasures of transience are sustained not just by the prospect of death but, more crucially, by Autumn's utter indifference to our anticipation of death. Like the urn, Autumn exhibits a coldness beyond coldness: colder than the death she foreshadows is the indifference with which she just happens to defer its onset when she might just as soon have delivered it directly. So Keats casts Autumn as death "sparing the next swath" and, with a Moneta-like blankness, "keeping steady [her] laden head across a brook, or by a cyder-press, with patient look, watching the last oozings hours by hours."

In this representation of the coldness not just of death per se but of death's indifference to its own event, we see the ethical imperative emerge from within the aesthetic object. In light of this compound coldness, the hours by hours with which we're arbitrarily indulged become akin to the serial discipline of sublime consumerism, a discipline reiterated on larger scales in Lamia's series of erotic conquests and in the series comprised in all the works of Keats's *annus mirabilis*. On micro- and macro-levels alike these series acknowledge implication in modernity's constitutive disciplinary sublimity and demonization of effeminate beauty. But Keats's poetic experiments of 1819 rechannel such discipline into scrupulously serving the demonized mistress herself. The effect is not to invert the normative objects of desire and disdain but to rewrite the very logic of desire: making it self-conscious of itself *as* a discipline even while opening it to wildly unregulated sensuality—which is to say, to sensuality per se: the wind and the rain as emanations not of supposedly comprehensible natural powers but of inscrutable, supernatural ones. Keats shows that this magical sensuality is accessed neither by mastering the cliffs and oceans of conventional sublimity nor by mastering the alterity of female sexuality, but by mobilizing the overlooked intensities of impotence itself, its stolen hours and illicit oozings. Such is the queer currency of modern sympathy. By functioning to put this into circulation, to render it fungible, the object of endless copying, Keats's art pioneers the immanent critique of consumer subjectivity, catalyzing a possibility of relatively autonomous ethical agency and social solidarity.

Levinson construes this accomplishment—Keats's ability to make a currency of queerness, his subversive intervention in his own culture, and his enduring significance for us today—as a poetics of arrested development: "The deep contemporary insult of Keats's poetry, and its deep appeal (and long opacity) for the modern reader, is its idealized enactment of the conflicts and solutions which defined the middle class at a certain point in its development and which to some extent still obtain. . . . In emulating the condition of the accomplished middle class (the phrase is itself an oxymoron), Keats isolated the constitutive contractions of that class. The final fetish in Keats's poetry is precisely the stationing tension." Keats's arresting poetic fetishes can have a remarkably transhistorical capacity for historicist critique because we and Keats's contemporaries are alike implicated in what Levinson terms the "oxymoron" of bourgeois selfhood, the promise of continuous, always unfinished, normative development, on the one hand, and assurance, on the other hand, that this promise is always already fulfilled or in Levinson's term "accomplished." While Jerome McGann defined the Romantic ideology as the tendency of latter-day Romanticists to disregard the historical difference separating us from our objects of study, Levinson suggests that there is a certain transhistorical master ideology of bourgeois development that lends a radically critical valence to this panel's title. Here I hope not to correct but to add particular details and texture to her account of how Keats's "forever feeling" manages such a contradictory feat of transhistorical historicist critique.

Levinson's emphasis on fetishism and arrested development can seem to imply a kind of isolated and impotent stuckness, emblematized by Prophro's fetishistic gazing on Madeline's empty dress and ineffectual masturbatory "musing," "entoiled in woofed fantasies." But Levinson attributes Keats's critical power to his carnivalesque pluralism, observing that "Keats's relation to the Tradition is better conceived as diologic (Bakhtin) than dialectic (Bloom). The poetry does not clear a space for itself by a phallic agon; it opens itself to the Tradition, defining itself as a theater wherein such contests may be eternally and inconclusively staged. The authority of this poetry consists in its detachment from the styles or voices it entertains. . . . All such masks, inauthentic and incomplete, are not ultimately mastered by the master-of-ceremonies. And because they remain external to authorial consciousness, theirs is the empowering virtue of the supplement. In these magic supplements, 'Things semi-real,' lies the terrific charm of Keats's poetry." Keats replaces the history of rivaling claims to master narratives with the magically "*eternal*" temporality of carnivalesque theater, the endless proliferation of allegory. If Paul de Man describes prosopopoeia as a "voice assum[ing] mouth, eye, and finally face, a *chain* that is manifest in the etymology of the trope's name . . . to confer a mask or face," then the Keatsian mask isn't a sign of personhood but an animating link of social life, perpetuating such conferrals.

Another term for the bourgeois ideology of development is the *Freudian subject*, and I would like to return, in this book's closing chapter, to the "fort-da" game explored in chapter 2 in hopes of taking some measure of the distance covered by the intervening discussions of the interplay between poetry and selfhood. There we noted Freud's prescriptive imposition of an empirically causal account of subjective development. Here I would question his more basic assumption that subjectivity is developmental. Freud's tendentious staging of his fort-da game makes vivid what it means to *suppress* the autonomous play of masks Levinson describes. For Freud, we recall, the "obvious interpretation" of the game is that it constituted "the child's great cultural achievement—the instinctual renunciation which he had made in allowing his mother to go away without protesting. He compensated himself for this by himself staging the disappearance and return of the objects within his reach" (*Beyond the Pleasure Principle* 14). Yet Freud's account suggests that this "staging" is haunted by an unacknowledged master of ceremonies behind the scene. What makes the boy's accomplishment "cultural," as Freud says, is that it is, also in Freud's sense although he disregards it here, "overdetermined," that it conjures up more meaning than it can account for, specifically the whole narrative of normative subjective development, the story of how one becomes a story-worthy subject, an agent of intentional action, in the first place. Freud acknowledges that construing the boy's initially inchoate utterance "oooo" as an attempt at the German word "*fort*" required an inference on his part: the disruptive behavior, which Freud had originally been able to grasp only as *indeterminately other* than that of a "good" boy, is retrospectively interpreted as an as-yet-incomplete attempt to *become* a good boy. Even while the child is uttering inarticulate "ooo" sounds, then, this indeterminately other behavior is retrospectively assimilated to the developmental trajectory: Freud masters the staging of the fort-da game so that the boy, having always implicitly *intended* to become a good boy, effectively already was a good boy even before officially accomplishing this.

By way of illustrating how a fort-da game might look in the absence of such a supervening master narrative, I'll briefly consider Keats's "On Seeing the Elgin Marbles" sonnets and "The Eve of St. Agnes." The masks of personification which expose egoistic selfhood as hollow, static artifice, nonetheless refract temporal, subjective expressions of desire in a manner suggested by Bill Brown's nondevelopmental or "unhuman (not antihuman) history." Darwinism is helpful here because the picture it offers is at least as disenchanted as Byron's, which itself deconstructs cultural illusions by way of an uncompromising, survival-of-the-fittest code that might be called proto-Darwinian. What used to be called *adaptive fitness* has been downgraded by modern Darwinism to "satisficing," an economic notion that basically mocks normative desire and satisfaction by construing adaptive success as irreducibly accidental. Following the term's coiner, Herbert Simon,[33] economists tend to oppose the supposed relative efficiency of satisficing to the higher costs of optimizing. Yet this just returns us to Fox's dilemma from chapter 1, that is, we can't measure the relative efficiency of either approach unless we have some privileged knowledge of the purpose or norm we're trying to fulfill, but this is just what participants (as opposed to observers) of evolutionary processes can never pretend to have. Hence Daniel Dennett writes, "Merely claiming that [satisficing is the basic structure of all real decision-making, moral, prudential, economic, or even evolutionary] is not necessarily saying that it is best."[34] Evolutionary success in this view is a matter not of *satisfying* any positively identifiable *norm* of fitness but of purely and simply escaping extinction, of contingently just *sufficing* to avoid death. Normative questions of why or how death is avoided always run the risk of obscuring the contingency of adaptation by insinuating that it does not merely satisfice but satis*fies* some more or less enduring norm of fitness. There are many wonderful recent texts that explore the undecidability of developmental norms in evolution and history.[35]

Such rhetorical distinctions are important because they implicitly effect much of the reality they can seem merely to describe. The ecological rationale of ecopoetics seems to hinge on this point. A great virtue of the biologist Joan Roughgarden's *Evolution's Rainbow*, for instance, is not only its sophistication on questions of Darwinian theory but also its attentiveness to the rhetorical figures by which these questions are framed. Specifically, Roughgarden advocates switching from the trope of "survival of the fittest" to a rather social rubric highlighting the relative productivity of various forms of cooperation. This rhetorical shift is not reducible to a theoretical claim but also promises to remove an obstacle to ecological thinking: namely, the undue essentializing of the individual who, whether on the level of the gene or the organism, would embody easily fetishized characteristics of "fitness." Instead of the trope of the fit individual, Roughgarden proposes that of the productive community as a

---

33. *Models of Man: Social and Rational.*
34. *Darwin's Dangerous Idea,* 504.
35. See, for instance, Michael Pollan, *The Botany of Desire*; Joan Roughgarden, *Evolution's Rainbow*; and Michel Serres, *The Parasite.*

much richer, more nuanced and capacious—and finally productive—"thing to think with."

Roughgarden doesn't propose a new trope as such; on the contrary, she suggests that the evolution of human society may result in a wide variety of family arrangements, "monogamy, polyandry, or polygyny," and even that the wildly unpredictable turbulence of social dynamics make "the outcome of social evolution . . . as uncertain as where a white-water stream deposits a floating leaf" (177). But her recourse to the leaf metaphor here seems instructive, because it implies that it is finally literary invention that stands to sustain our sensitivity to the diversity of potential social forms. If we can't unambiguously name or individually display what it is that keeps extinction at bay, we can try to speak in ways that keep us alive to the unpredictable tumult of the floating leaf.

Hence the kind of communal productivity described by Roughgarden paradoxically must involve a great deal of what cannot appear other than as unproductive, unaccountable expenditure (such as, for instance, poetic flourishes in works of evolutionary theory). Waste is itntegral to what George Bataille termed a *general* as opposed to a *restricted* economy. Like Roughgarden's productive collective of unfit individuals, the gift economy requires its participants to divest from the calculus of possessive individuality. Michel Serres suggests that his book *The Parasite* has a millennial mission based in Bataille's distinction: to reverse the world order, allowing a primeval gift economy to return and supplant the current economy of restrictive meaning and debt. "The world turns in one direction; history has its economy where exchange is fundamental: it is called the meaning of history. It stops a moment, turns in the other direction, and in this new story, exchange appears after everything was freely given. It is not a new story; on the contrary, it is an ancient one, lost in the dark recesses of memory. . . . There are only barely perceptible traces of the history of giving in texts and on monuments. Since then, we have been caught up in economic history, a time of calculation and exchanges and of making up for losses. Does this history have an outside? That is precisely the subject of this book" (30ff.).

Serres represents the parasite not just as the trace of a lost and perhaps future gift economy but concomitantly as a rhetorical figure uniquely adapted to acknowledging what Roughgarden calls the tumult of social dynamics. In both English and French the term can serve as a metaphor of itself: if its primary meaning is that of a biological parasite, in both cases its secondary meaning applies this by analogy to the notion of a social freeloader. In French, however, the term has a unique third signification—namely, "noise," or what surrounds and obscures the signal—which arguably describes the kind of contingencies that analogical transfers of meaning, for instance, from biological to social parasites, elide but also presuppose. In his account of the fable of the city mouse and the country mouse Serres makes much of the reversibility of the roles of guest and host: the roles are structural and provisional, and the individuals who fill them arbitrary. So the fable recounts how the city mouse plays guest to a man but host to the country mouse. It is the crucial role of the third term, *noise,* to disrupt the role-players and reveal the provisionality and arbitrariness of their roles. So when the country mouse's enjoyment of his host's hospitality is interrupted by the man's noise, the country mouse becomes a kind of host to that visitation. The man is accommodated by the country mouse without knowing it; he receives a hospitality of which he's oblivious, which, according to the logic of the gift, makes it all the more generous. As in a gift economy, the parasite economy is predicated upon overabundance. What circulates across this economy are not credits and debts in a stable currency akin to a standard of fitness, but ever new means of experiencing excess, of exploiting what according to any stable norm must appear illicit, wasteful, or otherwise unfit.

Serres writes that "one parasite chases another out. One parasite (noise), in the sense that information theory uses the word, chases another, in the anthropological sense. Communication theory is in charge of the system; it can break it down or let it function, depending on the signal. A parasite, physical, acoustic, informational, belonging to order and disorder, [is] a new voice, an important one, in the contrapuntal matrix" (6). Like the leaf in tumult, the parasite describes the merest form itself of subsisting—or communicating import—in the midst of chaos. Not unlike Roughgarden, Serres casts such subsistence less in terms of an abiding identity and more in terms of a paradoxical double negative: a defiance of disintegration, holding noise at bay just long enough to grasp it as noise rather than being consumed by it. It is because the leaf is utterly at the mercy of the tumult that it can figure the tumult as such. Like the floating leaf, the parasite is crucially a figure of the act itself of figuration, of the act of communication by which a community pragmatically constitutes itself as a group of participants in such acts, as transmitters and receivers of signals of this sort. After all, the terms *noise, contingency,* and *chaos* are finally no less figurative than terms like *parasite, tumult,* and *wind.* What's crucial is the two-part act itself of, in Ammons's terms, giving away: of, first, submitting to disruption, in order, second, for that disruption to be grasped as such. The individual voice is sacrificed to recover an impersonal grammar of communication per se. To give the wind away means, on the one hand, to cede, to forfeit the wind as something nameable or otherwise possessable, to acknowledge the irreducibility and autonomy of noise. However, on the other hand it is to give the wind a way, a means of effecting itself as such, a way of being not sheer tumult but specifically wind, of containing tumult in a name. Blowing a reed over gives wind a way to be wind. The parasitic power of Ammons's poem is to make the work itself of figuration just barely register or transmit this side of sheer tumult.

Likewise for Serres, the ulterior economy of the gift can be approached only from within the restrictive economy of debt; the chaos of noise may be engaged only by way of what Serres describes as a cascade of disruptions that at any moment can appear to flow in but one direction. "A human group is organized with one-way relations, where one eats the other and where the second cannot benefit at all from the first. . . . The flow goes one way, never the other. I call this semiconduction, this valve, this single arrow, this relation without a reversal of direction, 'parasitic'" (5); "The chain of parasitism is a simple relation of order, irreversible like the flow of the river" (182).

Serres's simile here recalls Roughgarden's of the floating leaf, but it turns the figure in a way that would seem to contradict her insistence on the unpredictability of evolution, implying that, regardless how tumultuous, the river must ultimately carry the leaf downstream. Serres's figure of the arrow in particular seems to underscore his commitment to approaching the parasite from within the same restrictive economy—the world of possessive, predatory, patriarchal individuals—that the parasite stands to dismantle. It is only in the context of normative demand for fitness that the generous excess of unfitness may manifest as such.

Leo Bersani and Adam Phillips bracingly consider the prevalence of certain sex practices, dangerous to humans, in the light of their positively *promoting* (the evolutionary success of) HIV.[36] This returns to the basically Burkean point that the weight around which our actions gravitate is not itself explainable in the same terms we use to justify our actions. Such weight is "unhuman" in Brown's sense, which is to say more disturbingly directionless than it would be were it "antihuman." As Timothy Morton puts it, "Strict Darwinism is profoundly anti-teleological (Marx liked it for that reason). Individuals and species don't abstractly 'want' to survive to preserve their form: only macromolecular replicators 'want' that. For the replicators' viewpoint, if it doesn't kill you ('satisficing'), you can keep it, whatever it is. A vast profusion of gender and sex performances can arise. As far as evolution goes, they can stay that way. Thinking otherwise is 'adaptationism.'"[37] This leads Morton to a provocation analogous to Bersani and Philips's, construing climate change

---

36. *Intimacies.*
37. Morton, *The Ecological Thought*, 84ff.

as they did HIV, as a "hyperobject" that for all its evident destructiveness is instructive insofar as it "undermine[s] normative ideas of what an "object" is in the first place."[38]

If this is the world picture that modernity has inherited, then one does not need apocalyptic futures to learn that the notion of *mastering suspicion* is a nonstarter. But this suggests how precisely the superfluous and symptomatic status of post-personal personification might have a key role in both recognizing this evolutionary reality and learning to live in a merely satisficing way. Satisficing must entail a lot of superfluity, because without norms of fitness it is never possible to know what is necessary and what isn't. Thus satisficing, strictly speaking, means doing significantly more than is necessary. Mauss's account of the gift is the most famous example of the role of waste in securing a kind of effective sociality. Leo Bersani's account of the sociality of cruising is another example. Both center on a certain rhythm of postindividualism: whether the rhythm of a gift economy in which my confidence that my gift will be reciprocated hinges not on an impersonal, instrumental, rational, and "thin" understanding that the recipient will repay me in kind but, on the contrary, on a nonrational but "thick" supposition that *the universe* somehow will repay me in kind, that I will eventually receive an analogously gratuitous gift precisely from someone who *does not owe it to me*.[39] The economy of the gift is postindividual in that it requires its participants to divest from the calculus of possessive individuality: it is an economy precisely of such displays of divestment, an economy of waste. The crystallization of the materiality things independently of egoistically possessive relations to them—the brain beyond mind—unlocks an analogously postindividual experience of desire as the substrate of thinghood per se. For Bersani this discipline of impersonal intimacy heralds an "ecological ethics . . . in which the subject, having willed its own

---

38. contemporarycondition.blogspot.com/2010/03/hyperobjects-and-end-of-common-sense.html

39. As I discuss in Chapter 1, the philosopher Harry Frankfurt argues in implicitly Burkean terms that two kinds of commitments or promises simultaneously animate all intentional behavior which he labels *thin* and *thick*: thin promises rely on networks of explicit reasons to explain and justify them; thick promises by contrast are on some level self-justifying; they represent a certain explanatory end of the line. So, for instance, when one engages in a social practice like voting or playing a game of chess, one agrees to follow certain explicit rules: to vote in the right precinct, not to vote twice; to move the rook one way and the bishop another. Following such rules is impersonal in the sense that there is an impersonal script or rulebook dictating what adherence entails. But there is a whole other, overarching thick level of commitment involved in my choice to even play the game in the first place. So a robot could undertake actions adhering to the rulebook of democratic participation just as a computer can play chess, but it can't make the prior choice to *undertaking* those games. There's no rulebook and hence no way of mimicking the free choice to enter into the game in the first place.

lessness, can live less invasively in the world," making it "not only imperative but natural to treat the outside as we would a home."[40] This is what's entailed by finding oneself in the trellis of a working brain, in a climate model irreducible to weather, and in a Darwinian satisficing without normative satisfaction or fitness.

Perhaps the most nuanced account of satisficing developed in the Romantic period is Keats's account of Psyche, which is to say of a kind of love or desire according to which only the ghostly recoils of our own self-wasting suffice. Here is Keatsian Darwinism, from a letter he wrote in 1819:

> For in wild nature [if] the Hawk would loose his Breakfast of Robins and the Robin his of Worms The Lion must starve as well as the swallow—The greater part of Men make their way with the same instinctiveness, the same unwandering eye from their purposes, the same animal eagerness as the Hawk—The Hawk wants a Mate, so does the Man—look at them both they set about it and procure one in the same manner—They want both a nest and they both set about one in the same manner—they get their food in the same manner. The noble animal man for his amusement smokes his pipe—the Hawk balances about the Clouds—that is the only difference of their leisures.... Even here though I myself am pursuing the same instinctive course as the veriest human animal you can think of—I am ... young writing at random—straining at particles of light in the midst of a great darkness—without knowing the bearing of any one assertion of any one opinion. Yet may I not in this be free from sin? May there not be superior beings amused with any graceful, though instinctive attitude my mind may fall into, as I am entertained with the alertness of a Stoat or the anxiety of a Deer?[41]

Two not easily reconcilable things to note about this: Keats's endorsement of superfluity on the one hand and his cold, verging on sadistic, association of this with the predator's unique perspective on the suffering of prey. Only to the deer's predator is the luxury available to superfluously notice and ruminate upon the deer's anxiety. It is no accident that for Keats the human equivalent of animal predation involves smoking because smoking people, as in smoking them out, was the term of art at the time for cornering, mastering, and seeing through an adversary (for, in Prufrock's terms, formulating them, pinning them to the wall and watching them wriggle). Keats was himself famously smoked by his Tory reviewers, and he was highly attentive to his potential smokability.[42] As he wrote in another letter,

---

40. *Intimacies*, 62.
41. Hyder E. Rollins, ed., *Letters of John Keats*, 79ff.
42. For a different account of Keats on Psyche and smoking, to which I am greatly indebted, see Chandler, *England in 1819*, chapter 7.

> I will give you a few reasons why I shall persist in not publishing "The Pot of Basil"—It is too smokeable. . . . There is too much inexperience of life, and simplicity of knowledge in it. . . . I intend to use more finesse with the Public. It is possible to write fine things which cannot be laugh'd at in any way. Isabella is what I should call were I a reviewer "A weak-sided Poem."[43]

This notion of poetry as blood sport offers a completely disenchanted, cynical view of the cultural scene as basically a market economy in arbitrary prestige where resentful rivals fight to expose each other's fraudulence. It's hard to imagine Keats of all people endorsing such a view, but it is, in fact, only by recognizing how thoroughly resigned he is to it that we can begin to appreciate the kind of impersonal intimacy and erotic gratuitousness Keats associates with Psyche.

The "Ode to Psyche" itself hinges on many levels of skepticism at once: first, at the level of the story of the original legend itself, Psyche was *born of skepticism* in the sense that she was a mortal who became worshipped only because reverence for the truly worship-worthy god, Athena, was being neglected. Thus Psyche is a symptom of a time of irreverence. Moreover, Psyche herself is the apotheosis of the kind of skepticism that insists upon empirical verification: she can't resist shining a light on Eros to see his beauty for herself. But the remarkable thing about the ode is that it doesn't concern this legend at all but rather just its reception, which is arguably a way in which Keats intends to smoke the recently deceased Mary Tighe, whose popular "Psyche or the Legend of Love" does pretend to retell this legend. Keats's ode by contrast hinges on the fact that Psyche is made a goddess only to find out it is too late; Christianity has come and left the old gods bereft of worshippers. The same skepticism that elevates her to immortal status makes her in turn impossible to worship. She is created and destroyed by the same principle, which in the ode doesn't amount to a zero-sum game but instead throws in relief the gratuitousness of erotic striving, what Bersani described as the sheer movement of desire—of shooting for a target or straining to see—irrespective of the object to be captured or revealed. Psyche is the property precisely of a "*brain*" whose very inert materiality frees it up to experience its forms as gratuitous excess, to, as the ode concludes, "let the warm love in." However, Keats emphasizes that what coaxes this love in is precisely the "bright torch in a night casement," precisely the instrument by which Psyche skeptically seeks evidence of Eros's beauty. Keats's deepest investment is in the unresolvable tension, agitation, and irreducible movement of psychic self-suspicion.

---

43. Ibid., 174.

I will try to illuminate this movement by looking at the two sonnets Keats wrote after viewing the Elgin marbles.

*On Seeing the Elgin Marbles*

Haydon! Forgive me, that I cannot speak
Definitively on these mighty things;
Forgive me that I have not Eagle's wings—
That what I want I know not where to seek:
And think that I would not be over meek
In rolling out upfollow'd thunderings,
Even to the steep of Helciconian springs,
Were I of ample strength for such a freak—
(1–8)

So Keats is saying: forgive me *the audacity of my desire, precisely that I would thunder if I had the strength I don't, that "I would not be so meek" as I am*. But (unlike, for instance, Prufrock's ironic invocations of Lazarus and Prince Hamlet) this thundering is itself also already implicitly *seen through* or smoked, likened to a "freak" that rhymes with and refigures the meekness. Haydon prominently advocated for the government purchase of the Elgin marbles and hoped that taking Keats to see them would help to enlist Keats in a broader aesthetic and culture mission which the marbles symbolized. Haydon gratefully received these sonnets as a tribute both to himself and to that mission (although in another layer of passive-aggression Keats would ultimately publish the sonnets in the journal of Haydon's rival for Keats's affection, Leigh Hunt). I wouldn't say that Haydon completely misread Keats's gesture, but he radically oversimplified it, neglecting, for instance, the irony of the present sonnet's second half. For here Keats proceeds to offer precisely the supposedly *un*thundered thunder (that even in hypothesis isn't just thunderous but already associated with meek freakishness) as a token of contrition to the ostensibly legitimate worshipper Haydon. There's something extremely ironic and bitingly passive-aggressive about this: offering failed praise in apology for failing to praise is like saying, "I'm sorry for coming to your fancy dinner party all covered in mud, but as a token of my contrition allow me to spread it all over your furniture." But Keats here also adds another twist to the irony by *praising* Haydon for ostensibly actually possessing the strength Keats says he lacks, as if Keats had not made it clear he does not believe in such strength. In the dinner party example it's as if one then were to then to praise the host for having such a clean and nice suit while running one's dirty hands across it. Keats mocks precisely the untouchable integrity he is ostensibly praising:

> Think too that all those numbers should be thine;
> Whose else? In this who touch thy vesture's hem?
> For when men star'd at what was most divine
> With browless idiotism—o'erwise phlegm—
> Thou hadst beheld the Hesperean shine
> Of their star in the East, and gone to worship them.
> (11–16)

As a matter of historical record, Haydon *epitomized* precisely the legitimate worshipper with whom Keats apologetically contrasts himself. But in the sonnet it is precisely the ostensible legitimacy of Haydon's worship that sets him outside the scene of Keats's apology to him: "thou hadst gone" Keats says to Haydon in the past perfect, so Keats reveals in the last line that the addressee named in the first was *never even there to begin with*. In the final turn of the screw of the poem's irony Keats effectively says to the host whose suit and furniture he's just soiled, "Oh sorry: I believe I'm at the wrong address." Haydon's legitimate worship of the marbles finally represents an inert stasis that is just as absolutely cut off from the sonnet's ironic movements as the browless, phlegmatic idiots who don't worship the marbles at all. The reverent and irreverent are equally thoroughly smoked.

The second sonnet begins in the classic manner of his odes: complaining, like a stubborn, disconsolate child, that the poet is not up to his task:

> My spirit is too weak—Mortality
> Weighs heavily on me like unwilling sleep,
> And each imagin'd pinnacle and steep
> Of godlike hardship, tells me I must die
> Like a sick Eagle looking at the sky.
> (1–5)

Keats makes the eagle's sickness his own: a bird become a stranger to the very element of its existence. Continuing to elaborate this desolation, Keats doesn't narrate a resistance to growing up but just *relishes* this failure:

> . . . 'tis a gentle luxury to weep
> That I have not the cloudy winds to keep,
> Fresh for the opening of the morning's eye.
> (6–8)

Keats seems to strike a sentimentally elegiac pose but immediately subverts it: he registers the gentle luxury of bourgeois wistfulness in the face of museum pieces, but not without then extracting from that luxury any claim to legitimate mourning. The tears Keats weeps have no more connection to a genuine *sigh of mourning* than the sick eagle does with the cloudy winds at the opening of the morning's eye. Playing on the words' sounds in our ears, Keats likewise alienates us from our eyes. All this allegorical play showcases the poet, as Keats emphasizes, *luxuriating* in how cut off he is from the world of legitimate grief. In lieu of legitimate mourning, all Keats has is the orphaned artifact of the tear itself, unmagnanimous salt ore, a strictly material excretion akin to the oozings he invokes in "Ode to Autumn," where, likewise, material opacity becomes the catalyst of allegorical regeneration.

So self-loss is made expressive, not as a prelude to self-discovery, but *as such*; but what then is expressed if not a personal self? It's easy to take Keats's suspicious advocacy of unmagnanimous, unsmokable, orelike opacity as a signal that he pursued a proto-Symboliste, Mallarmean hermeticism, and many people, notably Helen Vendler, celebrate his achievement as a poet along these lines. Keats's famously malicious critics gave him cause to be self-protective. But as I've been suggesting it's instead the mark of his uncompromising historicism, his openness to the investment of his time in radical self-suspicion. He's attempting to transfigure this into something like what Bersani termed a new ecological ethics of impersonal intimacy. Here Keats's materiality is unmagnanimous but laden with affect, and there is something revealingly *moving* about Keats's strictly formal exchange, in the sonnet's conclusion, of plural terms not for definite but indefinite singular ones:

> Such dim-conceived glories of the brain
> Bring round the heart an undescribable feud;
> So do these wonders a most dizzy pain,
> That mingles Grecian grandeur with the rude
> Wasting of old Time—with a billowy main—
> A sun—a shadow of a magnitude.
> (9–14)

The grandeur, sun, and magnitude are implicitly all merely one of many such things. It is as if the bird has realized that it is not the only one to have lost a sky, that this sky is only one of many lost worlds. Here we begin to see the eternal temporality of a fort da game that *leads nowhere* but to endless rehearsals of itself. Projecting a self-allegorizing imagination into the bird makes the figure more conducive to affect even as it becomes more formally opaque. Recalling Wordsworth's account of active suffering, Keats makes the suffering of worldlessness inseparable from *the form itself of its allegorization*:

as the bird's passive suffering of its affliction becomes inseparable from its active manner of figuring it, the intimate particularities, the texture and feel, of affective content become correlated not with privative internality but with social sharability. This is like the experience Keats describes in a letter of being at a party and empathizing with people in a compulsive, serial way, moving insatiably from one individual to the next. Instead of connecting him with others, empathy alienates him from himself. Instead of taking narrative ownership of another's pain, this self-dissolution becomes a way of allegorizing it: actually *sharing* suffering means sharing its compulsion to allegorize itself, not to grow up but just laterally replicate.

If Keats's forever-young masks—or what we might term *youth culture*— represent a kind of transmodern mode of expression and empathy, then this is due not to enlightenment virtues of either penetrating insight or openness to questioning but, on the contrary, to resignation to unquestionable compulsions of affect, material, and form. In *The Ignorant Schoolmaster* Jacques Rancière propounds the democratizing effects of such compulsions, making the classroom less a top-down monologue of teacher to student than a level scene of endless paraphrase defined by Frances Ferguson as the material "exchange of what you mean for what I would say."[44] Such exchange becomes pluralistic dialogue in virtue of engaging what the philosopher Harry Frankfurt calls implicit "thick promises": in contrast to the thin promises which we can explicitly articulate and defend, thick promises represent our commitment to even participating in the game of linguistic exchange in the first place, to respecting what you say for no reason other than the event of your saying it: to experience that event as such is already to be implicated in that promise (175–76). As Rancière emphasizes, literary scholars are especially well advised to heed their students' instruction in such spontaneous, indefensible commitments; these stand to keep us honest and humble about the capacity of argument to stage-manage communication and compassion.

Turning in conclusion to "The Eve of St. Agnes," allegorical "mingling" is likewise a signature of that poem: Porphyro "mingles" with Madeline's "wild dream" and redoubles this figure in that of the blending odors of rose and violet. These mingling allegories of mingling bring the romance narrative to a virtual halt, not by actually arresting subsequent narrative development but by virtualizing it, the rest of the story merely elaborating these intermingling dreamworlds, with the couple gliding like phantoms through the suspended animation of the palace, all the revelers in drunken "be-nightmared" slumber, the beadsman finally silenced and asleep, and Angela dead and "deform." Like-

---

44. *Solitude and the Sublime*, 169.

wise, in "Ode on a Grecian Urn," the dream of music seen but not heard, of the kiss of lovers forever more about to kiss, is given an especially thorough formal autonomy and coherence by virtue of the urn's great stasis, blocking any hope of narrative payoff. As a radical obstacle to narrative development, the urn forces us to experience the fort-da game in the ways in which our desire compulsively stages itself in the absence of narrative warrantees. If the same can be said of the conclusion to the "Eve of St. Agnes," this is most commonly framed in Levinson's terms by giving positive valance to Byron's derisive references to Keats's masturbatory poetics: the romance narrative gives way to a masturbatory dream. But the account above of "On Seeing the Elgin Marbles" suggests an arguably more radical suspension of purpose. As "Ode on a Grecian Urn" likewise suggests, the sonnet's mingling figures of mingling are perpetuated not by the "burning forehead and parched tongue" of the masturbator alone but by the way in which this issues in a less isolated eroticism, a more expansive sense of connection with "other woes than ours." Correspondingly I would suggest that Prophyro's phallic throbbing and fetishism does not set the stage of the romance's version of such mingling—he after all reports himself a *successful* pilgrim, the confirmed hero of his romance narrative—but is rather a prop in the staging set by his appropriately *plural* set of female counterparts, Madeline, St. Agnes herself, and Angela, the actual stage designer of the lovers' dreams. This makes a difference not because Madeline's dream is necessarily less subject to the label *masturbation* but because it is more given to mingling, to pluralistic, allegorical dispersal rather than fetishistic containment, especially since Madeline herself is likened to the key figure of "Elgin Marbles," the sick bird, "a dove forlorn and lost with sick unpruned wing."

The term *masturbation* is not inapt for her disabled fantasy, but it is less precise than we need, especially in light of characterizations of affect shared under the signs of failure and waste, what Judith Butler, in *Subjects of Desire*, most succinctly calls "queer performativity." Leo Bersani describes the queer mechanics of a fort-da game without developmental purpose as a "discipline of *impersonal intimacy*": a pleasure "in being 'reduced' to an impersonal rhythm" that "doesn't satisfy conscious or unconscious desires; [but instead] testifies to the seductiveness of the ceaseless movement toward and away from things without which there would be no particular desire for *any* thing, a seductiveness that is the ontological ground of the desirability of all things." Particular material bodies and things, the stage props of desires, mediate our thick commitment to the very sharability of affect, that it's not something we do alone but together, as a precondition of, or stage setting for, all of the individuating narratives we, like Freud's master of ceremonies, retrospectively impose. A thing sustains its particularity *in virtue not in spite of* how it echoes off other things; allegory is how we sustain the game of affective particularity, the thick promise we make to one another that we are each particular things. This finally is why the fort-da game is consoling, just because it is a *game*, with rules and thick promises, that can give some order to overwhelming affect, not the anxiety-ridden order of the possessive containment promised but never delivered by bourgeois selfhood, but the order of the rhythm of social exchange, of dialogue, poetry, music, and dance, illuminating a logic to one's own body in and as the pattern of its echoing in other bodies.

Correspondingly the most compelling such disclosure in "St. Agnes" comes not with the intermingling of *dreams* that seal the success of Prophyro's pilgrimage but with a prior intermingling of *bodies* as Madeline guides the ailing Angela down the stairway to her room. On the level of narrative, this appears less an instance of mutually intoxicating visions than of the blind leading the blind. Angela, blinded by fear and groping for the stair, is guided by Madeline, who is possessed by visions of Agnes, the patron saint of virgins and rape victims, who was brutally murdered for her refusal to consummate her marriage. But a deeper and darker dialogue unites these stumbling women than the overtly gorgeous visions uniting the gliding lovers. Keats evokes an unheard melody, specifically the stifled song of a dying bird, to figure the eloquence of the pain Madeline feels in her heart. Extending these compound negations, Keats casts her heart as also the *auditor* of its own silent eloquence: "But to her heart, her heart was voluble, / Paining with eloquence her balmy side." The image of this silent and dark but eloquent interchange of a heart divided from itself cannot but evoke the interchange between the two blinded bodies jointly negotiating the stairs. But Keats evokes these two hearts by way of an epic simile that engenders a third, belonging to yet another dying bird, also female: "As though a tongueless nightingale should swell / Her throat in vain, and die, heart-stifled, in her dell."

The rhythm of this interheart eloquence, dark, painful, and silent, mingles indifferently among Madeline, Angela, Anges, and the proliferating sick figurations to which they do and do not give wing. Radically resistant of narrative and procreative purpose, it is nonetheless undeniably erotically and socially regenerative, perpetuating this series of nonsexual dreams of sex, queerly capable of embodying this paradox, and illuminating, thereby, what experience outside ideology is like, then and now and forever.

# BIBLIOGRAPHY

Abrams, M. H. *The Mirror and the Lamp: Romantic Theory and the Critical Tradition*. New York: Oxford University Press, 1953.

Adorno, Theodor W. *Minima Moralia; Reflections from Damaged Life*. Trans. E. F. N. Jephcott. London: New Left Books, 1974.

——. *Negative Dialectics*. Trans. E. B. Ashton. New York: Continuum, 1973.

Appadurai, Arjun. "Introduction: Commodities and the Politics." In *The Social Life of Things*. Ed. Arjun Appadurai. Cambridge: Cambridge University Press, 1986. 3–65.

Aristotle. "De Poetica (Poetics)." In *The Basic Works of Aristotle*. Ed. Richard P. McKeon. New York: Modern Library, 2001. 624–67.

Bamford, Samuel. *Passages in the Life of a Radical*. Oxford: Oxford University Press, 1984.

Bataille, George. *The Accursed Share*. New York: Zone, 1988.

Benjamin, Walter. *Charles Baudelaire: A Lyric Poet in the Era of High Capitalism*. Trans. Harry Zohn. London: Verso, 1983.

——. *The Work of Art in the Age of Its Technological Reproducibility, and Other Writings on Media*. Ed. Michael W. Jennings, Brigid Doherty, and Thomas W. Levin. Cambridge: Harvard University Press, 2008.

Bernstein, J. M. "Confession and Forgiveness: Hegel's Poetics of Action." In *Beyond Representation: Philosophy and Poetic Imagination*. Ed. Richard T. Eldridge. Cambridge: Cambridge University Press, 1996. 34–65.

Bernstein, Jay. "Conscience and Transgression: The Exemplarity of Tragic Action." In *Hegel's Phenomenology of Spirit: A Reappraisal*. Ed. Gary K. Browning. Dordrecht, Netherlands: Kluwer, 1997. 79–97.

Bersani, Leo. *Is the Rectum a Grave? and Other Essays*. Chicago: University of Chicago Press, 2010.

Bersani, Leo, and Adam Phillips. *Intimacies*. Chicago: University of Chicago Press, 2008.

Bewell, Alan J. "The Political Implications of Keats's Classicist Aesthetics." *Studies in Romanticism* 25, no. 2 (Summer 1986): 220–29.

Blake, William. *The Complete Poetry & Prose of William Blake*. Ed. David Erdman. New York: Anchor, 1982.

Bloom, Harold. *The Visionary Company: A Reading of English Romantic Poetry*. Ithaca: Cornell University Press, 1971.

Bloom, Paul. *How Pleasure Works: The New Science of Why We Like What We Like*. New York: W. W. Norton, 2010.

Borsch-Jacobson, Mikkel. *Lacan: The Absolute Master*. Stanford: Stanford University Press, 1991.

Bourdieu, Pierre. *Distinction: A Social Critique of the Judgement of Taste*. Trans. Richard Nice. Cambridge: Harvard University Press, 1987.

Brown, Bill. "The Secret Life of Things: Virginia Woolf and the Matter of Modernism." In *Aesthetic Subjects*. Ed. Pamela R. Matthews and David McWhirter. Minneapolis: University of Minnesota Press, 2003. 397–430.

———. "Thing Theory." *Critical Inquiry* 28 (2001): 1–22.

Burke, Edmund. *A Philosophical Enquiry into the Origin of Our Ideas of the Sublime and Beautiful*. Ed. T. Boulton. Notre Dame: University of Notre Dame Press, 1968.

———. *Reflections on the Revolution in France*. In *Selected Writings and Speeches*. Ed. Peter J. Stanlis. Brunswick, NJ: Doubleday, 1963.

———. *Reflections on the Revolution in France*. Ed. and with an introduction by Leslie G. Mitchell. New York: Oxford University Press, 1993.

Butler, Judith. *Antigone's Claim: Kinship between Life and Death*. New York: Columbia University Press, 2000.

———. *Subjects of Desire: Hegelian Reflections in Twentieth-Century France*. New York: Columbia University Press, 1987.

Byron, George G. "Marino Faliero, Doge of Venice: An Historical Tragedy in Five Acts." In *The Complete Poetical Works: Volume 4*. Ed. Jerome J. McGann. Oxford: Oxford University Press, 1986. 299–446.

———. *Lord Byron: The Complete Poetical Works: Volume 2*. Ed. Jerome J. McGann. Oxford: Oxford University Press, 1980.

———. *The Major Works*. Ed. Jerome J. McGann. Oxford: Oxford University Press. 2008.

Campbell, Colin. *The Romantic Ethic and the Spirit of Modern Consumerism*. Oxford: Basil Blackwell, 1987.

Cannon, John. *Aristocratic Century: The Peerage of Eighteenth-Century England*. New York: Cambridge University Press, 1984.

Chandler, James. *England in 1819: The Politics of Literary Culture and the Case of Romantic Historicism*. Chicago: University of Chicago Press, 1998.

———. "Hallam, Tennyson, and the Poetry of Sensation: Aestheticist Allegories of a Counter-Public Sphere." *Studies in Romanticism* 33, no. 4 (Winter 1994): 527–37.

———. "Moving Accidents: The Emergence of Sentimental Probability." In *The Age of Cultural Revolutions*. Ed. Colin Jones and Dror Wahrman. Berkeley: University of California Press, 2002. 137–70.

———. "Romantic Allusiveness." *Critical Inquiry* 8, no. 3 (Spring 1982): 461–87.

Chandler, James, and Maureen McLane, eds. *The Cambridge Companion to British Romantic Poetry*. New York: Cambridge University Press 2008.

Christensen, Jerome. *Lord Byron's Strength: Romantic Writing and Commercial Society*. Baltimore: Johns Hopkins University Press, 1992.

Climate Central. *Global Weirdness: Severe Storms, Deadly Heat Waves, Relentless Drought, Rising Seas, and the Weather of the Future.* New York: Pantheon Books, 2012.

Cooper, John, ed. *Plato: Complete Works.* Indianapolis: Hackett, 1997.

Cosgrove, Peter. "Edmund Burke, Gilles Deleuze, and the Subversive Masochism of the Image." *English Literary History* 66, no. 2 (Summer 1999): 405–37.

Cronin, Richard. *The Politics of Romantic Poetry.* New York: St. Martin's Press, 2000.

Curran, Stuart. "Romantic Elegiac Hybridity." In *The Oxford Handbook of the Elegy.* Ed. Karen Weisman. Oxford: Oxford University Press, 2010. 238–50.

Deleuze, Gilles, and Leopold Sacher-Masoch. *Masochism: Coldness in Cruelty and Venus in Furs.* Trans. Jean McNeil. New York: Zone Books, 1991.

Dennett, D. C. *Darwin's Dangerous Idea: Evolution and the Meanings of Life.* New York: Simon & Schuster, 1995.

Deresiewicz, William. "Faux Friendship." *The Chronicle of Higher Education.* December 6, 2009. http://www.chronicle.com/article/Faux-Friendship/49308/.

Derrida, Jacques. "The Ends of Man." In *Margins of Philosophy.* Trans. Alan Bass. Chicago: University of Chicago Press, 1982. 109–36.

———. "From Restricted to General Economy." In *Writing and Difference.* Trans. Alan Bass. New York: Routledge, 2001. 251–94.

———. *Of Grammatology.* Trans. Gayatri Chakravorty Spivak. Baltimore: Johns Hopkins University Press, 1998.

———. *Points . . . Interviews, 1974–1994.* Trans. Peggy Kamuf. Ed. Elisabeth Weber. Stanford: Stanford University Press, 1995.

Earle, Bo. "Hegel's Poetics of History: Tragic Repetition and Comic Recollection." *Philosophy and Literature* 38, no. 2 (October 2014).

Erdman, David V., ed. *The Complete Poetry and Prose of William Blake.* With a New Foreword and Commentary by Harold Bloom. Newly rev. ed. Berkeley: University of California Press, 2008.

Evans, G. Blakemore, ed. *The Riverside Shakespeare.* 2nd ed. Boston: Houghton Mifflin, 1997.

Ferber, Michael. *The Poetry of Shelley.* New York: Penguin, 1994.

Ferguson, Frances. *Pornography, the Theory: What Utilitarianism Did to Action.* Chicago: University of Chicago Press, 2004.

———. *Solitude and the Sublime: Romanticism and the Aesthetics of Individuation.* New York: Routledge, 1992.

Frankfurt, Harry. *The Importance of What We Care About.* Cambridge: Cambridge University Press, 1988.

Freud, Sigmund. *Civilization and Its Discontents.* Trans. and ed. James Strachey. New York: W. W. Norton, 1962.

———. "Mourning and Melancholia." In *General Psychological Theory: Papers on Metapsychology.* Ed. and introd. Philip Rieff. New York: Touchstone, 1997. 164–79.

———. *The Standard Edition of the Complete Psychological Works of Sigmund Freud.* Trans. and ed. James Strachey. Vol. 3, *Early Psychoanalytic Publications (1893–1899).* London: Hogarth Press and Institute of Psychoanalysis, 1962.

———. *The Standard Edition of the Complete Psychological Works*. Trans. and ed. James Strachey. Vol. 18, *Beyond the Pleasure Principle, Group Psychology, and Other Works (1920–1922)*. London: Hogarth Press, 1961.

———. *The Standard Edition of the Complete Psychological Works*. Trans. and ed. James Strachey. Vol. 22, *New Introductory Lectures and Other Works (1932–36)*. London: Hogarth Press, 1961.

Freud, Sigmund, and Joyce Crick. *The Interpretation of Dreams*. Oxford: Oxford University Press, 1999.

Frye, Northrop. *Fearful Symmetry: A Study of William Blake*. Princeton: Princeton University Press, 1947.

Gill, Stephen, ed. *William Wordsworth: The Major Works*. Oxford: Oxford University Press, 2000.

Girard, René. *Deceit, Desire, and the Novel: Self and Other in Literary Structure*. Trans. Yvonne Freccero. Baltimore: Johns Hopkins University Press, 1976.

———. *Things Hidden since the Foundation of the World*. Trans. Michael Metteer (Book I). Trans. Stephen Bann (Books II and III). Stanford: Stanford University Press, 1987.

Hamilton, Clive. *Requiem for a Species*. New York: Earthscan, 2010.

Hartman, Geoffrey. *The Fateful Question of Culture*. New York: Columbia University Press, 1998.

Hegel, Georg W. F. *Phenomenology of Spirit*. Trans. Arnold V. Miller and J. N. Findlay. Oxford: Clarendon Press, 1977.

Henrich, Dieter. *Hegel Im Kontext*. Frankfurt: Suhrkamp, 1971.

Hill, Alan G., ed. *The Letters of William Wordsworth: A New Selection*. Oxford: Oxford University Press, 1984.

Hogg, T. J. *The Life of Percy Bysshe Shelley*. London: Routledge, 1906.

Horkheimer, Max, Theodor W. Adorno, and Noerr G. Schmid. Trans. Edmund Jephcott. *Dialectic of Enlightenment: Philosophical Fragments*. Stanford: Stanford University Press, 2007.

Hughes, D. J. "Potentiality in "Prometheus Unbound." *Studies in Romanticism* 2, no. 2 (1963): 107–26.

Jameson, Fredric. *The Political Unconscious: Narrative as a Socially Symbolic Act*. Ithaca: Cornell University Press, 1981.

Johnson, E. D. H. "A Political Interpretation of Byron's *Marino Faliero*." *The Modern Language Quarterly* 3, no. 3 (1942): 417–25.

Kaufman, Robert. "Negatively Capable Dialectics: Keats, Vendler, Adorno, and the Theory of the Avant-Garde." *Critical Inquiry* 27, no. 2 (Winter 2001): 354–84.

Keach, William. "Obstinate Questionings: The Immortality Ode and *Alastor*." *The Wordsworth Circle* 12 (1981): 36–44.

Keats, John. *Keats's Poetry and Prose*. Ed. Jeffrey Cox. New York: Norton: 2008.

Kermode, Frank. *The Sense of an Ending*. New York: Oxford University Press, 2000.

Khalip, Jacques. *Anonymous Life: Romanticism and Dispossession*. Stanford: Stanford University Press, 2009.

Kripke, Saul A. *Wittgenstein on Rules and Private Language: An Elementary Exposition*. Cambridge: Harvard University Press, 1984.

Laplanche, Jean. *Life and Death in Psychoanalysis*. Baltimore: Johns Hopkins University Press, 1976.

Latour, Bruno. "Hegel's Poetics of History: Tragic Repetition and Comic Recollection." *Philosophy and Literature* 38, no. 2 (October 2014): 314–31.

———. *Politics of Nature.* Cambridge: Harvard University Press, 2004.

Lear, Jonathan. *Happiness, Death, and the Remainder of Life.* Cambridge: Harvard University Press, 2000.

———. *Love and Its Place in Nature: A Philosophical Interpretation of Freudian Psychoanalysis.* New Haven: Yale University Press, 1998.

Levinson, Marjorie. *Keats's Life of Allegory: The Origins of a Style.* Oxford: Blackwell, 1988.

Lloyd, David, and Paul Thomas. *Culture and the State.* New York: Routledge, 1998.

Locke, John. *An Essay Concerning Human Understanding.* Ed. Peter H. Nidditch. Oxford: Clarendon Press, 1975.

Lukács, Georg. *History and Class Consciousness.* Trans. Rodney Livingstone. Cambridge: MIT Press, 1971.

Lukács, György. "Reification and the Consciousness of the Proletariat." In *History and Class Consciousness: Studies in Marxist Dialectics.* Trans. Rodney Livingstone. Cambridge: MIT Press, 1971. 183–222.

Macpherson, C. B. *The Political Theory of Possessive Individualism: Hobbes to Locke.* Oxford: Clarendon Press, 1962.

Makdisi, Saree. *William Blake and the Impossible History of the 1790s.* Chicago: University of Chicago Press, 2003.

Manning, Peter. "Childe Harold in the Marketplace: From Romaunt to Handbook." *The Modern Language Quarterly* 52, no. 3 (June 1991): 170–90.

Martin, Phillip. *Byron: A Poet before His Public.* Cambridge: Cambridge University Press, 1982.

Marx, Karl. *Capital: A Critique of Political Economy.* Vol. 1. Trans. Ben Fowkes. London: Penguin 1990.

McGann, Jerome J. *Fiery Dust: Byron's Poetic Development.* Chicago: University of Chicago Press, 1968.

———, ed. *Lord Byron: The Major Works.* Oxford: Oxford University Press, 2000.

———. *The Romantic Ideology: A Critical Investigation.* Chicago: University of Chicago Press, 1983.

Mellor, Anne K. *Romanticism & Gender.* New York: Routledge, 1992.

Mills, Jagentowicz. "Hegel's Antigone." In *The Phenomenology of Spirit Reader: Critical and Interpretive Essays.* Ed. Jon Stewart. Albany: State University of New York Press, 1998. 243–71.

Mitchell, W. J. T. *Blake's Composite Art: A Study of the Illuminated Poetry.* Princeton: Princeton University Press, 1978.

Morton, Timothy. "The Dark Ecology of Elegy." In *The Oxford Handbook of the Elegy.* Ed. Karen Weisman. Oxford: Oxford University Press, 2010. 251–71.

———. *The Ecological Thought.* Cambridge: Harvard University Press, 2010.

———. *Hyperobjects.* Minneapolis: University of Minnesota Press, 2013.

———. "*Hyperobjects* and the End of Common Sense." *The Contemporary Condition.* March 18, 2010. contemporarycondition.blogspot.com/2010/03/hyperobjects-and-end-of-common-sense.html

Nagel, Thomas. *The View from Nowhere.* New York: Oxford University Press, 1989.

Ngai, Sianne. *Our Aesthetic Categories*. Cambridge: Harvard University Press, 2012.

Nietzsche, Friedrich. *Beyond Good and Evil*. Trans. R. J. Hollingdale. New York: Penguin, 1990.

———. *Twilight of the Idols*. Trans. Michael Turner. New York: Penguin, 1990.

Nussbaum, Martha C. *The Fragility of Goodness: Luck and Ethics in Greek Tragedy and Philosophy*. Cambridge: Cambridge University Press, 1986.

O'Rourke, James. "Introduction." In "Ode on a Grecian Urn": *Hypercanonicity and Pedagogy*. Ed. James O'Rourke. *Romantic Circles Praxis* (October 2003). http://www.rc.umd.edu/praxis/grecianurn/2003.

Perelman, Bob. "Fake Dream: The Library." In *Ten to One: Selected Poems*. London: Wesleyan University Press, 1999. xiv.

Pippin, Robert B. "The Death of God and Modern Melancholy." In *Modernism as a Philosophical Problem: On the Dissatisfactions of European High Culture*. 2nd ed. Oxford: Blackwell, 1999. 144–54.

Plutarch. *Plutarch's Lives: The Translation Called Dryden's*. Trans. John Dryden. Rev. A. H. Clough. New York: Bigelow, Brown & Co, 1911.

Pollan, Michael. *The Botany of Desire: A Plant's-Eye View of the World*. New York: Random House, 2002.

Praz, Mario. *The Romantic Agony*. 2nd ed. Trans. Angus Davidson. Oxford: Oxford University Press, 1978.

Proust, Marcel. *Illuminations*. Trans. Harry Zohn. New York: Schocken, 1968.

Quinney, Laura. *William Blake on Self and Soul*. Cambridge: Harvard University Press, 2010.

Rancière, Jacques. *The Emancipated Spectator*. Trans. Gregory Elliott. New York: Verso, 2009.

———. *The Ignorant Schoolmaster*. Stanford: Stanford University Press, 1991.

———. *Staging the People*. Trans. David Fernbach. New York: Verso, 2011.

Reik, Theodor. *Masochism in Modern Man*. Trans. Margaret H. Beigel and Gertrud M. Kurth. New York: Farrar, Straus and Company, 1941.

Reiman, Donald H., ed. *Shelley's Poetry and Prose: Authoritative Texts, Criticism*. 2nd ed. New York: Norton, 2002.

Revkin, Andrew. "The Greenhouse Effect and the Bathtub Effect." http://dotearth.blogs.nytimes.com/2009/01/28/the-greenhouse-effect-and-the-bathtub-effect/

Ricoeur, Paul. *Freud and Philosophy: An Essay on Interpretation*. Trans. Denis Savage. New Haven: Yale University Press, 1977.

Rollins, Hyder E., ed. *The Letters of John Keats, 1814–1821*. Vol. 2. Cambridge: Harvard University Press, 1958.

Rose, Gilliam. "The Comedy of Hegel and the Trauerspiel of Modern Philosophy." In *Hegel's Phenomenology of Spirit: A Reappraisal*. Ed. Gary K. Browning. Dordrecht, Netherlands: Kluwer, 1997. 105–12.

Roughgarden, Joan. *Evolution's Rainbow: Diversity, Gender, and Sexuality in Nature and People*, 2nd ed. Berkeley: University of California Press, 2009.

Rousseau, Jean-Jacques. *Basic Political Writings*. Trans. and ed. Donald A. Cress. Indianapolis: Hackett, 1987.

Rovee, Christopher. "Trashing Keats." *English Literary History* 75, no. 4 (Winter 2008): 993–1022.

St. Clair, William. *The Reading Nation in the Romantic Period*. Cambridge: Cambridge University Press, 2004.

Sartre, Jean-Paul. *Search for a Method*. Trans. Hazel E. Barnes. New York: Knopf, 1963.

Sedgwick, Eve Kosofsky. *Between Men: English Literature and Male Homosocial Desire*. New York: Columbia University Press, 1985.

Serres, Michel. *The Parasite*. Trans. Lawrence R. Schehr. Minneapolis: University of Minnesota Press, 2007.

Shakespeare, William. *King Lear*. In *The Riverside Shakespeare*. Ed. G. Blakemore Evans. 1249–1306.

———. *The Tragedy of Hamlet, Prince of Denmark*. In *The Riverside Shakespeare*. Ed. G. Blakemore Evans. Chicago: Houghton Mifflin. 1135–202.

———. *The Tragedy of Macbeth*. In *The Riverside Shakespeare*, by G. Blakemore Evans. Ed. Harry Levine. 1307–47.

Shelley, Percy. *Shelley's Poetry and Prose*. 2nd ed. Ed. Donald H. Reiman and Neil Fraistat. New York: Norton, 2002.

Shelley, Percy Bysshe. "A Defense of Poetry." In *Romanticism: An Anthology*. Ed. Duncan Wu. Malden, MA: Blackwell, 2006. 944–56.

———. *Prometheus Unbound: A Lyrical Drama in Four Acts, with Other Poems*. Cambridge: Cambridge University Press, 2013.

Shklar, Judith. "Hegel's Phenomenology: An Elegy for Hellas." In *Hegel's Political Philosophy—Problems and Perspectives: A Collection of New Essays*. Ed. Z. A. Pelczynski. Cambridge: Cambridge University Press, 1971. 73–89.

Simon, Herbert A. *Models of Man: Social and Rational; Mathematical Essays on Rational Human Behavior in Society Setting*. New York: Wiley, 1957.

Smith, Adam. *The Theory of Moral Sentiments*. Amherst: Prometheus Books, 2000.

Smith, Charlotte. "The Emigrants." In *Selected Poems*. Ed. Judith Willson. New York: Routledge, 2003.

Strachan, John, ed. *The Poems of John Keats: A Sourcebook*. London: Routledge, 2003.

Towsey, David. "Platonic Eros and Deconstructive Love." *Studies in Romanticism* 40, no. 4 (2001): 511–30.

Ulmer, William. *Shelleyan Eros*. Princeton: Princeton UP, 1990.

Vendler, Helen. *The Music of What Happens: Poems, Poets, Critics*. Cambridge: Harvard University Press, 1988.

Wasserman, Earl R. *Shelley: A Critical Reading*. Baltimore: Johns Hopkins University Press, 1971.

Watkins, Daniel P. *Keats's Poetry and the Politics of the Imagination*. Rutherford, NJ: Fairleigh Dickinson University Press, 1989.

Williams, Raymond, *Modern Tragedy*. Ed. Pamela McCallum. Peterborough, ON: Broadview Press, 2006.

Wittgenstein, Ludwig. *Remarks on the Philosophy of Psychology: Vol. 2*. Translated by C. G. Luckhart and M. A. E. Aue. Edited by G H. von Wright and Heikki Nyman. Oxford: Blackwell, 1980.

———. *Wittgenstein's Lectures: Cambridge; 1932–1935*. Ed. Alice Ambrose. Chicago: University of Chicago Press, 1982.

Wolfson, Susan J. *Borderlines: The Shiftings of Gender in British Romanticism*. Stanford: Stanford University Press, 2006.

———. *Formal Charges: The Shaping of Poetry in British Romanticism*. Stanford: Stanford University Press, 1997.

———. *The Questioning Presence: Wordsworth, Keats, and the Interrogative Mode in Romantic Poetry*. Ithaca: Cornell University Press, 1986.

Wollstonecraft, Mary. *Vindication of the Rights of Men*. New York: Prometheus, 1996.

Wonkblog. Kevin Schaul. https://www.washingtonpost.com/graphics/business/wonkblog/mass-shooting-definition/.

Wordsworth, William. *The Fourteen-Book Prelude* (1850). Book Seventh. In *William Wordsworth: The Complete Poetical Works*. London: Macmillan and Co., 1888.

———. *The Major Works*. Ed. Stephen Gill. New York: Oxford, 2008.

———. "Resolution and Independence." In *William Wordsworth: The Major Works*. Ed. Stephen Gill. 118–19.

———. "The Tables Turned: An Evening Scene on the Same Subject." In *William Wordsworth: The Major Works*. Ed. Stephen Gill. 131.

———. *The Thirteen-Book Prelude* (1805). Book VII. In *William Wordsworth: The Major Works*. Ed. Stephen Gill. 597–622.

Žižek, Slavoj. *The Sublime Object of Ideology*. London: Verso, 1989.

# INDEX

Abrams, M. H., 57, 60, 82n35
Adams, Hazard, 58
Adorno, Theodor W., 71n15, 74–76, 82n35, 84, 104, 179, 180–81, 182; *Dialectic of Enlightenment*, 6, 17, 77, 79, 104, 105, 163, 164, 179n22
*Alastor, or The Spirit of Solitude* (Shelley), 116–25, 134, 135, 135n8, 137–40, 146, 161n11
All Lives Matter, x
Althusser, Louis, 4, 14
*Angelus Novus* (Benjamin), xii
*Antigone* (Sophocles), 65–69, 90–93, 95, 98, 100, 102
Appadurai, Arjun, 18
Arendt, Hannah, viii
Aristotle, viii, 65, 66, 66n7, 89, 90, 91, 94, 99
"À une passante" (Baudelaire), ix, 156–57, 160–61, 170

Bamford, Samuel, 1, 2
Bataille, George, 11, 13, 188
Baudelaire, Charles, 21, 165, 169, 175, 175n21, 176, 180; "À une passante," ix, 156–57, 160–61, 170
Benjamin, Walter, ix, 19, 20, 21, 30, 157, 170, 175; *Angelus Novus*, xii
Bergson, Henri, 26
Bernstein, J. M., 89–93, 95, 98, 99, 101, 102
Bersani, Leo, 112, 190, 191, 193, 196, 198
Bewell, Alan, 172n16

Blake, William, viii, 35–62, 143, 150; *The Book of Thel*, 36, 37, 42, 43, 46–49, 55–59, 62; *The Visions of the Daughters of Albion*, 36, 37, 42–43, 48, 49–50, 54–57, 60–61
Black Lives Matter, ix
Bland, Sandra, vii, viii, ix, xi, xii
Bloom, Harold, 44, 46, 60, 115, 125, 135, 166
Bloom, Paul, 47n22
*Book of Thel, The* (Blake), 36, 37, 42, 43, 46–49, 55–59, 62
Bourdieu, Pierre, 106, 107, 167, 169
Brown, Bill, 18, 19, 20, 26, 186, 190
Burke, Edmund, 8, 16–23, 82, 89, 141, 154, 168, 180, 190
Burke, Kenneth, xi, 5
Butler, Judith, 93, 112, 198
Byron, 63–113, 115, 123, 135, 167–68, 170–71, 173–75, 181, 187, 198; *Childe Harold's Pilgrimage*, 64, 65, 68–88, 104–6, 108, 111, 112, 113, 115, 135; "Darkness," 65, 110, 113; *Don Juan*, 65, 77, 87–89, 102, 103, 105, 106, 108, 111, 113, 114, 115; *Marino Faliero*, 64, 65, 87, 102, 103–10, 113

*Cambridge Companion to British Romantic Poetry* (Chandler and McLane), 26–32
Campbell, Colin, 64, 107
Chandler, James, 2n1, 3, 5–6, 18, 19, 82n35, 105, 172n16; *Cambridge Companion to British Romantic Poetry*, 26–32; *The Questioning Presence*, 6, 6n8
*Childe Harold's Pilgrimage* (Byron), 64, 65, 68–88, 104–6, 108, 111, 112, 113, 115, 135

209

Christensen, Jerome, 67–73, 71n15, 75–76, 79–81, 84, 84n36, 90
Climate Central, 12, 12n18
Coleridge, Samuel Taylor, 82, 82n35, 84, 116, 117, 130, 139, 140; *Hymn before Sunrise*, 82, 125–28, 131–33, 136–37
Cosgrove, Peter, 171
Cronin, Richard, 2, 3
Curran, Stuart, 63, 85

"Darkness" (Byron), 65, 110, 113
Darwin, Charles, 186, 187, 192
"Defense of Poetry, A" (Shelley), 48, 87, 116, 117, 120, 123, 124, 129, 139, 140, 145, 155
Deleuze, Gilles, 171, 179
de Man, Paul, 112, 185–86
Dennett, Daniel, 187
Deresiewicz, William, 88n41
Derrida, Jacques, 11, 12, 13, 70, 108
*Dialectic of Enlightenment* (Adorno and Horkheimer), 6, 17, 77, 79, 104, 105, 163, 164, 179n22
*Don Juan* (Byron), 65, 77, 87–89, 102, 103, 105, 106, 108, 111, 113, 114, 115

Eliot, T. S., 36
"Emigrants, The" (Smith), 7–9
"Eve of St. Agnes, The" (Keats), 110, 176–77, 185–86, 197–99

"Fake Dream: The Library" (Perelman), 32–33
*Fall of Hyperion, The* (Keats), 143, 175–76, 178, 179, 180
Ferber, Michael, 115
Ferguson, Frances, 111, 112, 168, 182, 197
Foucault, Michel, viii, 4, 14, 36, 182
Fox, Charles James, 16–18, 187
*Frankenstein, or the Modern Prometheus* (Shelley), 158–60
Frankfurt, Harry, 191n39, 197
Freud, Sigmund, 35, 36, 39–42, 43–46, 47n20, 48, 50–53, 56, 61–62, 75, 93, 95, 119–20, 128, 134, 148, 161, 186
Frye, Northrop, 59, 60

Gibbons, Edward, 73
Girard, Rene, 171, 180

Hamilton, Clive, 4, 12, 24
*Hamlet* (Shakespeare), 66, 68, 69, 70, 73, 76, 81, 82, 101, 102, 103, 104, 109, 146, 194
Hartman, Geoffrey, 136–39, 156
Haydon, Benjamin, 194–95
Hegel, Georg Wilhelm, ix–xi, 7, 15n25, 16, 24, 25, 27, 28, 39, 39n10, 50, 64, 64n2, 65, 66–67, 110, 112, 136; *The Phenomenology of Spirit*, 89–101, 114
Heidegger, Martin, 16, 36, 75, 82
Henrich, Dieter, 100–101
Holocaust, xi
Horkheimer, Max: *Dialectic of Enlightenment*, 6, 17, 77, 79, 104, 105, 163, 164, 179n22
Huckabee, Mike, xi
Hughes, D. J., 135n8
Hunt, Henry, 1
Hunt, Leigh, 140, 141
*Hymn before Sunrise* (Coleridge), 82, 125–28, 131–33, 136–37
*Hyperion* (Keats), 143

*Ignorant Schoolmaster, The* (Rancière), 197
"Intimations Ode" (Wordsworth), 22, 70

James, Henry, 30, 32
Johnson, E. D. H., 102n55
Joyce, James, 36

Kant, Immanuel, 146, 149, 154–57, 160–63, 165, 166, 180
Kaufman, Robert, 139–40, 175n21
Keach, William, 122n3
Keats, John, xi, 6n8, 143, 166, 167–99; "The Eve of St. Agnes," 110, 176–77, 185–86, 197–99; *The Fall of Hyperion*, 143, 175–76, 178, 179, 180; *Hyperion*, 143; "Lamia," 173–78; "Ode on a Grecian Urn," 169n6, 183, 198; "Ode on Melancholy," 177, 179, 182; "Ode to Autumn," 184, 196, "Ode to Psyche," 193; "On First Looking into Chapman's Homer," 172–73; "On Seeing the Elgin Marbles," 186, 194–97; *Venus in Furs*, 179–80
Kermode, Frank, 23
Khalip, Jacques, 182n32
*King Lear* (Shakespeare), 76, 161
Klein, Naomi, 24

Kripke, Saul, 58

Lacan, Jacques, 36
"Lamia" (Keats), 173–78
Laplanche, Jean, 42
Latour, Bruno, 4, 14, 15, 32
Lear, Jonathan, 41, 42, 45, 46, 51, 52–53, 61
Levinson, Marjorie, 174, 175, 175n21, 185, 186
Levi-Strauss, Claude, 25
Liu, Alan, xii
Lloyd, David, 127n4
Locke, John, 35–39, 41, 48, 51, 54, 57, 58, 59, 60, 148
Lukács, Georg, 18, 69, 169

*Macbeth* (Shakespeare), 73, 74, 76, 78, 79, 81, 82, 84, 85, 123, 135, 165
Macphearson, C. B., ix, 39
Makdisi, Saree, 35, 36
Manning, Peter, 77n29
*Marino Faliero* (Byron), 64, 65, 87, 102, 103–10, 113
Marx, Karl, ix, 4, 36, 65, 78n29, 79
*Mask of Anarchy, The* (Shelley), 2, 140–44, 153–66
McGann, Jerome J., 23, 28, 39, 39n11, 64, 64n3, 68, 71, 71n15, 73, 105, 106, 114, 115, 185
McLane, Maureen: *Cambridge Companion to British Romantic Poetry*, 26–32
McLuhan, Marshall, xii
Mellor, Anne, 175
Mills, Jagentowicz, 93
Milton, John, 144, 145, 151
Mitchell, W. J. T., 47n21
"Mont Blanc" (Shelley), 125, 126, 132, 133, 133n7
Morton, Timothy, 6–7, 111, 112, 190

Nagel, Thomas, 37
Napoleon, 1, 73
Ngai, Sianne, 30–33
Nietzsche, 33, 36, 50, 79, 95, 130, 147, 154–57
Nussbaum, Martha, 66

"Ode: Intimations of Immortality" (Wordsworth), 125, 135–38, 156

"Ode on a Grecian Urn" (Keats), 169n6, 183, 198
"Ode on Melancholy" (Keats), 177, 179, 182
"Ode to Autumn" (Keats), 184, 196
"Ode to Psyche" (Keats), 193
"On First Looking into Chapman's Homer" (Keats), 172–73
"On Seeing the Elgin Marbles" (Keats), 186, 194–97
"On the Extinction of the Venetian Republic" (Wordsworth), 85
O'Rourke, James, 169n6
"Ozymandias" (Shelley), 158, 159

*Parasite, The* (Serres), 188–90
Perelman, Bob: "Fake Dream: The Library," 32–33
Peterloo Massacre, 1–3, 26, 167
*Phenomenology of Spirit, The* (Hegel), 89–101, 114
Phillip, Martin, 77n29
Phillips, Adam, 190
Pippin, Robert, 95
Plato, 14, 15, 66n7, 124, 125, 130, 131, 133, 134, 139, 140, 142, 143, 148; *Symposium*, 14, 124–34, 137
Praz, Mark, 115
*Prelude, The* (Wordsworth), 8–10, 21–22, 25
*Prometheus Unbound* (Shelley), 133n6, 135n8, 143–53, 159, 164
Proust, Marcel, 19–20

*Questioning Presence, The* (Chandler), 6, 6n8
Quinney, Laura, 37, 54–55, 57, 58, 59, 60

Radcliffe, Anne, 85
Rancière, Jacques, 26; *The Ignorant Schoolmaster*, 197; *Staging the People*, 2n3
Reik, Theodor, 171–72
"Resolution and Independence" (Wordsworth), 8, 22, 23
Ricks, Christopher, 175n21
Ricoeur, Paul, 26, 27, 36, 45
Rose, Gillian, 90, 93, 95, 98, 100, 112
Roughgarden, Joan, 187–90
Rousseau, Jean-Jacques, 2n3, 3, 71, 72, 74, 103n57, 105–8, 111, 170
Rovee, Christopher, 180–81, 181n28

Sartre, Jean-Paul, 105
Sedgwick, Eve, 171
Serres, Michel: *The Parasite*, 188–90
Shakespeare, William: *Hamlet*, 66, 68, 69, 70, 73, 76, 81, 82, 101, 102, 103, 104, 109, 146, 194; *King Lear*, 76, 161; *Macbeth*, 73, 74, 76, 78, 79, 81, 82, 84, 85, 123, 135, 165
Shelley, Mary: *Frankenstein, or the Modern Prometheus*, 158–60
Shelley, Percy, xi, 2, 5, 6, 23, 24, 27, 28, 29, 32, 33, 48, 87, 108, 114–66; *Alastor, or The Spirit of Solitude*, 116–25, 134, 135, 135n8, 137–40, 146, 161n11; "A Defense of Poetry," 48, 87, 116, 117, 120, 123, 124, 129, 139, 140, 145, 155; *The Mask of Anarchy*, 2, 140–44, 153–66; "Mont Blanc," 125, 126, 132, 133, 133n7; "Ozymandias," 158, 159; *Prometheus Unbound*, 133n6, 135n8, 143–53, 159, 164; "To Wordsworth," 23, 27
Shklar, Judith, 98
Simon, Herbert, 187
"Simon Lee" (Wordsworth), ix, xii, 8, 9
Smith, Adam, ix, 168, 169
Smith, Charlotte, 7–9, 11, 63, 85; "The Emigrants," 7–9
Socrates, 125–31, 133–34, 137
*Staging the People* (Rancière), 2n3
St. Augustine, 118–20, 122, 129, 139, 140
St. Clair, William, 76
Stevens, Wallace, 166
Strand, Mark, 61, 62
*Symposium* (Plato), 14, 124–34, 137

Thomas, Paul, 127n4
Tighe, Mary, 193
"Tintern Abbey" (Wordsworth), 25

"To Wordsworth" (Shelley), 23, 27
Towsey, David, 131n5
Trump, Donald, vii, x

Ulmer, William, 121, 123, 131

Vendler, Helen, 175n21, 196
*Venus in Furs*, 179–80
*Visions of the Daughters of Albion, The* (Blake), 36, 37, 42–43, 48, 49–50, 54–57, 60–61
Voltaire, 73, 147

Wasserman, Earl, 133n7
Watkins, Daniel, 172n16
"We are Seven" (Wordsworth), ix
Whitman, Walt, 180
Williams, Raymond, 88n40
Wittgenstein, Ludwig, 23, 36, 58–61, 141
Wolfson, Susan, 6, 19, 141–44, 153–55, 164, 166, 170n8, 171, 175
Wollstonecraft, Mary, 19
Woolf, Virginia, 36
Wordsworth, William, ix, xii, 1–34, 60, 70, 71, 72, 73, 75, 85, 86, 88, 116, 117, 118, 121, 123, 124, 125, 135, 136, 137, 138, 139, 140, 156, 196; "Intimations Ode," 23, 70; "Ode: Intimations of Immortality," 125, 135–38, 156; "On the Extinction of the Venetian Republic," 85; *The Prelude*, 8–10, 21–22, 25; "Resolution and Independence," 8, 22, 23; "Simon Lee," ix, xii, 8, 9; "Tintern Abbey," 25; "We are Seven," ix; "The World Is Too Much with Us," 24, 26

Žižek, Slavoj, 39n12

www.ingramcontent.com/pod-product-compliance
Lightning Source LLC
Chambersburg PA
CBHW020653230426

43665CB00008B/424